ENVIRONMENTAL LAW IN INDIA

Dr. R.B. Singh, currently a U.G.C. Research Scientist 'B' (Associate Professor) is a faculty member of the Department of Geography, University of Delhi. The UNESCO/ISSC (Paris) awarded 1988 Research and Study Grants Award in Social and Human Science on his Project Himalayan Highland-Lowland Interactive Systems. Dr. Singh was trained in the Geographical Information Systems Technology in the field of Environment under Training Programme of the UNEP/UNITAR in Switzerland. He has visited and lectured at several universities abroad under scientific exchange programme and participated in International Seminars in over two dozen countries.

He specializes in Environmental studies, Remote Sensing, GIS Tech. and Regional Development, and has to his credit six research volumes and a large number of research papers published in national and international journals. Presently, he is working on two prestigious projects sponsored by UGC and Ministry of Agriculture, Government of India.

Dr. Suresh Misra (b. 1958) holds M.A. in Political Science from J.N.U., New Delhi and D. Phil. from Allahabad University, Allahabad in 1990. He was associated with the Indian Institute of Public Administration, New Delhi as a Research Officer until 1992. After a years stay at the G.B. Pant Social Science Institute, Allahabad, he was a fellow at the Development study Centre, Rehovot, Israel to study Rural Cooperative Settlements in Israel.

Currently Dr. Misra is Associate Professor and Head, Faculty of Public Administration, Haryana Institute of Public Administration, (HIPA) Gurgaon.

Dr. Misra is a highly perceptive and talented academic whose major interests centre around Indian Government and Politics particularly rural politics. He has published a number of papers in reputed journals on themes related to Panchayati Raj institutions, agrarian reforms, and socio-cultural aspects of environmental problems. Among his major publications (books) are: *Politico-Peasantry Conflict in India: Dynamics of Agrarian Change;* and *Legislative Framework of Panchayati Raj Institutions in India;* and *Legislative Status of Panchayati Raj Institutions.*

ENVIRONMENTAL LAW IN INDIA

Issues and Responses

R. B. SINGH
Department of Geography
University of Delhi,
Delhi

SURESH MISRA
Haryana Institute of Public
Administration, Gurgaon
Haryana

CONCEPT PUBLISHING COMPANY, NEW DELHI-110059

ISBN 81-7022-575-2

First Published 1996

Published and Printed by
Ashok Kumar Mittal
Concept Publishing Company
A/15-16, Commercial Block, Mohan Garden,
New Delhi-110059 (INDIA)
Phones : 5504042, 5554042

FOREWORD

This book is the outcome of a National Sumposium on Environmental Ethics held at Gandhi Bhavan, University of Delhi on 1-3, March 1992. An important session of this symposium discussed the issue of Ethical Foundations of Environmental Law. Papers presented in the symposium constitute the main body of the book. Some of the relevant laws of India having direct implications for environmental policy and planning have been reproduced to make the book complete in coverage of the theme. The volume has finally emerged as a very timely contribution to environmental studies.

Environmental law provides the legal framework for action. All over the world, there is a growing tendency to use nature for economic benefits of individuals or corporate bodies. Nature, in economics is a resource for exploitation. This resource may be land, water, air, plants, minerals, fuels or animals. They are all at the disposal of man.

The Industrial Revolution in Europe was based on coal as an energy resource. Iron ore laid the foundation of steel industry. Subsequently other natural resources brought agricultural and industrial prosperity in the West. Laws enacted then were designed to encourage extensive and intensive exploitation of natural resources. Almost every country of Europe and later of other continents passed laws bestowing ownership of natural resources on individuals and private companies.

For the last 25 years or so, the mood of the people appears to have changed. It is now being increasingly realized that nature is not a resource alone, it is also a global womb for life to evolve, survive and prosper. This global womb too has certain degree of flexibility and resilience, as does the mother's womb. Over exploitation of nature destroys this resilience, jeopardizing the survival and evolution of life.

Laws have now come up to control the use of nature by man. Nature is no longer a resource for exploitation: It is a resource to be used judiciously and in conformity with the laws of ecology. There are laws which prohibit the setting of new industries without environmental clearance. Supreme Court of India has ordered closure of not a few but hundreds of factories which pollute rivers and other natural or cultural heritages. The Supreme Court and State High Courts in India have done Yeomen's service to protect the environment.

The central government has also played a leading role in environmental protection. Almost every year, some stringent legislation is being passed. Some of the old acts are being reviewed to plug the loopholes. Major schemes like Ganga Action Plan have been launched with appropriate financial backing to restore the ecological balance disturbed during the last two hundred years or so.

However, the progress towards eco-development is still slow. Developed countries, which are the major polluters have not taken the responsibility commensurate with their contribution to environmental. Nor have they helped the developing countries which lack resources to do the same. It is unfortunate that the developing countries have now to pay the price for what the developed countries did and are still doing.

Depletion of azone layer, green house effect, acid rain, etc. have not been caused by activities in developing countries. They are the consequences of Industrial Revolution to which now the developing countries also have been lured. They too are trying to industrialize themselves following the footsteps of the West.

In these countries, the problems of environment have acquired more serious proportions. While the West in its early stages of industrialization had the resources of the whole world at its disposal; the developing countries do not have adequate control over their own resources. Western countries could sell their industrial products in the captive markets of Asia, Africa and Latin America the developing countries cannot protect their own goods in their own markets. The West could syphon off the exess population (due to high birth rate and labour surplus agriculture) to new lands; the developing countries have no such avenues. These countries have now reached a point of crisis. If they industrialize themselves, they further pollute the already polluted environment; and if they do not industrialize, they cannot provide even the basic needs to their ever growing population.

It is this dilemma which makes environmental laws less effective in these countries. The laws and the courts can curb environmental destruction caused by corporate bodies; but they are unable to curb poverty which is the greatest polluter in these countries. It cannot take care of millions of individuals who cut the trees, destroy the soil, pollute the air, and contaminate the water day in and day out. Arms of the law can reach the culprits only if they are few. When almost everyone breaks the law, courts can do precious little. This is exactly the situation in which poverty stricken developing countries find themselves today.

I, therefore, feel that in order that the legal measures really become effective, two steps need to be taken in developing countries to improve the situation. The first step calls for a new style of development, a style different from that of the West. It should curb conspicuous consumption and lay stress on wage goods. The second step falls in the area of environmental Education. The aim of environmental education is to develop certain ethical standards which prompt people, without the fear of law, to protect the environment.

If these two steps are taken with seriousness they deserve, the laws protecting the environment will be more readily accepted by the people. The courts will thereby have time to deal with major offenders leaving the minor offenders to be dealt with by the people themselves.

I am confident that the look which has been so ably edited and produced will be welcomed by all those who are concerned with protection and management of the environment in India as well as abroad.

R. P. MISRA

New Delhi

PREFACE

Enactment and enforcement of environmental law is essential for sound environmental management. There are, however, not easily accomplished. Environment is not only natural but also cultural and civilizational. The existing laws cover only selected dimensions of environment. Further, the environmental problems requiring attention have different spatial coverages ranging from global to local. The laws have to enacted at a variety of territorial level. The multi-dimensional and multi-territorial nature of environmental law and its application aims (a) to collect and disseminate data on environmental law; (b) to promote the enforcement of international agreements on environmental law; (c) to promote the development or adoption of new agreements, principles or guidelines concerning environmental law; and (d) to provide assistance to states in matters of national legislation and the enforcement of environmental law. In the process of codification and implimention of environmental law particular attention must be paid to the interest and capabilities of a particular nation and its socio-economic and cultural realities. In accordance with the Directive Principles (Articles 48 and 51-A) of the Indian Constitution, the protection and improvement of the natural environment (including forests and wildlife) is an obligatory responsibility of the state and of every citizen of India. The overriding concern for ecological security has also been stressed in the National Policy for Economic Development. Several laws have been enacted from time to time which are directly or indirectly related to environmental protection. These legislations were not considered adequate. A comprehensive act was needed to cover all environmental resources. Therefore, the 1986 Environmental Protection Act was enacted. Subsequently, the Public Liabilities Insurance Act 1991 was enacted. Another key legislation was enacted in March 1991 relating to the labelling of environment friendly products. Recently Environmental Tribunal Act was also passed. The role of courts have been very helpful in environmental matters in India. It is well known fact that the Supreme Court of India has become a very important force for environmental protection in our country. However, success of such legislation will be ensured when there is adequate machinery to implement such laws at the national, state and local levels. More efforts will be directed towards development of institutional machinery for implementation of legislation in the future.

This book a compilation of papers presented in the National Symposium on Environmental Ethics at University of Delhi, is an attempt to update the available information on Environmental Law in India. The book contains nine of the papers presented which have been revised and updated. The authors deal with concepts, human right consideration, ethics and empirical case studies from various environmental Acts. Some of the relevant laws and acts of India have been reproduced to make the book holistic coverage on the environmental law. We are very grateful to Prof. R. P. Misra, President—Sustainable Development Foundation for providing us opportunity to work on such prestigious project. We will also like to express our sincere thanks to all contributors for taking keen interest for preparation of the paper. The contributions made by law-makers of India for formulation of the Acts are sincerely acknowledged.

R. B. SINGH
SURESH MISRA

CONTENTS

LIST OF CONTRIBUTORS

Ben Boer
School of Law,
Macquarie University, Australia

Vaclav Havel
Poet, A Play Right,
Ex-President of Czechoslovakia

R.P. Misra
Department of Geography,
Delhi School of Economics,
University of Delhi, Delhi

Suresh Misra
Haryana Institute of Public Administration,
Gurgaon, Haryana

R.G. Padia
Advocate and Part-time Lecturer,
Department of Law,
Allahabad University, Allahabad

P.S. Sangal
Faculty of Law,
University of Delhi, Delhi

I.C. Saxena
Retired Prof. of Law,
University of Rajasthan, Jaipur

Satish Shastri
Faculty of Law,
University of Rajasthan, Jaipur

R.B. Singh
Department of Geography,
Delhi School of Economics,
University of Delhi, Delhi

1

ENVIRONMENTAL LAW

R.B. Singh and *Suresh Misra*

Introduction

Environmental legislation is one of the major components of environmental management. The environmental law governs the man-nature relationship and thus the quality of human life. In the past, man considered nature as the sources of immediate satisfaction without considering long term perspectives and welfare of future generation. The earlier concept of "touch-me-not" has changed into "use-me-wisely". Man is considered custodian rather than the conqueror of nature. Law is an essential tool for the sound management of the environmental resources through ensuring proper implementation of approperiate policies.

TASK

The tasks of environmental law include-development of constitutional theory, formulating policies, introducing legislative measures and administrative regulations and providing opportunities for litigation to check environmental degradation and reorient the legal and administrative systems of governmental agencies (ESCAP). Environmental law consists of both "hard law", *i.e.*, international treaties and national legislations and soft law *i.e.* guidelines, standards, etc. Its elements are divided into two groups: *(i)* sectoral areas like air, water, soil and *(ii)* assessment.

NEED

Many countries have implemented a number of environmental laws, but effective enforcement and coordination have not been achieved uniformly.

The legislative measures require proper review to make it more responsive towards societal development and environmental enhancement. The holistic approach of environmental law may be considered as multi-level and multi-section concepts. The multi-level policy implementation includes governmental levels *i.e.* national, state and local. The multi-section includes three sectors *i.e.* government agencies, the private sector and the community at large. (Table 1.1)

TABLE 1.1: Environmental law as process (UNEP/IALS. 1979)

Practical Questions	What is the problem? What do we know about it?	What is possible desirable? How can we do it?	What do we decide to do?	How to make it work? How does it Work?
Conceptual Category	Data base	Policy development	Decision	Implementation
Comment in Plain Language	Obvious data Problem definition Additional information needed	Transform information into the best possible alternative solutions	Determine the course of action on basis of policy and political considerations	Draft, adopt and promulgate legislation(Re) organize institutions. Issue regulations Control/ enforce.
Specific Application	Multidisciplinary inventory of scientific, technical and legal information	Development of integrated national or sectoral environmental policy	Technical assistance to the political decision makers	Monitor results. Develop consolidated social indicators. Feed them back to Data, policy Implementation

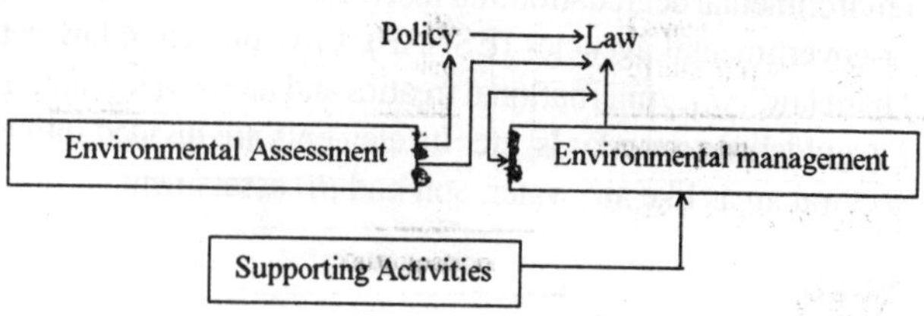

Stockholm Action Plan Matrix (1972)

NATURE OF INDIAN LAWS

In India, Tiwari Committee (of 1980) identifies a few defects of the environmental legislations as follows:

1. Majority of these laws are irrelevant.
2. Lacking statements of explicit policy orientation and societal needs.
3. Mutually inconsistent.
4. Inadequate provisions for helping the implementing machinery.
5. No procedure for reviewing the efficacy of the laws.

In recent years, many environmental protection acts have taken into consideration of above facts. In 1986, Environmental Protection Act was passed by Indian Parliament. The Government of India is actively considering various measures to increase the effectiveness of legislation. Such measures include tax relief and state supported credits in order to protect the environment and restore degraded ecosystems. It is also considered very useful in few cases to impose penalties to make the people and society more aware of the consequences of environmental degradation.

PLANNING-INSTRUMENTS

1. Development Plans

The Planning Commission of Government of India is responsible for preparing a national plans in India. Such five years plans incorporate environmental policies and management principles. Regional development plans and special areas programmes are prepared as policy statement regarding minimum environmental standards.

2. National Conservation Strategy

With the initiation of world conservation strategy, National Conservation Plans aim to achieve objective of integrating conservation with development plans. The National conservation strategy and policy statement on environmental concern and action points have been adopted by the Government of India in June 1992 on the eve of United Nations Conference on Environment and Development.

3. Environmental Impact Assessment

In many countries, development plan causes ecological degradation due to lack of consequences on the environment were not properly considered in projects planning, or implementation. Environmental Impact Assessment (EIA) is a planning instrument which assesses the possible impact of a proposed projects on the environment. Before implementing the project every country should develop its own approach, own political, constitutional and legal system. In the form of EIA, law has provided an excellent tool for environmental provision and protection as well as high powered integrated National Development Planning.

In India, a revised draft notification has been issued in January 1993, indicating the Government's intention to make environmental impact assessment a statuary requirement for all projects both in the public and private sectors. Major hydroelectric and irrigation projects, thermal power projects and industrial projects including refineries and petrochemical are subjected to environmental impact assessment. A high power committee constituted in the Department of Environment in order to analyse, *i.e.*, the environmental impact of projects. Out of the 242 projects appraised during the year in various sectors, 101 projects were granted environmental information has been sought for the remaining projects (Government of India, 1993). A review report of the Sardar Sarover Project has recommended that detailed assessments of social, human and environmental impacts need to be carried out for the project.

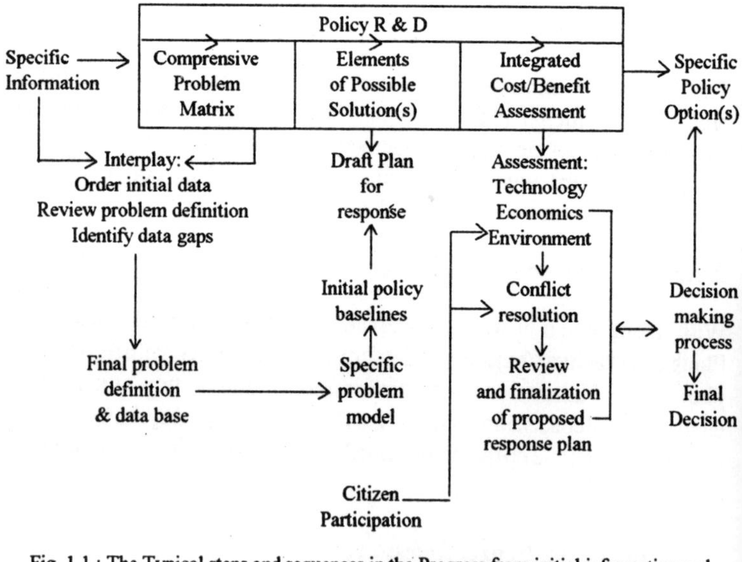

Fig. 1.1 : The Typical steps and sequences in the Progress from initial information and problem definition to final decision (Mayda, 1981a)

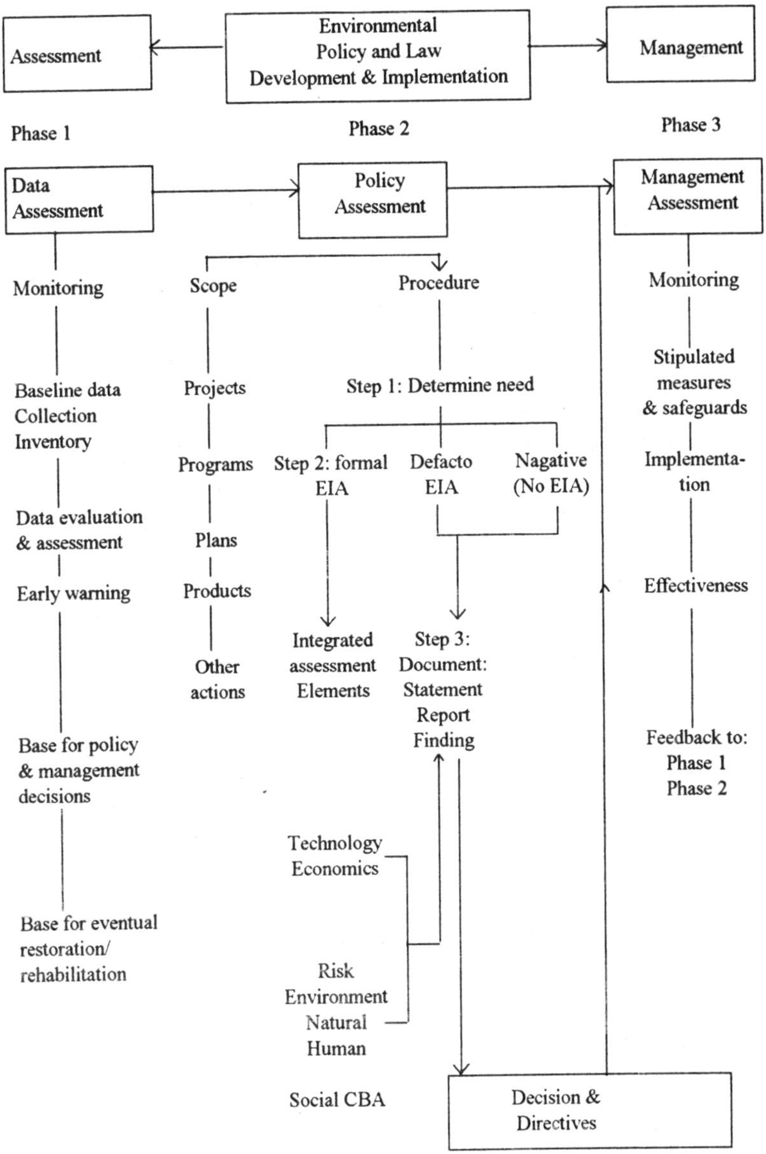

Fig. 1.2 Components and phases of environmental assessment (Mayada, 1981 b).

LAW : FUNCTIONS AND COMPONENTS

Law encompasses three discrete conceptual and functional categories (Mayda, 1986).

1. Positive law general rights and duties, procedural rules ways and means of resolving conflicts in a legal manner, in the form of decisions about particular, rights and duties of individuals.
2. Legal process.
3. Jurisprudence.

Mayda (1986) discusses the following principal categories of the ecomanagement : (Fig. 1.1 & 1.2)

1. Law framework : Power, standards and rules, institutions.
2. Mechanism for continuous policy development and adoption to new knowledge circumstances.
3. Planning and programming, including the necessary data generation.
4. Rational use of resources, including protection and prevention, conservation and rehabilitation quality control and improvement, optimization of—uses and procedures.
5. Support activities, education, passing, awareness building.
6. Monitoring for appropriate correction and innovation.
7. Budgetary means.

ENVIRONMENTAL LEGISLATION:CONCEPTS AND METHODS

1. Rules and Regulations

Regulatory measures are the most basic popular and political form of environmental control in India. It provides effective standard for all citizens. The administrative decision is needed in setting environmental standards which is based on scientific basis of human health and environmental sustainability. Environmental standards should be decided by interactive process of legal institutions, governmental organisations and the courts. There are two types of regulatory controls applied to point sources of pollution. These are specification standards and performance standards (ESCAP, 1985). Specific standards are regulatory controls which has been introduced in India regarding particular measures (anti-pollution devices or equipment). Such measures prevent environmental degradation particularly air and water pollution from industrial sources. Performance standard is a regulatory control which provides for a certain level of performance that must be achieved.

2. Incentives

Various incentives are being proposed in the from of preferential tax treatment like credits and concession in duty on import of pollution control facilities not locally available. The federal government subsidize partial cost of the installation of such facilities like sewage treatment plants to the state and local governments, tax deduction for installation of such equipment to industrial sector.

3. Disincentives

Many countries are implementing various disincentives measures to discourge the release of pollutants into the environment. The pollutants are destroyers of ecosystems. Disincentives also take the form of user and pollution taxes.

4. Economic Sanctions

In recent years, enforcement innovations deal with non-compliance regulations. Economic sanction is actually a penalties equal to the cost of compliance. This tool will cut delays and non-compliance. Through this government has to spend less for enforcement staff and less of the prosecutor's and judges time will be consumed.

5. Schemes for Settlement of Environmental Disputes

In many countries, courts' processes are very time-consuming financial-consuming. Thus settlement of disputes through administrative committees was therefore, resorted through reconciliation mediation and arbitration. This is considered as institutionalize measure to the settle of pollution grievances by local government.

REFERENCES

Baxi Upendra, 1985: Environmental law: Limitations and potential for Liberation, *India's Environment-Crises and Responses,* ed. J. Bandyopadhyay *et. al.,* Dehradun, Natraj Publication, pp. 291-309.

ESCAP, 1985: Status of Environmental Legislation in the ESCAP Region-Regional overview, *Integration of Environmental into Development: Institutional and Legislative Aspects*, Bangkok, pp. 133-145.

Government of India, 1981: the *Tiwari Committee's Report,* DST, New Delhi.

Government of India, 1993: *Annual Report 1992-93,* Ministry of Environment and Forests, New Delhi.

Mayda, Jaro, 1986: Law and Ecomanagement, *International-Social Science Journal,* Vol. 109, pp. 391-410.

2

ECOLOGICAL BALANCE AS A HUMAN RIGHT

R.P. Misra

Human Right has become a major concern of modern society. United Nations has established a Human Rights Commission. Several countries like India have moved in tune with the United Nations to set up their own Human Rights Commissions. A number of global, national and local level institutions have been formed to keep a watch at Human Right violations in different parts of the world.

The concept of human rights is not as recent as we often tend to think. Certain unalienable rights of individuals have been recognized in all societies. Equality before law of the land, freedom within a given social context and right to movement, to form associations of one's choice to profess only religion, and to livelihood have been recognized in all societies. Much of these rights were, however, never granted to those who were outside the clan, the caste and the religion of the dominant groups. Even among insiders, there were hierarchic divisions and the rights of those belonging to lower echelons of the society were marked by frequent violations.

One of the major events which triggered off democratic and humanistic values in Europe was the French Revolution. Man became the measure of everything. Liberty, equality and fraternity became the rallying points for the French to overthrow a feudal order. Similar changes swept over other parts of Europe of 18th and 19th centuries. But these were also the countries when Europe subjugated Asia, Africa and Latin America. Rights of individuals, communities and whole societies to govern themselves were taken away by force. Within the nations human rights of minorities and the so called less civilized were taken away. People were maimed as slaves, untouchables and antisocial elements. Within family structures, the rights of women and children as human beings were rarely respected.

The twentieth century was witness to a new phenomenon of misuse of state power at the cost of human rights of individuals and communities. Those who opposed or even disagreed with the state were dealt with severely. Not that it did not happen in medieval times. But in this century, it took a more violent and mass form. As wars and conflicts started having wider repurcussions, the violations of human rights also increased. It was a century of clash between colonial and nationalist forces. It was also a period of repression, mass killing and destruction. The Bolshevik revolution was too violent to herald a peaceful development of the Soviet Union. Many of the newly independent nations went through similar upheavels, and came to be ruled by dictators who were law by themselves. Discrimination on recial grounds continued. Aparthied in South Africa could see the sign of end only in the last decade of this century.

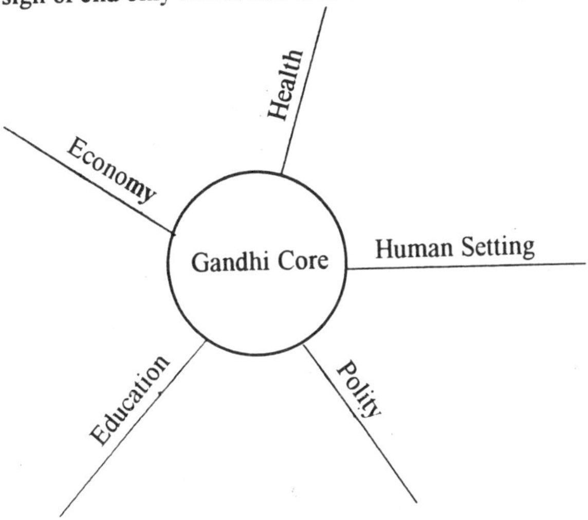

The great religions, cultures, philosophers, revolutions, and democratic ideals, were unable to stem the human rights violations for centuries and more so in the recent past. The consciousness of the people sensitive to these violations, led to the rearticulation of other organizations and rethinking about the basic human rights of individuals. Amnesty International has been pointing out the violations of human rights in different countries of the world. Its emphasis has exclusively been on the violation of rights by state agencies. In the recent past, it has started including cases of terrorist group violating the rights of individuals. Two aspects of these rights were prominently noted. First, no one should be punished except through due process of law, and second, no law should violate human rights to life and livelihood, to freedom of speech, to profess any religion, etc.

NEW DIMENSIONS OF HUMAN RIGHTS

While good progress has been made in the direction of protecting human rights, lot needs to be done. Violence against poor, women, children, social deviants, people pursuing certain occupations or having certain biological abnormalities, are common even today, one has to accept that the concept of human rights covers only a very restricted area of concern. New problems have now started coming up before humanity. The problem is no longer confined to the rights of individuals. The new problems raise the spectre of the anihilation of not only humanity but all forms of life from the surface of the earth. It is the problem of eco-disaster that man has incessantly worked for the last two to three centuries—perhaps unknowingly or because of his over confidence in his capacity to control nature.

One of the most fundamental human rights is the right to life. In fact all other rights of man are derivatives of this right. Right to liberty, property, belief and faith have no meaning if the very survival of man is at stake. And the need to incorporate human survival as a right which no individual or institution can violate, is now urgent because environmental dangers are real.

In this paper, an attempt is made to bring out the rationale for including ecological balance and environmental cleanliness as a human right.

ECOLOGICAL BALANCE AS A HUMAN RIGHT

According to the Qaice theory of the evolution of the earth, each phase and stage of evolution provided the basic conditions, *i.e.*, the environment for the next phase or stage. A particular life form emerged because favourable conditions—physical, chemical and biological, were present. Human being emerged as the ultimate product of the evolutionery process because other forms of life were already there. Without these less evolved forms of life, take gorillas, man would have not come into being.

He could have not evolved from fish or frog. Thus, man the most advanced form of life on the surface of the earth can trace his origin to unicell life.

He can exist only so long as the environment in which he evolved remains more or less the same. The land, the water, the air, the plants, the animals and everything else support man as man supports them. No element of the earth system can perhaps sustain itself for to long, without the rest of the elements. May be, in the short run, its ill effects may not be visible. But in the long run they cannot be avoided.

The evolutionary processes have also endorsed each life form with enherent carrying and assimilative capacities. There is built in flexibility and tolerance capacity. Environmental changes up to a limit do not affect the natural systems including human beings adversely in the short run. Any pollution at a minor scale is purified by the system. But if it goes beyond its assimilative capacity, it suffers damages which cannot be repaired.

Nature has developed, again through the evolutionary process, a critical balance in its various elements. *For example,* the air must have 21 per cent oxygen, 78 per cent nitrogen and 1 per cent other gases. Without this constitution, human life will not be possible. And before the human life came into being, such a mixture did not exist. The plants produce oxygen; they also absorb nitrogen. The production and consumption of various constituent of the air by different life forms is so steady and balanced, that the overall constitution of the air remains the same. What if plants do not release oxygen ? Or they do not absorb nitrogen? If the percentage of oxygen in the atmosphere declines, man will suffocate to death; if it increases fire will burn every thing. There is water balance, air balance, heat balance, etc. Is it unscientific to think of life balance also wherein all life forms are interdependent. None can live long without other life form. Only minor deviations within tolerable limits can be taken care of by the nature.

If right to life is the most basic of the human rights, and life depends on ecological balance and environmental quality, then any action that destroys ecology and environment is against human rights. Each individual and community has a right over the natural environment. This right is the most fundamental one. None can trample it without injuring the interests of other human beings. Thus for the survival of humanity, the maintenance of ecological balance is a must.

Laws are quite effective instruments to protect human rights. They might be international conventions, or local Panchayat rules, constitutions or parliamentary enactments. In the recent past, several international treaties have been signed and national governments have enacted laws to protect the environment. Agenda 21 signed by the members of the United Nations at Rio in 1992 and a plethora of laws to check air, water, land, noise, biospheric pollutions have been passed by the national governments. But their impacts are not great because ecology and environment has not yet became a part of human right. The laws passed so far, are only adhoc reactions of the society to the deteriorating living conditions. It is still customary to evaluate the damage caused to ecology and environment in terms of money. Those who have money can violate the inviolatable nature's laws. The term 'compensation' or 'polluters must pay' reflect the tendency to monetize human rights. Human rights are beyond monetized evaluation; they are invaluable and hence cannot be trampelled.

In civilizationally primitive but culturally advanced societies of yesteryears, nature was never treated as property. It was not owned by individuals nor anyone could sell it for profit. It was one area of human life wherein everyone was equal. Land belonged to the community, and so did the water, plants and the whole nature. Today, the situation is just the other way round. We call those communities which still adhere to the old principles as backward. Most of these communities have been anihilated. Millions of people have been not like birds so that their habitat could be alienated. Is it not tragic that the new world has been created on the graves of the old world; the old which lived in harmony with nature.

Man had acquired all necessary experimental knowledge to enable him to interact with nature and his fellow human beings positively. That experimental knowledge was interwoven in the religious tradition, folk .love and cultural values. There was no need for a law to prohibit tree cutting, *for example,* because no body will cut a tree. In fact emphasis was laid on planting trees, on rituals that indicated and expressed in day today life, the interdependence between man and nature.

In India, the natural phenomena were also the cultural and religious phenomena. Every mountain, hill, river forest, lake, and even tree was associated with some god, ancestor or a *rishi*. Defiling these phenomena was tantamount to religious sacrilege. The rituals which formed integral part of birth, marriage, death and other ceremonies, were not based on blindfaith, they all had scientific basis. But the naive belief in the virtues of rationalism and the scientific temper which flowed from the cartesian world view resulted in a tendency to regard all religious beliefs and practices as old fashioned and inconsistent with what has come to be known as 'modern' or 'scientific outlook'. It is unfortunate that the modern educated man is uncomfortable with his past traditions and values; he considers ancient religious texts to be irrelevant and he interprets them in modern contexts to debunk them as 'fresh' strange as it may seen there are people who burn *Manusmriti, Ramayan, Gita* and *Vedas* in India because they have references which have allegedly harmed interests of one group of people or the other, in the past. They rarely realize the advancements these text represented at the time of writing, and the internal value they contain in abundance. If nothing new has emerged to improve upon them in the light of the new social and cultural realities it is not their fault. By burning these books, they burn themselves, they burn their history and ancestry.

Laws to enforce ecological balance and environmental quality was not needed in the past. The lift style of the people ensured these basic human needs. The modern man having done away with his past tradition and freedom needs formal laws. He needs some one to tell him what to do and what not to do. He has become so irresponsible towards himself and his fellow brings that he needs policemen to stop him from doing wrong to his own future, to his own programmes, to his own race, and to himself.

He wants material goods at all costs, even at the cost of environment and his children's future. He, no more sees in long terms. He wants everything in the shortest possible time. He thinks future will take care of itself; and feels that future generations will be better equipped to handle their own problems.

The environmental laws which have been passed and enforced are not based on the recognition of clean environment as a human right. It is based on the fact pollution causes diseases, ill health and increases medical expenses. Because it is costly so it should be checked. It is being measured in terms of monetary cost and price. The question of biodiversity is important only because man is yet to know what benefits he can derive from the unknown plants and animals we do not see plants and animals as necessary elements of the total environment for better future of man.

CAN NATURE GO TO COURT ?

India has a law under which the temple properties belong to the diety. They cannot be alienated. They can only be used. In the event of any dispute, one of the two contestants is the diety. Someone who manages the temple property on behalf of the diety fights the case. The final decision is in favour or against the diety. The diety represents the faith of the people. Freedom to choose one's faith is a human right.

Similarly, clean environment represents being the basic survival need of humanity, it is a human right. Clean environment cannot be ensured without ecological balance, and hence ecological balance is a human right.

No one can take away the ecological rights of others. In fact, no one can own nature. It must belong to all people and all living things, and it must be managed by human beings as custodians of the earth.

There is thus a need to broaden the scope of human rights to include in it the right to ecological balance and clean environment. Fortunately, the NGO's all over the world consider nature as commons property and have been fighting against governments and private companies who treat nature as Real Estate. Once, nature is accepted as a human right, the cause of humanity will be served better.

NEED FOR ENVIRONMENTAL EDUCATION

Compliance of laws connot be ensured without appropriate education. Many of this environmental laws the world over are known for breach more than for compliance. People consider these laws to be irritants and hinderances in the success of their pet projects. They try to circumvent them; beneath the superficial compliance, there is substantive breach.

Even human rights, as they are conceived at present, are not observed well. Hence so much ontery. Violence is the major source of breach of human rights and laws. Our TV, radio and other mass media preach violence, and show how violence is perpetrated day and night. This is informal education that we get from our early childhood.

When we look at the family education, the situation is getting from bad to worse. Earlier, we had joint families. The new generation had its roots in the past. We then became nucleated family. When the children of these famalies grew up, they know the grand parents only by pictures, if at all. They lost touch with the past. Now there is a trend of single parent families, leaving the children to the care of the orphonage and governmental institution. The children of such families tend to lose their present as well as the future. Will such children, on becoming adults, care for the law and human rights? What type of education these children receive ?

Here is a dilemma for education in general and environmental education in particular. Environmental education is not confined to man-nature relationship alone; it also takes care of the relationship of man with his fellow human beings. Without education, seen in its broader perspectives, there can be no way of enforcing a moral and ethical code of conduct which alone can ensure compliance with protect the human rights no matter how one defines it.

3

POLITICS WITH CONSCIENCE

*Vaclav Havel**

As a boy, I lived for sometime in the country and I clearly remember an experience from those days : I used to walk to school in a nearby village along a cart track through the fields and, on the way, see on the horizon a huge smokestack of some hurriedly built factory, in all likelihood in the service of war. It spewed dense brown smoke and scattered it across the sky. Each time it saw, it, I had an intense sense of something profoundly wrong, of humans soiling the heavens. I have no idea whether there was something like a science of ecology in those days; if there was, I certainly knew nothing of it. Still that 'soiling the heavens' offended me spontaneously. It seemed to me that, in it, humans are guilty of something, that they destroy something important, arbitrarily disrupting the natural order of things, and that such things cannot go unpunished. To be sure, my revulsion was largely aesthetic; I knew nothing then of the noxious emissions which would one day devastate our forests, exterminate game and endanger the health of people.

If a medieval man were to see something like that suddenly on the horizon—say, while out hunting—he would probably thing it the work of the Devil and would fall on his knees and pray that he and his kin be saved.

What is it, actually, that the world of the medieval peasant and that of a small boy have in common? Something substantive, I think, both the boy and the peasant are fare more intensely rooted in what some philosophers call 'the natural world', or *Lebenswelt,* than most modern adults. They have not yet grown alienated from the world of their actual

* Vaclav Havel is a poet, a play right. He was the President of Czechoslovakia until its division in 1992.

personal experience, the world which has its morning and its evening, its *down* (the earth) and its *up* (the heavens), where the sun rises daily in the east, traverses the sky and sets in the west, and where concepts like 'at home' and 'in foreign parts', good and evil, beauty and ugliness, near and far, duty and work, still mean something living and definite. They are still rooted in a world which knows the dividing line between all that is intimately familiar and appropriately a subject of our concern, and that which lies beyond its horizon, that before which we should bow down humbly because of the mystery about it.

The natural world, in virtue of its very being, bears within it the presupposition of the absolute which grounds, delimits, animates and directs it, without which it would be unthinkable, absurd and superfluous, and which we can only quietly respect. Any attempt to spurn it, master it or replace it with something else, appears, within the framework of the natural world, as an expression of *hubris* for which humans must pay a heavy price, as did Don Juan and Faust.

To me, personally, the smokestack soiling the heavens is not just a regrettable lapse of a technology that failed to include 'the ecological factor' in its calculation, one which can be easily corrected with the appropriate filter. To me it is more, the symbol of an age which seeks to transcend the boundaries of the natural world and its norms and to make it into a merely private concern, a matter of subjective preference and private feeling, of the illusions, prejudices and whims of a 'mere' individual. It is a symbol of an epoch which denies the binding importance of personal experience—including the experience of mystery and of the absolute—and displaces the personally experinced absolute as the measure of the world with a new, man-made absolute, devoid of mystery, free of the 'whims' of subjectivity and as such, impersonal and inhuman. It is the absolute of so called objectivity : the objective, rational cognition of the scientific model of the world.

Modern science, constructing its universally valid image of the world, thus crashes through the bounds of the natural world which it can understand only as a prison of prejudices from which we must break out into the light of objectively verified truth. The natural world appears to it as no more than an unfortunate left-over from our backward ancestors, a fantasy of their childish immaturity. With that, of course, it abolishes as mere fiction even the innermost foundation of our natural world; it kills God and takes his place on the vacant throne so that henceforth it would be science which would hold the order of being in its hand as its sole legitimate guardian and be the sole legitimate arbiter of all relevant truth. For after all, it is only science that rises above all individual subjective truths and replaces them with a superior, trans-subjective, trans-personal truth which is truly objective and universal.

Modern rationalism and modern science, though the work of man that, as all human works, developed within our natural world, now systematically leave it behind, deny it, degrade and defame it—and, of course, at the same time colonize it. A modern man, whose natural world has been properly conquered by science and technology, objects to the smoke from the smokestack only if the stench penetrates his apartment. In no case, though, does he take offence at it *metaphysically* since he knows that the factory to which the smokestack belongs manufactures things that he needs. As a man of the technological era, he can conceive of a remedy only within the limits of technology—say, a catalytic scrubber fitted to the chimney.

Lest you Misunderstand : I am not proposing that humans abolish smokestacks or prohibit science or generally return to the Middle Ages. Besides, it is not by accident that some of the most profound discoveries of modern science render the myth of modern science render the myth of objectivity surprisingly problematic and, via a remarkable detour, return us to the human subject and his world. I wish no more than to consider, in a most general and admittedly schematic outline, the spiritual framework of modern civilization and the source of its present crisis. And though the primary focus of these reflections will be the political rather than ecological aspect of this crisis, I might, perhaps, clarify my starting point with one more ecological example.

For centuries, the basic component of European agriculture had been the family farm. In Czech, the older term for it was *grunt*—which itself is not without its etymological interest. The word, taken from the German Grund, actually means ground or foundation and, in Czech, acquired a peculiar semantic colouring. As the colloquial synonym for 'foundation', it points out the 'groundedness' of the ground, its indubitable, traditional and prespeculatively given authenticity and veridicality. Certainly, the family farm was a source of endless and intensifying social conflict of all kinds. Still, we cannot deny it one thing: it was rooted in the nature of its place, appropriate, harmonious, personally tested by generations of farmers and certified by the result of their husbandry. It also displayed a kind of optimal mutual proportionality in extent and kind of all that belonged to it; fields, meadows, boundaries, woods, cattle, domestic animals, water, toads and so on. For centuries no farmer made it the topic of a scientific study. Nevertheless, it constituted a generally satisfactory economic and ecological system, within which everything was bound together by a thousand threads of mutual and meaningful connection, guaranteeing its stability as well as the stability of the product of the farmer's husbandry. Unlike present-day 'ago-business', the traditional family farm was energetically self-sufficient. Though it was subject to common calamities, it was not guilty of them—unfavourable weather, cattle disease, wars and other catastrophes lay outside the farmer's province.

Certainly, modern agricultural and social science could also improve agriculture in a thousand ways, increasing its productivity, reducing the amount of sheer drudgery, and eliminating the worst social inequities. But this is possible only on the assumption that modernization, too, will be guided by a certain humility and respect for the mysterious order of nature and for appropriateness which derives from it and which is intrinsic to the natural world of personal experience and responsibility. Modernization must not be simply an arrogant, megalomaniac and brutal invasion by an impersonally objective science, represented by a newly graduated agronomist or a bureaucrat in the service of the 'scientific world view'.

That is just what happened to our country: our word for it was 'collectivization'. Like a tornado, it raged through the Czechoslovak countryside thirty years ago, leaving not a stone in place. Among its consequences were, on the one hand, tens of thousands of lives devastated by prison, sacrificed on the altar of a scientific Utopia about brighter tomorrows. On the other hand, the level of social conflict and the amount of drudgery in the countryside did in truth decrease while agricultural productivity rose quantitatively. That, though, is not why I mention it. My reason is something else : thirty years after the tornado swept the traditional family farm off the face of the earth, scientists are amazed to discover what even a semiliterate farmer previously knew—that human beings must pay a heavy price for every attempt to abolish, radically, once for all and without trace, that humbly respected boundary of the natural world, with its tradition of scrupulous personal acknowledgement. They must pay for the attempt to seize nature, to leave not a remnant of it in human hands, to ridicule its mystery; they must pay for the attempt to abolish God and to paly at being God.

The price, in fact, fell due. With hedges ploughed under and woods cut down, wild brids have died out and, with them, a natural, unpaid protector of the crops against harmful insects. Huge unified fields have led to the inevitable annual loss of millions of cubic yards of topsoil that have taken centuries to accumulate; chemical fertilizers and pesticides have catastrophically poisoned all vegetable products, the earth and the waters. Heavy machinery systematically presses down the soil, making it impenetrable to air and thus infertile; cows in gigantic dairy farms suffer neuroses and lose their milk while agriculture siphons of ever more energy from industry—manufacture of machines, artificial fertilizers, rising transportation costs in an age of growing local specialization, and so on. In short, the prognoses are terrifying and no one knows that surprises coming years and decades may bring.

It is paradoxical : people in the age of science and technology live in the conviction that they can improve their lives because they are able to grasp and exploit the complexity of nature and the general laws of its functioning. Yet it is precisely these laws which, in the end, tragically catch up on them and get the better of them. People thought they could explain and conquer nature—yet the outcome is that they destroyed it and disinherited themselves from it. But what are the prospects for man 'outside nature'? It is, after all, precisely the sciences that are most recently discovering that the human body is actually only a particularly busy intersection of billions of organic microbodies, of their complex mutual contacts and influences, together forming that increadible megaorganism we call the 'biosphere' in which our planet is blanketed.

The fault is not one of science as such but of the arrogance of man in the age of science. Man simply is not God, and playing God has cruel consequences. Man has abolished the absolute horizon of his relations, denied his personal 'pre-objective' experience of the lived world, while relegating personal conscience and consciousness to the bathroom, as something so private that it is no one's business. Man rejected his responsibility as a 'subjective illusion'—and in place of it installed what is now proving to be the most dangerous illusion of all : the fiction of objectivity stripped of all that is concretely human, of a rational understanding of the cosmos, and of an abstract schema of a putative 'historical necessity'. As the apex of it all, man has constructed a vision of a purely scientifically calculable and technologically achievable 'universal welfare', demanding no more than that experimental institutes invent it while industrial and bureaucratic factories turn it into reality. That millions of people will be sacrificed to this illusion in scientifically directed concentration camps is not something that concerns our 'modern man' unless by chance he himself lands behind barbed wire and is thrown drastically back upon his natural world. The phenomenon of empathy, after all, belongs with that abolished realm of personal prejudice which had to yield to science, objectivity, historical necessity, technology, system and the *apparat*—and those, being impersonal, cannot worry. They are

---

No evil has ever been eliminated by suppressing its symptoms. We need to address the cause itself.

abstract and anonymous, ever utilitarian and thus also ever a priori innocent.

And as for the future? Who, personally, would care about it or even personally worry about it when the perspective of eternity in one of the things locked away in the bathroom, if not expelled outright into the realm of fairy tales ? If a contemporary scientist thinks at all of what will be in two hundred years, he does so solely as a personally disinterested observer who, basically, could not care less whether he is doing research on the metabolism of the flea, on the radio signals of pulsars or on the global reserves of natural gas. And a modern politician? He has absolutely no reason to care especially if it might interfere with his chances in an election, as long as he lives in country where there are elections.

A Czech Philosopher, Vaclav Belohradsky, suggestively unfolded the thought that the rationalistic spirit of modern science, founded on abstract reason and on the presumption of impersonal objectivity, has, beside its father in the natural sciences, Galileo, also a father in politics—Machiavelli, who first formulated, albeit with an undetone of malicious irony, a theory of politics as a rational tenchnology of power. We could say that, for all the complex historical detours, the origin of the modern state and of modern political power may be sought precisely here, that is, once again in a moment when human reason begins to 'free' itself from the human being as such, from his personal experience, personal conscience and personal responsibility and so also from that to which, within the framwork of the natural world, all responsibility is uniquely related, his absolute horizon. Just as the modern scientists set apart the actual human being as the subject of the lived experience of the world, so ever more evidently, do both the modern state and modern politics.

As Belohradsky points out, the depersonalization of power and its conquest of human conscience and human speech have been successfully linked to an extra-European tradition of a 'cosmological' conception of the empire (identifying the empire, as the sole true centre of the world, with the world as such, and considering the human as its exclusive property). But, as the totalitarian systems clearly illustrate, this does not mean that the modern impersonal power is itself an extra-European affair. The truth is the very opposite : it was precisely Europe, and the European West, that provided and frequently forced on the world all that today has become the basis of such power : natural science, rationalism, scientism, the industrial revolution, and also revolution as such, as a fanatical abstraction, through the displacement of the natural world to the bathroom down to the cult of consumption, the atomic bomb and Marxism. And it is Europe—democratic western Europe—which today stands bewildered in the face of this ambiguous export.

The contemporary dilemma, whether to resist this reverse expansionism of its erstwhile export or to yield to it, attests to this. Should rockets, now aimed at Europe thanks to its export of spiritual and technological potential, be countered by similar and better rockets, thereby demonstrating a determination to defend such values as Europe has left, at the cost of entering into an utterly immoral game being forced upon it ? Or should Europe retreat, hoping that the responsibility for the fate of the planet demonstrated thereby will infect, by its miraculous power, the rest of the world ?

I think that, with respect to the relation of Western Europe to the totalitarian systems, no error could be greater than the one looming largest : that of a failure to understand the totalitatrian systems for what they ultimately are—a convex mirror of all modern civilization and a harsh, perhaps final call for a global recasting of that civilization's self-understanding. If we ignore that, then it does not make any essential difference which form Europe's efforts will take. It might be the form of taking the totalitarian systems, in the spirit of Europe's our rationalistic tradition, as some locally idiosyncratic attempt at achieving 'general welfare', to which only men of ill—will attribute expansionist tendencies. Or, in the spirit of the same rationalistic tradition, though this time in the Machiavellian conception of politics as the technology of power, one might perceive the totalitarian regimes as a purely external threat by expansionist neighbours who can be driven back within acceptable bounds by an appropriate demonstration of power, without having to be considered more deeply. The first alternative is that of the person who reconciles himself to the chimney belching smoke, even though that smoke is ugly and smelly, because in the end it serves a good purpose, the production of commonly needed goods. The second alternative is that of the man who thinks that it is simply a matter of a technological flaw, which can be climinated by technolocial means, such as a filter or a scrubber.

The reality, I believe, is unfortunately more serious. The chimney 'soiling the heavens' is not just a technologically corrigible flaw of design, or a tax paid for a better consumerist tomorrow, but a symbol of a civilization which has renounced the absolute, which ignores the natural world and disdains its imperatives. So, too, the totalitarian systems warn of something far more serious than Western rationalism is willing to admit. They are, most of all, a convex miror of the inevitable consequnces of rationalism, a grotesquely magnified image of its offshoot of its own development and an ominous product of its own crisis. Those regimes are not merely dangerous neighbours and evenless some kind of an avant-garde of world progress. Alas, just the opposite : they are the avant-garde of a global crisis of this civilization, first European, then Euro-American, and ultimately global. They are one of the possible futurological studies of the Western World, not in the sense that one day they will attack and conquer it, but in a far deeper sense—that they illustrate graphically to what the 'eschatology of the impersonal', as Belohradsky calls it, can lead.

It is the total rule of a bloated, anonymously bureaucratic power, not yet irresponsible but already operating outside all conscience, a power grounded in an omnipresent ideological fiction which can rationalize anything without ever having to brush against the truth. Power as the omnipresent monoploy of control, repression and fear; power which makes thought, morality and privacy a state monopoly and so dehumanizes them; power which long since has ceased to be the matter of a group of arbitarary rulers but which, rather, occupies and swallows up everyone so that all should become integrated within it, all least through their silence. No one actually possesses such power, since it is the power itself which possesses everyone; it is a monstrosity which is not guided by humans but which, on the contrary, drags all persons along with its 'objective' self-momentum—objective in the sense of being cut off from all human standards, including human reason and hence entirely irrational—to a terrifying, unknown future.

Let me repeat : it is a great reminder to contemporary civilization. Perhaps somewhere there may be some generals who think it would be best to dispatch such systems from the face of the earth and then all would be well. But earth and then all would be well. But that is no different from an ugly woman trying to get rid of her ugliness by smashing the mirror which reminds her of it. Such a 'final solution' is one of the typical dreams. of impersonal reason—capable, as the term 'final solution' graphically reminds us, of transforming its dreams into reality and thereby reality into a nightmare. It would not only fail to resolve the crisis of the present world but, assuming anyone survived at all, would only aggravate it. By burdening the already heavy account of this civilization with further millions of dead, it would not block it essential trend to totalitarianism but would rather accelerate it. It would be a Pyrrhic victory, because the victors would emerge from a conflict inevitably resembling their defeated opponents far more than anyone today is willing to admit or able to imagine. Just as a minor; *example:* imagine what a huge Gulag Archipelago would have to be built in the West, in the name of country, democracy, progress and war discipline, to contain all who refuse to take part in the effort, whether from naivety, principle, fear or ill-will !

4

SOCIAL ECOLOGY AND ENVIRONMENTAL LAW

*Ben Boer**

INTRODUCTION

(i) Environmental Law and Policy

In environmental decision-making, it is often difficult to keep legal and policy issues separate. Lawyers representing the various interests in any given environmental dispute often find themselves venturing into the realm of policy, because many decisions, made within a legal framework, tend to turn on what type of environmental/social/economic policy should be pursued by government, industry and the community. Because of this blurring of the distinction between law and policy the values of an affected community can and arguably ought to play a fundamental role in environmental decision making. This is not to say that the distinction between law and policy is always clear in other areas of law. However, environmental law, by its very nature, makes the distinction less clear.

The fact that *value questions are involved* is also the reason that environmental decision-making so often causes deep social divisions and widespread conflict. One of the reasons for this is *that the "affected community" in environmental disputes is generally much more extensive than in other kind of legal disputes.* As will be seen later, the use of the term "community" can be extended from human community to the biotic

* Ben Boer is Senior Lecturer, School of Law, Macquarie University.

community which includes human beings as well as the non-living elements of an environment. Environmental disputes often touch upon human feelings rather than, or in addition to, property or financial interests. These feelings do not necessarily depend on any physical proximity or financial connection, and can be "experienced" simply by hearing about an environmental problem, for example through the media.

Given that value questions are often central to environmental disputes, it is appropriate for *lawyers and others involved in environmental decision making to investigate existing decision-making processes in order to determine how adequately these value questions are addressed* and whether or not they ought to be conceived of in different framework from the present one.

(ii) Definitions and Distinctions

Some distinctions must be drawn here between the terms "Enviroment", "environmentalism" and "ecology". "Environment" has become a popular term which from a scientific point of view is taken to mean everything that is physically external to the organism; organisms of course include human beings.[1] When taking of the social environment metaphysical and aesthetic aspects are called into play, to do with human relationships, perceptions of natural beauty and human-created beauty (buildings, etc.). In the philosophical literature, there seem to be two streams of thought on environment and environmentalism. *For example,* Naess identifies a *shallow environmentalism* where conservationist and preservationist policies are *based on considerations of human welfare and human interest, and a deep environmentalism. where nature is said to have an intrinsic value.*[2] *The shallow type of environmentalism is depicted by Bookchin as "a mechanistic, instrumental outlook that see nature as a passive habitat composed of objects such as animals, plants, minerals, and the like that must merely be rendered more serviceable for human use," thus reducing nature to a storage bin of "natural resources" or "raw materials"*. Bookchin goes on to state:

> "Environmentalism does not question the most basic premise of the present society, notably, that humanity must dominate nature; rather it seeks to facilitate that notion by developing techniques for diminishing the hazards caused by the reckless despoaliation of the environment."[3]

These conflicts have also been analysed in terms of shallow and deep ecology. Shallow ecology reflects the idea that humans can control and manage the physical world, and should do so. Deep ecology takes a broader approach; it views the environment from the perspective of the universe and the earth where humans are only one element in the system.[4]

The term "ecology" has been discussed as follows

> "... ecology deals with the dynamic balance of nature with the interdependence of living and nonliving things. Since nature also includes humanity's role in the natural world-specifically, the character, form, and structure of humanity's relationship with other species and with the inorganic substrate of the biotic environment. From a critical viewpoint, ecology opens to wide purview the vast disequilibrium that has emerged from humanity's split with the natural world. One of nature's very unique species, *homo sapiens,* has slowly and painstakingly developed from the natural world into a unique social world of its own. As both worlds interact with each other through the highly complex phases of evolution, it has become as important to speak of a social ecology as to speak of a natural ecology."[5]

Thus at present we have two divergent branches of ecology, one being the interrelationship between organisms and their environment, known as scientific or natural ecology, the other being the interrelationship of humans with their environment, known as human or social ecology.[6]

The term "ecological values" as used here is broadly defined to mean those values associated with both human and non-human perspectives of the environment. It thus encapsulates the "deep" environmental perspective and is co extensive with the concept of ecocentrism. The terms "ecological values" and "ecological ethic" are generally used in the body of this work in order to reflect an integrated view of human and the natural realm, not withstanding that many of the writers referred to use the terms "environmental values" and "environmental ethic".

Ecocentrism and technocentrism (or anthropocentrism) must also be properly distinguished. The ecocentric mode is said to be based on the supposition of a natural order where all things moved according to the natural law and a delicate and perfect balance was maintained up to the point where humans entered the scene "with all their ignorance and presumption."[7] Ecocentrism would define environment as a community or system which includes all living things as well as the air, water and soil that is their habitat. The technocentric mode is characterised by the application of rational and "value-free" scientific and managerial techniques by a professional, elite, who regard the environment as neutral stuff from which humans can properly shape their destinies.[8] It dictates that decisions are centred on human needs and on the human environment which are more immediately important for humans). Thc technocentric mode is reflected in most legal defnitions of the environment, to be discussed later.

These positions of ecocentrism and technocentrism are of course not fixed and immutable. Within each position there are degrees of perception and attitude. O'Riordan and Turner point out that the unbridled technocentrist, who is interventionist, optimistic about human capabilities, and resistant to alternatives, is a dying breed, even though he or she helped make possible the prosperity found in many industrialised nations. They maintain that not only is a broader and more detailed scientific understanding necessary for future technocentrists, but with that understanding "must come a sympathy if not wholehearted support for the feeling of groups identified as 'ecocentrists'.[9]

The concept of social ecology advanced in this article, in which human and natural realms are seen as part of the same ecological order, may well be able to accommodate the various positions found within the technocentric or anthropocentric modes.

The concept of "values" presents a number of problems when dealing with environmental issues. There is a tendency to look at those values which can be measured in some "concrete" way as being the most important. *For example,* Hundloe[10] identifies three broad categories: social value, economic value and financial value. However, he recognises that :

> There is, obviously, what we might term 'ecological' value or 'intrinsic' value associated with natural environments. As the aim of this paper is to deal with 'human' values (how human beigns value natural environments) ecological value will only be considered in the context of human values. It is for others to put the case for ecological value.

This omission of ecological values is at once an illustration of the general thrust of this article, the ecological values are often excluded from the decision-making process as well as representing a confusion—as to what ecological values are and how they can be evaluated. It will be seen that the values made explicit through the concept of social ecology are not, and should not be seen as, separate from the "human" values.

(iii) The Environmental Debate

In the past two decades there has been a proliferation of legislation, policy statements, conferences and seminars on environmental decision-making throughout the world. With the introduction of the National Environmental Policy Act, 1969 (NEPA) in the United States, environmental management was no longer seen to be limited to matters of physical resources but was extended to the effect of decisions on both the human population and the rest of the biological community. It could be said that we are in a critical stage of transformation from the period of the "economic human", represented by the several hundred years of industrial revolution, to the time of the "ecological human". Transformations have been identified in a whole range of human endeavours, including politics, economics and philosophy. Just what such transformations entail, or should entail, is the subject of a good deal of debate amongst philosophers. Some of this debate centres on the question of "paradigm shifts".[11]

A paradigm can be defined as a scheme for understanding and explaining certain aspects of reality.[12] Paradigm shifts can be described by models which detail, for example, the dominant paradigms found in a society or community. These models list a range of assumptions about human society and human attitudes towards particular matters, this is often done by means of a table or chart. Opposite the assumptions are found the changes that are seen to be taking place over a particular period. These changes or paradigm shifts strive to demonstrate that new attitudes and attributes are being formed or acquired.

In the environmental area, these paradigms are depicted by Cotgrove and Duff as a dominant social paradigm in conflict with an alternative environmental paradigm. They hypothesise "that these two belief structures are internally consistent and strongly held, so that conflict between advocates of each is inevitable." Thus

> the debate about environmental issues becomes a dialogue of the blind talking to the deaf. It is such experiences ... which contribute to the decline in political legitimacy, a falling off in support for traditional political parties and processes, and an increase in direct action.[13]

Many decisions have become more significant because of the vastly increased capacity of human beings to influence the nature of their environment, seen most graphically in pollution of the air, water, sea and land. Even though some of the technology exists to control if not eliminate this pollution (the most significant exception being disposal of nuclear waste), more often than not the political will to apply this technology through rigorously-enforced standards is lacking. This reluctance is coupled with inadequate techniques for assessing the effect of environmental degradation, and a consequent ignorance on the part of decision-makers of the long-term implications. Even where the effects are known, the present decision-making processes and administrative arrangements work to prevent the affected community from having access to sufficient information to allow individuals and groups to protest. This has resulted in insufficient pressure being placed on politicians and agencies concerned with environmental control to ensure compliance with statutory requirements or to make those requirements more stringent. In addition, belief in the "technological flx" means that when some environmental disaster looms, decision-makers can rely once again on "science" to solve the problem. The irony is that where science might be able to solve the problem, it often could have prevented the problem in the first place if the correct motivation had been present. Thus one question to be answered is, what is the correct motivation for obtaining the proper design of, *for example,* production processes which otherwise produce pollution or other environmental degradation?[14] A further and more far-reaching question is, do we need the products which necessitate polluting proudction processes ?

Narrow y-based assessment systems have resulted in decision-makers not accounting for all the relevant factors in any particular environmental issue. In many countries this has led to the degradation of ecosystems and has severely affected the natural bases on which both human and non-human life depends. This is particularly, so in relation to matters such as soil erosion,[15] forest depletion over-fishing and pollution.[16] Many governments seem to fall into the trap, particularly in hard times, of trying to justify more, and more rapid, development of finite resources *(for example,* minerals and fossil fules) and the over-use of so called renewable resources, on the assumption that those resources are renewable promptly and automatically, and without significant environmental degradation. Perhaps the best example of this is in forestry.[17]

Early warnings given by such bodies as the Club of Rome[18] the United Nations Conference on the Human Environment[19] the editors of *The Ecologist*[20] and the International Council of Scientific Unions[21] among others, have resulted in widespread debate and concern. More recently the publication of the *World Conservation Strategy*[22] has sparked many national governments into initiating their own strategies *(for example,* in Australia, the National Conservation Strategy for Australia[23]).

The Global 2000 Report to the President[24] commissioned by President Carter in 1977, has had a profound effect in the United States and elsewhere, although the Reagan administration has down played its importance.

(iv) Multi-dimensional Issues

The modern environmental debate is inherently interdisciplinary in nature. Without this fundamental understanding, analysts working in various fields will miss vital implications of their work. *For example,* lawyers working in enviromental law need to become more aware of the ecological, sociological, political and economic dimensions of this area.[25] We also need to realise that the legal approach is not necessarily the most useful one in arriving at ecologically-acceptable decisions.

On the other hand, it is also necessary for workers in other fields to come to grips with the formal and informal decision-making processes embodied in environmental legislation and government policy at federal, State and local level, which can prohibit, control or encourage activities which impact on the environment. Certainly in Australia there is still a tendency for those working in disparate fields connected with the environment not to communicate effectively with one another, nor to attempt to gain an integrated understanding of the various elements which can be found in an issue of environmental concern. A recent report *Integrated Engergy-Economic-Environmental Model for Australia*[26] recognises and demonstrates the need for such an approach. In introducing their model the authors state at p. 2:

> Energy-economic-environmental systems need to be planned in the context of resource availability, social goals, and technical, economic and environmental values .... Difficulties of planning arise from problems of resolving conflicts in goals, institutional factors, and the synthesis of diverse types of data. Integrated models are designed to assist an understanding of interconnected economic, energy and environmental systems, and to generate policy alternatives.

We need to recognise that environmental decision-making is multi-dimensional, involving a choice of both social values and the weight to be given to those values :

> Environmental issues are "polycentric" and can be the subject of intense social conflict. Environmental values compete with other

> social, economic and political values in the making of policy. The identification of environmental values and the weight given to them is critical in the decision-making process. Technological and social change this century has necessitated a re-appraisal of old environmental values and the formulation of new ones. Environmental policy issues should be resolved in a forum which allows the representation of affected interests in the decision making process, and which allows debate on environmental values and their priority with respect to other values in the decision. The choice of values should be made by a majority of the representatives. This process will accommodate the changing social values in our community.[27]

A consequence of such a recognition is that new and more effective ways must be found to discern what the values of the community are. In the formulation of environmental policy as with any other, it can be argued that effective participation by broad cross-sections of the affected community can be vital in coming to an "acceptable" decision. By spreading the input, it is more likely that ecological values of a community will be represented and given weight. In order to arrive at the stage where effective community participation can take place, it will be necessary for the community to gain a more comprehensive understanding of the issues. This process of environmental education had been in train for quite some time, with the growth in number of environmental conservation organisations throughout the world, the introduction of environmental education programmes in schools and the proliferation of programmes in the mass media.[28]

In recent times, more people have become aware of the need for and the effect of political lobbying as an aspect of community participation. In the United States, *for example,* conservation organisations, such as the Sierra Club, have taken on a much more political role particularly in the face of drastic budget cuts and policy changes within the Environment Protection Agency.[28] Environmental law organisations such as the Natural Resources Defence Council have come to realise that direct political lobbying is as important as fighting actions in the courts. (See, *for example,* the launching through a national press conference by a broad coalition of groups of the document *Indictment : The Case Against Reagan's Environmental Record;* see also *The Reagan Energy Plan : A Major Power Failure.*[30])

In Australia, the Franklin-Lower Gordon dam issue prompted the Australian Conservation Foundation to enter into the political arena in the 1983 Federal election, threatening to stand conservation candidates in political seats if necessary.[31] On the same issue, the Tasmanian Wilderness Society also recognised the necessity of taking political action both in the building of the dam, primarily to gain media attention, and in lobbying activities. The director of that organisation personified this two-pronged approach by stepping out of goal on a charge of trespass on Hydroelectricity Commission—controlled land and into a seat in the Tasmanian Parliament. In short there is mounting demand for much broader community participation in environmental decision making.

EVALUATION PROCESSES AND DECISION-MAKING

This section outlines some of the problems with present processes of measuring the values represented by any particular environment or ecosystem. It is argued that the techniques of monetary cost-benefit analysis, shadow pricing and the methods of evaluation found in modern environmental impact assessment are often unsatisfactory because they have a tendency to reduce the range of factors taken into account in the decision making porcess. In Tribe's words, they can squeeze out "soft" but crucial information merely because it seems difficult to render commensurable with the "hard data".[32] That crucial information, as we will see, needs different techniques of evaluation, entailing deeper and broader forms of inquiry and an expanded understanding of what is included in "environment".

A. Limitations of the Economic Approach

(i) *Economics and Cost-Benefit Analysis*

The words "ecology" and "economics" share a common words Greek root *oikos* meaning "household"[33] O'Riordan contends that the original but now obsolete role of economics was the management of the household, a concept which could be applied to dispersed human communities, where management meant careful husbandry of resources (especially effort) within a harmonious pattern of relationships between interacting parties. He notes that there is a growing number of environmental economics who are pleading for a return to this obsolete economics, in the belief that sustained economics growth as currently practised is inimical to human well-being and incongruent with fundamental biophysical laws.[34] From the point of view of understanding some of the differences between the concerning of economists and ecologists it is useful to note the following

> Disagreements between economists and ecologists hinge largely on their differing perspectives of time, in general, 5-10 years is considered to be a long period by economists, but a short period by ecologists.[35]

Use of monetary cost-benefit analysis as a major basis for environmental decision-making has become rather old-fashioned being a relic of the 1950s and 1960s before other values were able to be more broadly understood by policy-makers, industrialists, the scientific community and the public generally.[36] The main problem of monetary cost-benefit analysis obviously lies in the difficulty of placing a monetary value on the various elements of the enviroment. As part of the environmental impact assessment process, however, cost-benefit analysis is often seen to play an important, though misplaced role.[37] (O'Riordan, *op. cit.*, p. 171; Daly, *op. cit.*, p. 172; Tribe, *op. cit.*, at 1319-20).

Pearce and Nash discuss the rationale of modern cost-benefit analysis, stating that it relates not to individual rational decisions about the gain or advantage and loss or disavantage, but to social decisions about matters which affect a group of individuals, whether the group inhabits a locality, region, state or nation. They argue that the characteristic of rationality of the individual faced by a decision extends to the social context :

> "if we leave a whole group of individuals to carry out their own 'personal' CBAs (cost benefit analyses) in respect of a given context we can simply aggregate the results to secure a social evaluation. Of course, we must know what it is we are aggregating. As we shall see it is not a set of political votes, and for very good reasons. What is being aggregated is a set of money valuations—all positive valuations would indicate that the persons expressing them reckon that the project has net benefits for them: all negative valuations would reflect net costs to the persons expressing them".[38]

In recognising that cost-benefit analysis rests on value judgments, they advocate a "value sensitivity" approach. This is basically done by making explicit the implicit value judgments found in conventions cost-benefit analysis and then showing how the outcome of a cost-benefit analysis varies with different value judgments. They argue that a process of monetary voting for and against a proposal in a way which allows individual preferences to be weighted by some "intensity" factor which is correlated with the individual's income is apparently superior to a political system of voting which is unable to reflect the intensity factor.

Pearce and Nash, whilst presenting perhaps one of the most advanced systems of cost-benefit analysis available, do not come to grips sufficiently with the problem of monetary evaluation of subjective environmental values. Cost-benefit analysis as practised is premised entirely on the values important to humans, for humans. It does appear not to admit of the possibility that non-human objects can be judged in any framework outside the human want-oriented perspective. In other words, any intrinsic value that a non-human object may be accorded is distorted or flattened into an aspect of human self-interest.[39] Nevertheless, within this monetary framework, Pearce has recognised that :

> "There are indications, no more than that, that an ethical shift is taking place. The new ethic commands us to consider the fact that trade-offs are all to easy to make when the gain is ours and the cost is someone else's. For the current generations, a situation where A gains and B loses at least implies a potential for A and B to negotiate or to establish protective laws. But the nature of the bargain is now one where the losers are future generation who, by definition, have no voice and hence no chance to alter the behaviour of current generations. In short, without an ethic of concern for the future, future generations near and distant may have to bear a disproportionate share of the costs of actions taken now."[40]

(ii) Shadow Pricing and Non-monetary Valuation

Application of cost-benefit techniques by, way of denoting monetary value to things that have no market prices, through "shadow-pricing" is also unsatisfactory. The calculation of shadow prices, after all, rests on the same basis as market prices: the desires of individuals. It is arguable that the only way in which the intensity of those desires can be effectively determined is by interviewing a representative sample of people.[41]

The intensity valuation by non-monetary means has been developed recently by Bennett to measure the "existence benefits" of continued preservation of a natural ecosystem; the area under study was the Nadgee Nature Reserve near Canberra. The methodology employed was to interview over 500 people in Canberra regarding their willingness to pay for the preservation of the area on the basis that they would not be likely to make any direct or indirect "use" of the area whatsoever.[42] Although, a Bennett recognises, there can be problems of bias evident in this kind of analysis, it appears that the results obtained can be useful to decision-makers when deciding to "manage" an area for natural values. The methodology can of course be extended to other kinds of environmental issues. One needs to bear in mind that there can be a real difference in the amount that a person is willing to pay for an "environmental good", which is related to income, and the amount for which a person is willing to sell or be compensated for an "environmental good". The latter can be much higher because it is more likely to include "irrational" desires such as emotional attachment to a view, the protection of wildife habitat, etc.[43] It is worth noting in passing that other non-monetary methods of evaluating visual qualities of landscape have recently been developed.[44]

(iii) Reduction to Dollars

Thus the use of a monetary-based value system of cost-benefit analysis as a basis for decision-making generally reduces ecologial values to the lowest common denominator of exchange: money.[45] That which cannot be reduced in such a way is in danger of being perceived as having no value and thus cannot be taken into account in any effective way in the decision-making process. Of course it is recognised that whether the monetary or non-monetary valuation is used, these methods are undeniably anthropocentric.

(iv) Cost-benefit Analysis and Environmental Impact Assessment

A reasonable amount of work has been done in Australia on the use of cost-benefit analysis in environmental impact assessment. A workshop organised by the Department of Home Affairs and Environment proposed in 1982 "that guidelines be produced to help in the application of cost-benefit techniques to improve environmental impact statements."[46] In the United States, these matters have progressed a little further. The Regulations to the National Environmental Policy Act 1969 (U.S.) (promulgated in 1978) make it explicit that cost-benefit analysis must, where appropriate, be included in environmental impact statements, as an aid in evaluating the environmental consequences of Federal agency actions. In addition, it should

> "discuss the relationship between that analysis and analysis of unquantified environmental impacts, values and amenities. Further, the weighing of the merits and drawbacks of the various alternatives need not be displayed in a monetary cost-benefit analysis and should not be when there are important qualitative considerations."

Finally,

"an environmental impact statement should at least indicate those considerations, including factors not relating to environmental quality, which are likely to be relevant and important to a particular decision."[47]

Thus at least in Frederally-required environmental impact statements in the United States, cost-benefit analysis is limited to the monetary kind, that is, it should be applied to those matters that can easily be quantified in dollars and cents. Other methods should be used for evaluating those matters which cannot be so translated.

(v) A Wilderness Example : South-West Tasmania

In evaluating a proposal for a dam in a wilderness area, such as in South-West Tasmania, there are particular factors which can be easily quantified, and thus easily subjected to cost-benefit analysis. These include the costs of initial planning, expenses related to political campaigns to convince the public of the merits or demerits of the proposal, costs of policing the dam site against protesters and costs of setting up special courts to deal with charges against protesters. The costs of construction are a separate expense which may or may not turn into a benefit, depending on the profitability of the development as a whole. The benefits include employment of construction workers, police and magistrates. Benefits also accrue to airlines, bus companies and railways, as well as fishing and tourboat operators hiring out their boats to demonstrators and others. Local commerce in close proximity to the dam site can supply foodstuffs and other commodities. Primary and secondary industries would also benefit directly through supply of construction materials. Conservation societies involved in organisation of protests employ more people, and in the longer term, local communities and the State benefit from tourism attracted to the wilderness area through this activity. All of these effects can potentially be subjected to monetary cost-benefit analysis, and certain conclusions may be able to be drawn for and against to proposal to build a dam.[48]

Some of the economic factors were the subject of a study by Kirkpatrick, for the Tasmanian Department of the Environment.[49] Kirkpatrick urged that the potential losses of wilderness areas which would result construction of the Lower Gordon dam :

> "...must be seen in the context of a rapidly growing number of wilderness users whose contribution to the Tasmanian economy is far from insignificant. At least 12,300 Tasmanians and 26,000 visitors ... ventured into the wilderness in 1978. If each user spent 100 dollars to gain access to and survive in the wilderness, and each of the dollars-spent generated another dollar through multiplier effects, approximately 8 million dollars would have been led into Tasmania".[50]

Studies of this kind can be of importance to preservation or conservation arguments. In the short-term at least, hard economic data is often seen to be best way to convince legislators and other decision makers of the demerits of a particular proposal. Therein lies a danger of legitimating

> "a system of discourse which so structures human thought and feelings as to erode, over the long run, the very sense of obligation which provided initial impetus for his own protective efforts."[51]

However, it is not only conservationists who employ this approach. *For example,* the Senate Select Committee on South West Tasmania Report and other Matters 1982 spends eight chapters on analysing the largely economic data on demand and supply of electricity and two chapters on "Other Matters". Yet it is precisely these "other matters" which the Senate Select Committee was in reality most concerned about. those "other matters" which are difficult, if not impossible, to quantify in this situation include the importance of archaeological finds in relation to Aboriginal occupation of the area[52] the value of the wilderness of fish, bird and other non-human life, and the psychological need for and emotional attachment of present and future human generations to the wilderness value of the area.[53]

In terms evalutating whether or not to retain a wilderness area of wild-wide significance, many conservationists would argue that the economic considerations are irrelevant. Yet the fact that these natural values are relegated to the category of "other matters" and dealt with after the economic considerations are spelled out reflects the conventional approach of adopting these considerations as the first tool for justifying a particular course to decision makers. This is not surprising, in terms of the distortions which Tribe describes as flowing from the human want-oriented perspective, discussed previously.[54]

B. Limitations of the Environmental Impact Approach

(i) The Anthropocentric Limitation

Environmental impact assessment has become a familiar technique since the passing of the National Environmental Policy Act (NEPA) in the United States in 1969. This technique is still regarded by many as the most comprehensive, effective and efficient method of evaluating the effects on the environment of development proposals. The method involve a much broader analysis than the weighing of monetary costs and benefits, although as we have seen, it can include it. The central section of NEPA is a 102. It says :

> "The Congress authorizes and directs that, to the fullest extent possible : (1) the policies regulations, and public laws of the United States shall be interpreted and administered in accordance with the policies set forth in this Act, and (2) all agencies of the Federal Government shall :
>
> (A) Utilize a systematic, interdisciplinary approach which will insure the integrated use of the natural and social science and the environmental design arts in planning and in decision-making which may have an impact on man's environment;
>
> (B) Identify and develop methods and procedures, in consultation with the Council on Environmental Quality established by Title II of this Act, which will insure that presently unquantified environmental amenities and values may be given appropriate consideration in descision-making along with economic and technical considerations;
>
> (C) Include in every recommendation or report on porposals for legislation and other major federal actions significantly affecting the quality of the human environment, a detailed statement by the responsible official on :
>
> *(i)* the environmental impact of the proposed action;
>
> *(ii)* any adverse environmental effects which cannot be avoided should the proposal be implemented;
>
> *(iii)* alternatives to the proposed action;
>
> *(iv)* the relationship between local and short-term uses of mans environment and the maintenance and enhancement of long term productivity, and

(v) any irreversible and irretrievable commitments of resources which would be involved in the proposed action should it be implemented."

The "detailed statement" [s. 102(C)] refers to what is now commonly called an environmental impact statement (EIS). In an early case under NEPA, Calvert Cliffs[55] the Atomic Energy Commission had continually asserted prior to NEPA that it had no statutory authority to concern itself with the adverse environmental effects of its actions.

> "Now, however, its hands are no longer tied. It is not only permitted, but compelled, to take environmental values into account."[56]

Notwithstanding this obligation, it becomes clear, on analysing NEPA and its regulations, that the legislation is largely anthropocentric. This is made quite explicit in the definition of "human environment" (reg. s. 1508. 14) :

> "Human Environment shall be interpreted comprehensively to include the natural and physical environment and the relationship of people with that environment. [See the definition of 'effects' (s. 1508. 8)]. This means that economic or social effects are not intened by themselves to require preparation of an environmental impact statement. When an environmental impact statement is prepared and economic or social and natural or physical environmental effects are interrelated, then the environmental impact statement will discuss all of these effects on the human environment."

The definition is not only anthropocentric, but narrowly so; economic and social effects are not intended by themselves to require an EIS. The legislation places humans apart from the natural order, as trustees of the environment for future generations, as planners and controllers of the earth[57] at least as far as jurisdiction allows.[58] This does not mean that the non-human aspects of the American environment are not to be protected; quite the contrary. What it does mean is that the non-human aspects are to be protected, preserved and enhanced through the Act only insofar as it suits the human members of the earth's community.

The Australian legislation does not fare much better. The definition of "environment" in the commonwealth and New South Wales Legislation as including "all aspects of the surroundings of man, whether affecting him as an individual or in his social groupings," (see Environment

Protection) (Impact of Proposals) Act 1975 (Cth) (Impact Act) and Environmental Planning and Assessment Act 1979 (N.S.W.) (E.P.A. Act) puts a decidedly humancentred stamp on the issue of environmental protection, planning and assessment. As Bates notes, definitions of "environment" in State legislation (with the exception of New South Wales), are cast more widely than the Commonwealth definition.[59] Whilst the Commonwealth and New South Wales definition is an example of the narrower concept of environment, it should be said that in examining the legislation in both jurisdictions, and the administrative procedures made under the Impact Act, it is clear that there is some concern for ecological, intrinsic values. For instance, in making a determination as to whether an EIS is required pursuant to the Impact Act, the administrative procedures require that the Minister or Department on behalf of the Minister shall take into account whether the proposed action may result in :

> "3.1.2 *(c)* a substantial impact on the ecosystems of an area;
> *(d)* a significant diminution of the aesthetic, recreational, scientific or other environmental quality, or value, of an area;
> *(f)* the endangering or further endangering of any species of fauna or flora;
> *(g)* important long term effects on the environment;
> *(h)* the degradation of the quality of the environment."

The other subclauses are to greater or lesser degrees, directly concerned with environment protection from a human-centred viewpoint. Of course there is no real quibble with the thrust of those remaining sections. The point at issue is what weight teach of these environmental and human effects or impacts will be given in any environmental impact statment that might be drawn up pursuant to these procedures, and more importantly, what weight teach will be given in the final decision.

In the New South Wales Legislation, the objects of the EPA Act (s. 5) are again largely anthropocentric. The objects of the Act, so far as is relevant here, are :

> "*(a)* To encourage—
> *(i)* the proper mangamement, development and conservation of natural and man-made resources, including agricultural land, natural areas, forests, minerals, water, cities, towns and villages for the purpose of promoting the social and economic welfare of the community and a better environment;

(ii) the promotion and co-ordination of the orderly and economic use and development of land;
(iii) the protection, provision, and coordination of communication and utility services;
(iv) the provision of land for public purposes;
(v) the provision and co-ordination of community services and facilities; and
(vi) the protection of the environment."

Where environment is mentioned (*(i)* and *(vi)*), it seems almost as if it has been tacked on as after thought in order to lend the legislation some validity. The emphasis certainly seems to be on "development".

One might not be tempted to accord this any great significance, if the former New South Wales Minister for Planning and Environment had not made the following statement :

> "Because of the sheer size and complexity of the system, and because planning controls often remain in force for many years, one can easily end up with a situation in which those controls no longer reflect present-day circumstances and present-day political priorities. This potentially gives rise to pressures and tensions. In recent years *for example,* employment has become a major public and political concern. Inevitably this has had implications for the planning system. It would appear that there are some people who seem to think that the major purpose of the Environmental Planning and Assessment Act is to provide a means of delaying or preventing development. In reality, s. 5 of the Act refers to 'promoting the social and economic welfare of the community and a better environment'. Therefore, *stimulating job-creating development is just as valid an object of the Act as is protecting the environment.* Ultimately, the balance between those objects (if they are in conflict) is a matter of political choice. One would be blinkered if it were not appreciated that because of the current economic climate, the Government has chosen to place a good deal of emphasis on job-creation".[60] (emphasis in original).

The use of "and" in the phrase "and a better environment" makes it clear that "a better environment" cannot be used as an alternative to "social and economic welfare;" rather the phrases should be read conjunctively.[61] The Minister's speech is certainly an example of the cavalier attitude that the New South Wales Government appears to have to its own environmental planning legislation.[62]

Examining the regulations under the EPA Act governing environmental impact assessment, the matters listed for inclusion have some conern for ecological values as well as values important for humans. (See, for example, regs 34, 56, 57). The question to be asked here is whether the environmental consultants and others involved in the preparation of EISs ought to be subjected to much closer direction as to what emphasis should be placed on ecological values. The judgments inherent in this process will largely reflect the subjective biases of the evaluators. Many would argue that complete objectively in these matters is impossible, even where the most "purely" scientific questions are involved.[63] Craig has analysed the concept of objectivity in terms of it having become a form of technological domination.[64] Her discussion leasds on the Bookchin's fundamental premise that "the domination of nature by man stems from the very real domination of human by human".[65] The upshot of these arguments is that in order for environmental decision-making processes to "properly" reflect ecological values, we should recognise that the evaluation of enviromental impacts is inherently subjective. Having established this, methods might then be evolved in order to put this principle into practice. The main difficulty here is the gap between the anthropocentric, utilitarian conception of the environment and the ecocentric intrinsic conception. How these conception, might be bought together is addressed below:

TECHNICAL AND LEGISLATIVE MODELS

Given the increasing awareness of environmental issues in the community and the increasing sophistication of techniques for evaluation of proposals, it is clear that no single strategy is in itself sufficient to answer the multi-dimensional problems confronting decision-makers. An integrative approach is certainly needed. To date we have largely operated in what Graig has characterised as the "technical" model of environmental decision making.[66] This model assumes that the issues involved can be treated as largely technical issues. It is based upon specific assumptions about the nature of citizens and society. Citizens are seen as alienated and privatised, primarily interested in acquisition of material goods. The technical model thus places the citizen in the role of a consumer, a role contrary to broad citizen participation in environmental decision-making. In analysing the in adequacies of the technical model she states.

"The application of a technical model of environmental policy-making has important implications for a modern democracy. In the first place, it inadequately identifies and under-represents policy issues in an environmental decision. Thus environmental problems, which affect the lives of many citizens, can be ignored or distorted by the technical model. The capacity to evolve long term environmental policy may be impeded. In the second place, there is little scope for citizen participation in decision-making and the ability of existing legislatures to reflect citizen values in these decisions can be seriously questioned."

Craig argues for a particular kind of "legislative" model of environmental decision making based on theories of participatory democracy which have the effect of—improving environmental decision-making :

> "The environmental and social consequences of policy decisions are integrally related. It is necessary for citizens and governments to depart from the consumer concept of citizenship in order for us to develop a non-exploitative approach to environmental issues. The involes a re-instatement of the ethical aspect of public life by applying a developmental of democracy. The developmental theory of democracy is directed to restoring the legitimacy of a dialogue on values amongst a politically active citizenry. It should provide a means for communication between all parties who participate in a decision, and gradually rebuild the importance of public life."[68]

The next section outlines some of the ways in which we can escape from the human-centred instrumentalist approach (the technical model of Craig's analysis) by means of ethical and possibly legal transformations.

SOCIAL ECOLOGY AND LAW

(i) Introduction

One of the central problems of evolving an ecocentric approach to environmental decision making is the separation between the realms of nature and human society. As Bookchin observes.

> "In view of the enormous dislocations that now confront us, our own era needs a more sweeping and insightful body of knowldege—scientific as well as social—to deal with our problems. Without renouncing the gains of earlier scientific and social theories, we must develop a more rounded critical analysis of our relationship with the natural world. We must seek the foundations for a more reconstructive

approach to the grave problems posed by the apparent 'contradictions' between nature and human society. We can no longer afford to remain captives to the tendency of the more traditional sciences to dissect phenomena and examine their fragments. We must combine them, relate them, and see them in their totality as well as their specificity."[69]

Bookchin goes on note the discipline of social ecology has been formulated to achieve this integration.

In applying social ecology to the environmental decision making process, it must be remembered that the role of law is only one factor in the multi-dimensional framework. Indeed, in its present stage of development, environmental law as a mechanism which functions to "administer" the environment, could be seen as being incompatible with the concept of social ecology. In order to achieve compatibility, environmental law, as it is found in legislation, policy and practice, needs to be informed by a clearly articulated ethic which is closely identified with and arises out of the concept of social ecology.

(ii) The Need for an Ecological Ethic

The concept of ecological ethics is not new.[70] However, with the notable exception of Tribe, there has been very little transference from philosophy to law in this area. Much of the environmental legislation that we have seen throughout the world in the past decade or two has been pragmatically oriented towards protection of the human environment, limited more by economic and political considerations than by technological inadequacies. Here, some recent conceptualisations of ecological ethics are analysed and evaluated.

In their work on *Human Chauvinsim and Environmental Ethics,* R. and V. Routley[71] state that the dominant Western ethical views concerning human relations with nature divide into three important traditions.[72]

> "a dominant tradition, the despotic tradition, with man as despot (or tyrant) and two lesser traditions, the stewardship position, with man as custodian, and the co-operative position, with man as perfector. Nor are these the only traditions; primitivism is another, and both Romanticism and mysticism have influenced Western views."

They argue that the dominant Western view

> "is simply inconsistent with an environmental ethic; for according

to it nature is the dominion of man and he is free to deal with it as he pleases (since-at least on the mainstream Stoic-Augustinian view, it exists only for his own sake), whereas on an environmental ethic man is not so free to do as she/he pleases".[73]

They posit that an alternative ethic is needed

"by a growing number of valuers because they have values, interests and new concerns of ecological sorts which do not fit in with, but conflict with, central features of prevailing Western ethics".[74]

They identify far-reaching cultural and ethical changes which could be said to represent a transformation of human consciousness in relation to valuation of the environment.

Thompson[75] argues that scientific theories have made if possible to challenge the human chainist view of the world, thus encouraging a new way of valuing ecology in stressing our dependence on natural systems and our close relationship with other forms of life, leading us to see ourselves as part of an interdependent web of living things and that our survival is bound up with that of the "lowliest" plants and animals.[76] Thompson goes on the argue that ethical revolution presupposes a social critique, the essence of which is summed up in the belief that the social world is linked to the domination of nature in such a way that the disappearance of one form of domination requires the removal of the other.[77] This is essentially the argument that Bookchin also puts forward.[78]

Birch and Cobb also discuss why a new ethic is necessary and why this ethic should go beyond anthropocentrism to include animal rights, human riths and the rights of the biosphere in general. They conclude :

"Despite the restricted role that ethical principles and arguments play in shaping behaviour, they remain important. It is unwise for those who are critical of inherited ethical and legal systems simply to abandon the field of ethics and law to anthropocentrism and to take up the task of formulating principles which do not depend on it.".[79]

(iii) Transcendence and Immanence

Social ecology would recognise that humans exist within the natural order. This recognition opens up the possibility of overcoming the difficulties of the dominant, anthropocentric approach to decision-making as well as avoiding the problems of ecocentrism ignoring the needs of humans.

Tribe,[80] discusses this possiblity in terms of a synthesis between transcendence and immanence. Transcendent consciousness :

> "characterisically perceives God as an other-wordly entity-one standing apart from and above the world. Genesis proclaims the sovereignty of God over the physical universe: it is but a small step to infer the dominion of man, as God's representative on earth, over all life ... so long as man is thought to stand apart from nature, and the universally divine in individual man apart from this more particular manifestation as a concrete social being, the manipulative stance toward the world of physical process and social structures, expressed respectively through the media of 'technology' and 'public policy', is likely to prove invincible."[81]

The opposite concept is that of immance, which

> "was exemplified by the pantheistic belief that all objects and places in the natural world possessed guardian spirits demanding propitiation as security against unspeakable harm".[82]

Neither conception was perceived as being satisfactory; transendence implied human manipulation of the world, whereas immanence implied that the existing order was to be treated as sacred, thus effectively

> "freezing the social evolution of humanity into its contemporary mold ... Unless evolving human consciousness and will are recognised as legitimate and indeed vital parts of the natural order, there can exist only sterility and paralysis, negating all possibility of critique and progress."[83]

He thus agrued for a synthesis of transcendence and immanence, of sacred observer and grand manipulator, thus allowing for evolving processes of interaction and change, the processes being made possible by a legal and constitutional framework for choice which should incorporate procedures for its own evolution. This synthesis would need to cut across what Tribe called the received categories of nature and culture, "for implicit in that classic dichotomy is a denial of any possible union between the immanent and the transcendent". He goes on to say :

> "To recognise that humanity is a part of nature and the natural order a constituent part of humanity is to acknowledge that something deeper and more complex than the customary polarities must be

articulated and experienced if the immanent and the transcendent are somehow to be united. At that crossoroads, conceptions like harmony, rootedness in history, connectedness with the furture, all seem more pertinent than the ultimately conventional concept of the natural."[84]

Up to this point, Tribe and Bookchin are more or less congruent with each other. What Tribe does not make explicit and Bookchin does, is that the present ecological crisis is a reflection of a crisis in social relations and that the human crisis finds its roots in the domination exercised by humans over each other. Liberating humans from domination by other humans as well as the human domination of nature is, Bookchin's formulation, a necessary precondition for the development of an ecological ethic which may in turn contribute to the evolution of an ecological society.

(iv) A New Ethic Outlined

In any ecological ethic that is evolved as a foundation for environmental law and environmental decision making, it would seem to be essential to be able to accommodate natural, human-built and social environments, in order to be consistent with the concept of social ecology. The beginnning of an answer might be found in Leopold's analysis.

> "An ethic, ecologically is a limitation on freedom of action in the struggle for existence. An ethic, philosophically, is a differentiation of social from antisocial conduct. These are two definitions of one thing. The thing has its origins in the tendency of interdependent individuals or groups to evolve modes of co-operation. The ecologist calls these symbioses. Politics and economics are advanced symbioses in which the original free-for-all competition has been replaced, in part, by co-operative mechanisms with an ethical content."

Leopold called for an extension of ethics to the land, so that human connection with the land is no longer a strictly economic relation entailing privileges but not obligations. He argued that all ethics so far evolved rest upon the single premise that individual humans are part of a community of interdependent parts; instinct prompts him or her to compete for a place in that community, but ethics prompts him or her to co-operate. "The land ethic simply enlarges the boundaries of the community to include soils, waters, plants and animals or collectively the land." A land ethic, in Leopold's formulation, could not prevent the alteration, management and use of soils, waters, plants and animals, but it affirmed their right to continued existence and in parts at least, in a natural state :

> "In short, a land ethic changes the role of *Homo sapiens* from conqueror of the land-community to plain member and citizen of it. It implies respect for... fellow members and also respect for the community as such."[86]

Put another way, the environment is not a commodity belonging to humans, but rather a community to which humans belong.[87] This is the ecocentric or social ecology approach, which is

> "characterised by the wholeness and integrity of humans and nature and by ecological egalitarianism or the equality of humans with other members of the Earth's ecosystem."[88]

Leopold's formulation of the land ethic is given practical application in this passage[89]

> "The 'key-log' which must be moved to release the evolutionary process for an ethic is simply this: quit thinking about land-use as solely an economic problem. Examine each question in terms of what is ethically and esthetically [sic] right, as well as what is economically expedient. *A thing is right when it tends to preserve the integrity, stability, and beauty of the biotic community. It is wrong when it tends otherwise."* (Emphasis added.)

An ethic such as this for the natural or non-human ernvironment could also be extended to the human environment, both built and social. However, there are a number of difficulties with this ethic as it stands. *For example,* natural ecosystems do not necessarily remain "stable" nor might it be desirable for them to do so. "Beauty" is apparently an entirely human conception and can change as the beholder changes. This is not to say that beauty should not play any role. Rather, it could be assumed that any particular natural environment has its own aesthetic qualities. "Integrity" would, however, seem to be worth retaining. In addition, related concepts such as cohesion and interdependence between parts of a community sufficient to keep it "whole" might provide a more adequate basis for such an ethic.

Thus if we adopted as a principle

> "that a decision is right when it tends to accord with a duty on humans to preserve the integrity, cohesion and interdependence of any community, including its human elements,"

then we may be moving towards an acceptable ethic which comprehends the whole environment. Such a formulation incroporates Tribe's idea that

> "the impulse that is felt by many as awe and respect for a vast canyon or a spider's web, has much in common with the sense of sanctity felt by others as they stand before the structures at Stonenge or the cathedral at Chartres."[90]

Such an ethic would not only be relevant to a decision as to whether or not to dam a river for hydro electric power generation, *for example,* but also whether or not an historic building ought to be preserved. It would extend to human social impact, so that any environmental decision which keeps a human community integrated, cohesive and interdependent is a "right" decision. There are obviously many definitional, value and valuation problems with such a formulation.

One matter that should be stressed here is that any ethic adopted must be developed within the affected community. It is for this reason that the ethic outlined above is necessarily a tentative one. An implication of social ecology advanced by Bookchin would seem to be that the forms of democracy we currently practise in societies such as Australia would need to undergo a substantial transforamation from representative democracy to a form of participatory democracy,[91] or "developmental democracy" which may allow such a transformation go take place, which will in turn lead to the kind of "legislative" forms of environmental decision making outlined previously.[92]

Once an ethic has been developed, it follows from the above that it should be open to further volution, to accommodate the changing values of the community. Implementation of education, policy formulation and legislation should also be seen in this light. It is probable that, as Hardin has argued,[93] an appeal to conscience is not enough. Hardin saw that

> "individualistic self-interest was leading us to disaster and believed that the only way to bring human conduct into line with environmental needs was by stringent legal controls."[94]

He advocated a mutual coercion, mutually agreed upon by the people affected. The history of environmental legislation in the past decade shows that many governments agree with the Hardin line of reasoning. A real problem facing us is how far we can or should go in enacting legislation to protect ecological values, bearing in mind the arguments put above in relation to the development and implementation of an ecological ethic.

LEGAL RAMIFICATIONS OF EVOLVING AN ETHIC

The introduction of an ethic, on the basis of social ecology, into the present legal framwork, if this is both theoretically possible and politically realistic, could have broad ramifications, including the rewriting of legislation having environmental implications to reflect changed and changing environmental policy objectives. Foremost amongst legislative amendments might be the redefinition of "environment", formulation or reformulation of the "objects" of Acts, implementation of community participation systems and importation of wide-standing provisions where at present they do not exist. The enactment of new legislation to more adequately protect various elements of the environment and to promote environmental quality would also be needed.

(i) The World Conservation Strategy and Legislative Reform

The World Conservation Strategy implicitly calls for an ecological ethic in relation to the rewriting of legislation. If we are to take its injunctions seriously we are obliged to look at the statute books in order to identify all the legislations which has any impact on the environment, with a view to changing it to achieve ecological value objectives more directly. The World Conservation Strategy states in this respect :

> Each country should review and consolidate its legislation. concerning living resources to ensure that it provides sufficiently for conservation. Each country should also review and if necessary strengthen—its capacity to implement its conservation legislation, both existing and required. Ideally a commitment to conserve countries' living resources should be incorporated in the constitution or other appropriate legal instrument. The commitment should lay down the obligation of the state to conserve living resources and the systems of which they are part, the rights of citizens to a stable and diversified environment, and the corresponding obligations of citizens to such an environment.

> There should be specific legislation aimed at achieving the objectives of conservation by providing for both the sustainable utilisation and protection of living resources and of their support systems. Comprehensive conservation legislation should provided for the planning of land and water uses and should regulate both direct impacts on the resource, such as exploitation and habitat removal, and indirect ones such as pollution or introduction of exotic species. In addition it should include requirements to undertake ecosystem evaluations, environmental assessments, and like mechanisms to ensure the incorporation of ecological considerations into policy making. The law should also provide for the participation of citizens in the elaboration of policies, for the provision of sufficient information for participation to be effective, and for legal resources to implement these rights. In addition there is a need to revise traditional concepts of the law of remedy, which currently envisage compensation only for economic loss, narrowly or long term damage to individuals and communities through the depletion of species or the destruction or degradation of ecosystems.[95]

There are, in the light of the concerns of this article, a number of, serious problems with both the World Conservation Strategy and the National Conservation Strategy for Australia, particularly in terms of the human-centred approach, and the question of "use" and "resources". Also problematic are terms such as "living resource management." The emphasis on "living resources rather than reference to the ecosystem as a whole, whether in terms of human utilisation or otherwise, is a fundamental limitation of otherwise, is a fundamental limitation of both the World Conservation Strategy and the National Conservation Strategy for Australia. Apart from these difficulties, however, they represent at least a few steps in the right direction and every effort should be made to ensure that the processes recommended in them be implemented, incorporating a capacity to adapt to changing cirumstances and perceptions.[96]

(ii) Redefinition of "Environment"

In order to more explicity reflect ecological values, a beginning could be made with the redefinition of "environment". Instead of environment including all aspect of the surroundings of humans, whether, affecting them as individuals or in their social groupings (see Environmental

Planning and Assessment Act, 1979 (N.S.W.), Environment Protection (Impact of Proposals) Act 1974 (Cth), we could develop the ecocentric definition referred to above (environment as a community or system which includes all living things as well as the air, water and soil that is their habitat). A new definition could be along the following lines :

> "Environment includes all aspects of the living community of earth and the natural, human-made and social surrounndings of that community."[97]

The phrase "all aspects" thus to longer refers merely to the surroundings of humans, but also to humans themselves, as well as non-human life forms and the other elements of the earth. By including humans within the definition, it can thus refer to the interaction between human and human (social aspects), humans and other life forms, and non-living elements of the earth (social ecological aspects), as well as the interaction of non-human life forms with non-living elements, and the interaction of non-living elements with other non-living elements (ecological aspects). Such a definition allows for the realisation that human beings, rather than being at the apex of an ecological pyramid, are simply members of the biophysical community of the earth and of the universe. It places natural communities and human communities together rather than separating them, thus conforming the Bookchins' model of social ecology. It might also be appropriate to the Australian Aboriginal concept of relationship to environment as a spiritual connection.[98]

Taking this definition as a more acceptable description of environment for the moment, what implications might this have for environmental decision-makers and the rest of the human community ?

If human beings are seen and can be seen as part of the environment attitudinal changes could follow which will allow human beings to speak more easily for the trees, the animals, the birds and other, non-living elements of the community of earth. It is possible that the concept of the public trust[99] would then be more broadly recognised in Australia, as well as the novel concept introduced by Stone that Natural objects should having standing to sue in much the same way as corporations.[100] Although this may seem rather odd at first it is not as far fetched as it seems. We already have legislation in many jurisdictions directed at protection of trees (generally in the form of tree-preservation orders)[101] and conservation of the environmental heritage, including both the built environment and natural areas.[102] In addition, legislation exists in many countries protecting animals from cruelty, and protection of native flora and fauna through national parks and wild life legislation. This legislation seems to recognise the moral duty on human beings to protect the natural elements of the community as well as aesthetic values. It can immediately be objected, of course, that the legislation has been formulated primarily for the benefit of human beings. *For example,* cruelty to animals provisions could be said to relate to the feelings of human beings rather than a concern for the animals themselves.

(iii) Objects of Environmental Legislation

A number of pieces of legislation in Australian jurisdictions can be identified as incorporating "objects". Perhaps the best known of these are the object section of the *Environment Protection* (Impact of Proposals) Act, 1947 (Cth):

> "s. 5(1) The object of this Act is to ensure, to the greatest extent that is practicable, that matters affecting the environment to a significant extent are fully examined and taken into account in and in relation to :
>
> *(a)* the formulation of proposals;
> *(b)* the carrying out of works and other projects;
> *(c)* the negotiation, operation and enforcement of agreements and arrangements (including agreements and arrangements with and with authorities of the states;
> *(d)* the making of or the participation in the making of, decisions and recommendations; and
> *(e)* the incurring of expenditure, by or on behalf, of the Australian Government and authorities of Australia, either alone or in association with any other government, authority, body or person".

The phrase, "to the greatest extent that is practicable" requires some examination. It could be construed narrowly by a Minister (s. 8), or an advisor to a Minister, in deciding what lengths should be gone to in order to enusre that matters significantly affecting the environment are fully examined. Practicability of analysis might be used as an excuse to put aside those environmental impacts that are difficult at first sight to analyse. Bates remarks that "factually practicable" is probably what is meant. He suggests that "practicable" should be read as "to the fullest extent possible."

Allowing for a slight difference in meaning, the American learning on the phrase "to the fullest extent possible", found in s. 102 of NEPA, might shed some light on how the Australian provision should be interpreted, or how it should be defined in the future.

> "Of course, all of these, s. 102 duties are qualified by the phrase 'to the fullest extent possible'. We must stress as forcefully as possible that this language does not provide an escape hatch for foot-dragging agencies; it does not make NEPA's procedural requirements somehow 'discretionary'. Congress did not intend the Act to be such a paper tiger. Indeed, the requirement of environmental consideration 'to the fullest extent possible' sets a high standard for the agencies, a standard which must be rigorously enforced by the reviewing courts."[103]

The phrase "to a significant extent" has a similar problem to that of "to the greatest extent that is practicable." There is no guidance as to what "significant" means, leaving it open for a decision making to exercise a broad discretion. In addition, there is the problem that a trivial effect for human beings might be a devastating effect for other elements of the ecological community. Lurning to the NEPA regulations, the word "significantly" is comprehensively defined in terms of both context and intensity.[104] It may well be useful to review the provisions of the Australian jurisdictions in the light of the regulations now enacted under NEPA, in order to be able to spell out more precisely when and how environmental assessment procedures are to be implemented.

More stringent regulations would seem to be needed in order to take into account the concerns implicit in the new definition of "environment". For ecological values to be properly assessed, however, evaluation will need to be carried out on a much broader basis, this is a major role of community participation in environmental planning.

COMMUNITY PARTICIPATION : SOME POSSIBILITIES

Mention has already been made of the rationale for broad community participation in environmental decision making. Here a number of areas are examined to illustrate what changes could be made if community participation based on a new ecological ethic of the kind envisaged were to be more fully accepted. It should be noted that in order to be consistent with the concept of social ecology, the acceptance of an environment ethic means that community participation is not just a strategy for implementation of the ethic, but quite possibly the strategy for implementation. Community participation in the sense in which it is used here would then become central to the methods by which environmental decisions are made and disputes resolved. In other words, the evaluation of environmental impacts as well as the making and implementation of policy would directly involve people of the affected community.[105]

(i) A Community Conslutation Policy

In its simplest form, community participation in environmental decision-making can be introduced by making departments of government more open and accessible to individuals and groups. If there is a rationale for a Department of Mineral Resources seeing the mining industry as its "constituency", there is no reason why an Environment Department is not able to view individuals and groups concerned with conservation and preservation as its "constituency". An example of this way of thinking is seen in Canada. Environment Canada has instituted a policy for public consultation. The policy is divided into four parts :

(a) Public consultation, which will assure a regular and predictable opportunity for the public to meet with departmental officials in order to discuss environmental issues and concerns;

(b) regulation-making, which will require that all significant new regulations and guidelines will be subject to an explicit procedure that allows for public comment at all stages of their development;

(c) information availability, which will make most departmental information accessible to the public; and

(d) contribution to transportation expenses, which will provide assistance to help qualifying groups attend designated meetings.

As a general framework, the policy will assure a consistent approach to public consultation and information availability throughout the department. At the sametime it will allow for each operational sevice and region to develop its programme activities in a way that best meets particular needs and circumstances. In this way the dual objective of consistency and flexibility will be achieved.[106]

Some of the ways in which the consultation policy is being carried out are in the provision of office space, telephones and printing and typing services for interested groups and individuals. Contact with other departments of government and with other conservation groups is facilitated by Environment Canada. The public relations Section of Environment Canada sees this as a two-way process; the voluntary and other non-governmental groups which receive assistance from Environment Canada are seen to be achieving the objectives of that department and are able to input a good deal of information and analysis.[107]

With suitable modifications there is no doubt that a consultation policy of this kind could be implemented in Australia. Administration of environmental policy at the local, State and federal decision-making levels could be considerably enhanced by implementation of such a policy, perhaps contributing to a significant reduction in conflicts between government and industry with environmental groups. If the decision-making processes were opened up in these ways then the amount of money that is spent by environmental groups, government and industry in format dispute resolution tribunals and direct confrontation could be put to much better use. *For example,* the thousands of dollars that it cost to maintain a police force to keep members of the public off public land in South West Tasmania in 1982-83 could have been used for developing other environmentally more acceptable alternatives for power generation and the saving of energy for that region.[108]

(ii) Statutory Committees : Community Input

The statutory advisory committees that already exist under some legislation (for instance Environmental Planning and Assessment Act, 1979 (N.S.W.) are usually designed to have an independent input into the department to which they are attached. The first matter to be addressed is whether these committees ought to be "advisory" or have some real decision making power. More often than not statutory advisory committees are no more-than what Arnstein[109] would call "therapeutic" elements in a participation process, if not purely "manipulative". Another matter is how members of these committees ought to be selected. For example, the Environment and Planning Advisory Committee under the EPA Act consist of the Director of the Department of Environment and Planning together with twelve persons from various government and non-government bodies, all appointed by the Minister. There is no guarantee that any of these people represent the interests of the "constituency" from which they come, or whether they are under any obligation to do so. There are no regulations as to who fixes the agenda and there is no provision for members of the public to make sub missions to the committees. There is also no obligation for agenda and minutes to be made publicly available nor are the meetings open.[110] A contrast to this can be found in the Netherlands, where a national committee composed of some fifty representatives is drawn from every level of the community, representing industry, government, unions and universities. The committee meets bimonthly with an independent chairperson and secretariat financed by the Ministry for the Environment. The agènda is set by the committee itself although the Ministry has an input. Agenda and minutes are publicly available and the meetings are open to observers.[111] Although this committee functions in an advisory capacity, the fact that the meetings are open and the input broad, puts a serious on us on the relevant Minister to heed the advice.

In examining the possibilities of such a committee in the Australian context, a way would need to be found to ensure that they can be made accountable to their constituencies, so that any policies formulated within them reflected the articulated needs and desires of those constituencies.

(iii) Community Participation Through Public Environmental Inquiries

The role of the public inquiry in environmental decision making is often underestimated. Properly conducted, it can perform a vital function in ensuring that the interests of all parties involved in a particular proposal are adequately represented and given weight in the decision making process.

Carew-Reid[112] has identified a wide range of problems to do with the procedural and substantive operation of public environmental inquiries in Australia. Three major weaknesses identified were their susceptibility to procedural *rigor mortis,* insensitivity to environmental significance of their terms of reference, and failure to facilitate effective representation of all affected interests. He remains confident that the public inquiry has nevertheless a significant role to play in environmental planning and decision making :

> "a public inquiry may provide the only opportunity for `live participation. An environmental inquiry which applies a diversity of involvement methods can do much more than EIS to raise public consciousness. It enables value judgments to be formed and reflected in the assessment process. Value judgments and the application of commonsense are vital ingredients in resolving many environmental controversies. For this reason, the public arena is the place where the associated decisions must be made and debated. Given access to all the necessary information, anyone is an expert in value judgments"[113]

Carew-Reid maintains that participation should be provided as of right at all stages in the environmnetal decision making process, form policy-making to the approval and oversight stages. The first requirement would be to entrench in all relevant legislation a proper public inquiry procedure, open to anyone who wishes to contribute, on behalf of any individual group or other living or non-living member of the bio-physical community. Solutions need to be found to the problem of ensuring that public inquiries are truly "public". Although official and voluntary legal aid-agencies have contributed greatly to the breaking down of barriers to official tribunals, there is as yet no tradition of assistance to individuals and groups for representation at public environmental inquiries. One of the problems here is that legal aid is generally accorded to individuals for individual legal problems, rather than to groups representing wider interests such as a concern for the preservation of a wilderness area, etc.[114]

(iv) Standing to Sue and Community Participation

An expensive form of community participation in environmental decsion-making is by taking action in the courts. However, for those willing and able to take this course, the significant barrier of standing to sue exists in many jurisdictions. In the Australian context, the case of Australian Conservation Foundation *v.* Commonwealth of Australia illustrates the problem of a group of concerned citizens (the Australian Conservation Foundation) in trying to influence and participate in an environmental planning decision where there are no specific statutory provisions or common law rights available.[115] The High Court found that the foundation needed to have "a special interest" in the preservation of the environment and that a mere intellectual or emotional concern was not sufficient for this purpose. Although the case of Onus and Frankland *v.* Alcoa of Australia is said to have loosened up the standing requirements a little, major obstacles remain to bringing actions at the federal level and in most states before individuals and groups in the community can protect aspects of the environmental amenity.[116]

A number of suggestions have been made in recent years to open up the standing question by introducing legislation whereby any person is able to bring an action for a breach of an Act or regulations made thereunder. Two significant discussion papers by the Australian Law Reform Commission, access to the courts (I) Standing : Public interest suits; (II) Standing : Class actions, have stimulated a good deal of debate in Australia in relation to the question of standing. The Trade Practices Act, 1974 (Cth), the Environmental Planning and Assessment Act, 1979

(N.S.W.), and the Heritage Act, 1977 (N.S.W.) have standing provisions for any person to bring an action to remedy or restrain a breach of the Act.[117] The World Heritage Properties Conservation Act 1983 (Cth) represents quite a large step forward at federal level in terms of standing. Although not as wide as s. 123 of the EPA Act (N.S.W.) ("any person"), s. 14 (1) of the World Heritage Act allows the Attorney-Gerneral or any "interested person" to apply for an injunction to restrain an act that is proclaimed to be"unlawful."[118]

However, a more general standing provision, not related to the breach of any particular Act, would be desirable if an ecological ethic were to be evolved. A significant precedent is the Environmental Protection Act, 1970 of Michigan. In essence this legislation states that the Attorney-General, any political subdivision of the State, instrumentality or agency, any person, partnership, corporation, association or other legal entity may maintain an action for declaratory and equitable relief against the State, or any other of the bodies listed, for the protection of the air, water and other natural resources and the public trust therein from pollution imparment or destruction. Whilst early critics of the legislation believed that the Act would open the floodgates for environmental litigation so that the courts would not be able to cope with the number of suits that were brought, this has by no means been a reality.[119] A number of American States have now followed the Michigan example. The even broader standing concept discussed by Stone, that natural objects should have standing similar to corporations, remains an attractive one and conforms in large measure to the ethic outlined above.[120]

(v) Environmental Advocacy

Since the early 1970s a number of public interest environmental law firms have been operating in both Canada and the United States. The Canadian Environmental Law Association, the West Coast Environmental Law Association an the Alberta Environmental Law Association are three Canadian examples; among the best known organisations in the United States are the Natural Resources Defence Council, the Environmental Defence Fund and the Sierra Club Legal Defence Fund. In the Australian context, the Public Interest Advocacy Centre was established under the auspices of the Law Foundation of New South Wales in mid-1982. Although it has no specific environmental brief, it has to date taken various environmental cases onto its files. Also in New South Wales the Environmental Law Association is in the process of establishing an Environmental Defender's Office modelled in part on the Canadian and

United States precedents.[121] The objective of the Environmental Defender's Office is to provide legal advice and representation to those whose purpose in obtaining the advice or representation chiefly involves the conservation or preservation of the natural or built environment, or the environmentally responsible use of Australia's resources. The Environmental Defender's Office will be primarily available to individuals and groups who lack the knowledge and resources to cope in the "traditional way", that is by engaging private solicitors and paying them the scheduled fee.

Several American States have established environmental defenders on an official level. The experience of Rhode Island however, is instructive. The Rhode Island Environmental Rights Act, 1978 created the position of Environmental Advocate, but the office was never properly funded, apparently because of cuts in Federal funding by the Reagan administration. It was partly for this reason that the Act Relating to Environmental Rights, 1982 extended to private citizens the right to seek enforcement of that State's environmental laws in a way similar to that of the Michigan Environmental Protection Act of 1970, that is, to be an extra watchdog on the activities of both the private and public sectors.[122]

(vi) An Environmental Bill of Rights

The Canadian Environental Law Association began its activities in the early 1970s. One of its initial objectives was the formulation of an Environmental Bill of Rights for Canada. The main elements of this Bill of Rights were :

- *(i)* the law would state unequivocally that citizens have a right to a healthy and attractive environment;
- *(ii)* the law would give any citizen the right to defend any part of the environment in the courts;
- *(iii)* the law would require social and environmental impact statements and cost-benefit analyses prior to development decisions;
- *(iv)* the law would give citizens the right of access to all information pertaining to environmental issues and decisions;
- *(v)* the law would give citizens the right to participate in the setting of standards of environmental quality;
- *(vi)* the law would require that recreational areas (parks) be held in public trust and citizens should be able to prevent violation of that trust in the courts;
- *(vii)* the law would allow class actions; that is any citizen should be able to sue on behalf of other aggrieved citizens for

damages resulting from environmental destruction.[123]

An Environmental Bill of Rights may well be unacceptable to most legislators and others in Australia at this point. However, such a Bill of Rights can be used as an educational tool in order to form the basis of a multi-dimensional approach to environmental decision making as opposed to rather haphazard legislation which is too subject to the political and economic demands of a particular time span.[124] In social ecology terms, however, an Environmental Bill of Rights might neatly complement the Federal Bill of Rights currently under consideration.

(vii) Social Impact Assessment

The process of environment impact assessment as presently carried out allows little input from the community in terms of how a proposed development or planning policy will affect the social and natural environment. The concept of social ecology would seem to demand not only that the social impacts of a decision should be as carefully assessed as the impacts in the natural ecosystem, but that the two kinds of assessment should be seen as one process. In other words, the values that are placed on human and non-human ecosystems by a particular community should not be seen as separate and distinct, but as integrated elements in one value system. The emerging discipline of social impact assessment could perhaps be the beginning of an answer to this integration. Until recently, social impact studies have been seen as

> "little more than a cursory overview of census data, an anecdotal history of affected groups and individuals, a collection of narrow cost-benefit calculations, or weak conjecture about the significance of selected social trends."[125]

SIA, developed within a conceptually adequate framework, could more accurately reflect the wider social, economic, and ecological concerns of a potentially affected community, and thus allow it to influence decision making processes directly and consistently.

CONCLUSION

The incorporation of an ecological ethic into the current legal and administrative framework faces many obstacles. Among these is the inconsistency between the concept of social ecology and the way in which decisions are made in this area at the present time. Social ecology would seem to require a highly developed form of citizen participation which would run counter to the forms of representative democracy found in contemporary Western societies. A participatory form of democracy, where individual citizens have at least an option to directly influence the policy and decision making process, seems to be called for. Further, social ecology would seem to require that citizens develop a consciousness of their inherent interconnectedness with the natural realm, such that the way in which the non-human realm is valued is equal to the way in which the human realm is valued. This entails a revolution in thinking, from a human dominant conception to at least a coexistence conception of nature.

The development of new definitions, redrafted legislative objects or improved techniques of cost-benefit analysis, environmental impact assessment, public inquiries and expanded standing provisions, will largely serve to perpetuate the *status quo* of power relations in decision-making processes, unless the role of the ordinary citizen is also expanded and developed. The "key-log", to borrow Leopold's phrase, which must be moved to allow these processes to begin is the realisation that there are no environmental crises as such, but crises in human relations with the environment, which are in turn predicted on crises between humans themselves.

REFERENCES

1. See Gilpin, A., Dictionary of Environmental Terms (Queensland University Press). p. 51.
2. Naess, A., "The Shallow and Deep, Long-Range Ecology Movement : A Summary" (1973) 16 Inquiry 95-100, as referred to in Elliot, R. and Gare, A. *Environmental Philosophy* (Queensland University Press, 1983).
3. Bookchin, M., The Ecology of Freedom (Cheshire, 1982), p.21.
4. The "deep ecology" movement has become a widespread phenomenon since the 1970s. See, *e.g.*, Ecophilosophy I, II, III and IV (1979-82) George Sessions, Sierra College, Rocklin, California; The Deep Ecologist (Ballarat 1982-84) and Hooker, C.A., "On Deep versus Shallow Theories of Environmental Pollution" in Elliot, R. and Gare, A., op. cit., p. *xi*.
5. Bookchin, *op. cit.*, p. 22
6. See further, *Fontana Dictionary of Modern Thought* (Fontana 1977), pp. 186-87; and more generally, Wittman, J.S., Selected Articles in Social Ecology (MSS Info. Corp. New York, 1973); Moos, R.H., Insel, P.M., Issues in Social Ecology—Human Milieus (National Press Books, 1974).
7. O'Riordan, T., Environmentalism (Pion, 1981), p.1.
8. *Ibid.*
9. O'Riordan, T. and Turner, K., An Annotated Reader in Environmental Planning and Management (Pergamon, 1983), pp. 7-8.

10. Hundloe, T., "The Dollars and Sense of Preserving the Natural Environment"; paper delivered to the Second National Environmental Law Symposium, "Principles into Practice", Melbourne, October 1982, p. 10.
11. A good explanation and critique of paradigm shifts can be found in Routley, R., "Roles and Limits of Paradigms in Environmental Thought and Action" in Elliot and Gare; see also Ferguson, M., The Aquarian Conspiracy: Personal and Social Transformations in the 1980's (Tarcher, Los Angeles, 1980). For a discussion of paradigm shifts in economics see O'Riordan and Turner, op. cit., pp. 211-264.
12. Ferguson, *op. cit.*, p. 27
13. Cotgrove, S. and Duff, A., "Environmentalism, Middle Class Radicalism and Politics", 28 The Sociological Review 331-51, as referred to in O'Riordan and Turner, *op. cit.*, p.8.
14. See, *e.g.*, Bookchin, M., *op. cit.*, p.19; the question of proper design is addressed by Hooker, C.A., in "On Deep versus Shallow Theories of Environmental Pollution" in Elliot, R. and Gare, A., *op. cit.*, p. 58; see also McHarg, I., Design with Nature (Natural History Press, New York, 1969) for a more technocentric approach.
15. See, *e.g.*, Land Degradation in Australia, Department of Home Affairs and Environment (AGPS, Canberra, 1983). In this report, land degradation is identified "as the most significant single issue on the Austrialian environmental science today, affecting large areas of Australia and critically limiting the scope for sustainable development" (Foreword); see also, Sheridan, D., Desertification of the United States (Council on Environmental Quality, 1981).
16. See generally, *e.g.*, Brown, L., Building a Sustainable Society (Norton, New York, 1980), The Global 2000 Report to the President (Penguin, 1982).
17. See, *e.g.* Routley, R. and V., Fight for the Forests (3rd ed., Research School of Social Sciences, Australian National University, 1975); Rawlinson, P. and Penna I., "Timber : The overextended Resource", in Birrell, R., Hill, D., and Stanley, J. (eds), Quarry Australia? (Oxford, 1982).
18. Meadows, W.H., Meadows, D.L., Randers, J. and Behrens, W.W., Limits to Growth (Universe, New York, 1972).
19. Ward, B. and Dubos, R., Only One Earth (Penguin, 1972).
20. Editors of The Ecologist, Blueprint for Survival (Penguin, 1972).
21. Holdgate, M.W., and White, G.F., Environmental Issues, SCOPE Report No.10, International Council of Scientific Unions, 1977.
22. International Union for the Conservation of Nature and Natural Resources, and World Wildlife Fund, World Conservation Strategy (1980).
23. The National Conservation Strategory for Australia, as Proposed by a Conference held in Canberra in June 1983. (AGPS, Canberra, 1983).
24. *Op. cit.*; see also Barney, G.O., *et al.*, Global 2000: Implications for Canada, commissioned by Environment Canada.
25. See, *e.g.*, Green, H.P., "Cost-Risk-Benefit Assessment and the Law: Introduction and Perspective" (1977) 45 (5) George Washington Law Review 901.
26. James, D., Chambers, J., Gilbert, A. and Wright, H., Energy Research Group, Centre for Environmental and Urban Studies, Macquarie University, December 1983; see also James, D., Integrated Energy—Economic Environmental Modelling with Reference to Australia (AGPS, Canberra, 1983).
27. Craig, D.G., Citizen Participation in Environmental Policy Decisions, Master of Laws thesis, Osgoode Hall Law School, York University, Toronto (unpublished, 1982), p. 40; see also Craig, D.G., "Democracy and Environmental Planning", paper delivered to the Second National Environmental Law Symposium, Melbourne, October 1983, p. 12.
28. See generally, O'Riordan and Tumber, *op. cit.*, pp. 373-94; also Linke, R., Environmental

Education in Australia (Allen and Unwin, 1979).

29. "Aspiring to be Third Rate" The Amicus Journal, Natural Resources Defence Council, Winter 1982, 14. See also Costle, D.M., "Environmental Regulation and Regulatory Reform" (1982) 57 Washington Law Review 409 on the question of the so called regulatory relief introduced by the Reagan Administration, which attempts to return to the market place to achieve social goals. Costle maintains that this approach is misplaced in the areas of environmental, health, and safety regulation.

30. The Indictment was published in March 1982 by a coalition of Friends of the Earth, Natural Resources Defence Council, The Wilderness Society, Sierra Club, National Audubon Society, Environmental Defence Fund, Environmental Policy Centre, Environmental Action, Defenders of Wildlife and Solar Lobby; the *Reagan Energy Plan* was published in 1982 by the Centre for Renewable Resources, Cousteau Society, Enviornmental Action, Environmental Action Foundation, Environmental Defence Fund, Federation of American Scientists, Friends of the Earth, National Audubon Society, Natural Resources Defense Council, the Nuclear Club Inc., Nuclear Information and Resource Service, Sierra Club, Solar Lobby and Union of Concerned Scientists; this list gives a flavour of the diversity of interest groups pressing for changes in environmental policy in the United States.

31. Sydney Morning Herald, 11 and 13 Dec., 1982.

32. Tribe, I, II., "Ways Not To Think About Plastic Trees : New Foundations for Environmental Law" (1974) 83 Yale L. J. 1312 at 1317-19. This article was written in response to Kreiger, M., "What's Wrong with Plastic Trees? (1973) 179 Science 446. For a critique of Tribe's article see Sagoff. M., "On Preserving the Natural Environment" (1974)84 Yale L. J., 205. and tribes reply, "from Environmental Foundations to constitutional structurers: Learning from Nature's Future" (1975)84 Yale L.J. 545. See also Arup, C., "Soft Values, Policy Analysis and the Legal Process" (1982) 1 Australian Journal of Law and Society 10 at 15, on the under-representation of environmental values in policy analysis.

33. O' Riordan, *op. cit.*, p. 85

34. *Ibid.* See also Daly, H.E., Steady-State Economics, The Economics of Biophysical Equilibrium and Moral Growth (Freeman, San Francisco, 1977), at p.99 et seq. for a critique of growth economics; and Gorz., A, Ecology as Politics (South End Press, 1980, Boston) passim.

35. SCOPE Report, 1975, p. 16

36. Johnstone, I.M., Comment on Environmental Considerations in Energy Production, American Bar Association Conference, Sydney 1980 (Monograph); see also Pearce, D.W., and Nash, C.A., The Social Appraisal of Projects (Macmillan, London, 1981), pp. 1-4, Passmore, J., Man's Responsibility for Nature (Duckworth, 1974), and Hooker, C.A., in Elliot and Gare, *op. cit.*, at p.62 and Sinden, J.A. and Worrell, A.C., Unpriced Values (Wiley, 1979).

37. O, Riordan, *op. cit.*, p. 171; Daly, *op. cit.*, p. 172, Tribe, *op. cit.*, p. 1319-20

38. Pears and Nash, *op. cit.*, p. 4

39. Tribe, *op. cit.*, at 1332. This approach has also been characterised as anthropocentric utilitarianism; see *e.g.*, Seidler, S., Justifications for Preserving the Natural Environment: The Moral Philosophy Underlying Environmental Decision making in the Modern West; the Anthropocentric Utrilitarian Basis of Cost—Benefit Analysis, Environmental Ethics Research Paper (University of Michigan Law School, 1982, upublished). James *et al.* (see n.23, *supra*) do not use the monetary cost-benefit approach in formulating their energy-economic-environmental model, favouring a cost-effectiveness analysis, which they consider to be more feasible. This is a method "in which environmental standards (either

discharge or ambient concentration) are met at minimum economic costs" (at p. 36). Whilst the study as a whole represents a considerable advance in its area it is still largely fixated on the primacy of monetary-based evaluation techniques.

40. Pearce, D., "Accounting for the Future", (1977) 9 Futures 365, as quoted in O'Riordan and Turnner, *op. cit.*, pp. 117-18. See also Pearce, D, "The Nature of Cost-Benefit Analysis" in Economics and Environment Policy : The Role of Cost Benefit Analysis; Department of Home Affairs and Environment (AGPS, Canberra, 1983), p. 6.
41. Seidler, *op. cit.*, p. 35
42. Bennett, J.W., "Valuing the Existence of a Natural Ecosystem" (1982) Vol. 13, No.10 Search 232.
43. See Hammack, J. and Brown, G.M. Waterfowl and Wetlands: Towards Bioeconomic Analysis (John Hopkins Press for Resources for the Future, 1974), as referred to in Knetch, J. L. and Sinden, J. A. "Willingness to Pay and Compensation Demanded : Experimental Evidence of an Unexpected Disparity in Measures of Value" (unpublished paper, Simon Fraser University, British Columbia, 1982).
44. Deardon, P., "A Statistical Technique for the Evaluation of the Vishal Quality of the Landscape for Land-use Plannning" (1980) 10 Journal of Environmental Management 51; "Landscape Evaluation: The Case for a Multi-disciplinary Approach" (1981) 13 Journal of Environmental Management 95, and "Public Participation and Scenic Quality Analysis" (1981) 8 Landscape Planning 3.
45. Tribe, *op. cit.*, p. 1331
46. Annual Report, Department of Home Affairs and Environment, 1982-83, 11, and Economics and Environment Policy : The Role of Cost-Benefit Analysis, Department of Home Affairs and Environment, *op. cit.* For more discussion of the link between cost-benefit analysis and environmental impact assessment see O'Riordan and Turner, *op.cit.*, 156-57.
47. National Environmental Policy Act, 1969, Regulations. 1502.23
48. It is of course recognised that a number of items listed here would not appear in a conventional cost-benefit analysis; further, whether some items should be listed as costs or benefits depends on the viewpoint of the valuer.
49. Kirkpatric, J., Hydroelectric Development and Wilderness in Tasmania (Deptt. of Environment, Tasmania, 1979).
50. Kirkpatrick, J., "Development and Wilderness in Tasmania" (1980) 8 *Habitat* 12. In his study, Kirkpatrick also analysed the "wilderness values" that would potentially be lost by the construction of a dam.
51. *Ibid.*
52. See Jones, R., Submission to Senate Select Committee on South-West Tasmania; *Hansard,* 19 March 1982; and "The extreme climatic place" 26 *Hemisphere* 54.
53. The human psychological need for wilderness experience has been written about in many quarters; see, *e.g.*, Brower, D., "Wilderness' A Universal Concern— (The Wildness within us)" in Mosley, G., Australia's Wilderness (Australian Conservation Foundation 1978), Nash, R., Wilderness and the American Mind (3rd ed., Yale University Press, 1982).
54. *Ibid.*, p. 1329
55. Calvert Cliffs Co-ordinating Committee Inc. *v.* United States Atomic Energy Commission U.S. Court of Appeals DCC 1971, 449 F.2d 1109.
56. *Ibid.*, p. 1117
57. This is made clear in s. 101(a) "... to create and maintain conditions under which man and nature can exist in *productive* harmony, and fulfil the social, economic and other requirements of present and future generations of Americans" (emphasis added).
58. NEPA has been held to apply extra-territorially; see, *e.g.* Sierra Club *v.* Coleman 405 F.

Supp. 63 D.D.C. 1976 and Executive Order 12114 44 Fed. Reg. 1957 (1979).

59. Bates, G.M., Environmental Law in Australia (Butterworths, 1983), p.1.
60. Official opening of New South Wales Environmental Law Association Seminar "The First Thousand Days of The Environmental Planning and Assessment Act", by Mr. Eric Bedford, Minister for Planning and Environment (1983) 13 Environmental Law Newsletter 16-17.
61. Waterson, N., Environmental Impact Assessment in New South Wales; Theory, Practice and Directions, Legal Research Project Thesis (School of Law, Macquarie University, 1983, unpublished), p. 45.
62. Other examples have been detailed in Budavari, R., "Parramatta Park: Where Politics and the Environment don't mix" (1983) 8 Legal Service Bulletin 25 and Ball, M., "Circumvention of Environmental Law in NSW" (1983) 12 Environmental Law Newsletter 21. See also Ryan, P. (1984) I E. & P.L.J. 72-77.
63. The implication here is that no science can ever be "pure". As Bookchin sees it, science has been "permitted to live a lie. It has presupposed, with astonishing success, that nature is orderly, and that this order lends itself to rational interpretation by the human mind, but that reason is exclusively the subjective attribute of the human observer not of the phenomena observed "Bookohm, *op. cit.* p.235. See also Rolston. H., "Are Value in Nature Subjective or Objective" in Elliot and Gare, *op. cit.*, p. 135.
64. Craig, "Democracy and Environmental Planning", *op. cit.*, p. 6.
65. Bookchin, *op. cit.*, p. 1 See also Marcuse, II, "Nature and Revolution" in Counter Revolution and Revolt (Boston Press, Boston, 1972), p. 60.
66. Craig, Citizen Participation in Environmental Decision making *op. cit,* p. 153 et.
67. A list of some of the most significant writing might be Thoreau, H.D. Walden (Signet, 1960), Espaid, A. A. Sand Country (Ballantine, 1966), Schumacher, I.E. Small is Beautiful (Abacas, 1973), Passmore, J., Man's Responsibility for Nature (Duckworth, 1974), Routley, R., and Routley V., "Human Chauvman and Environmental Ethics" in Mannison, D., McRobie. M and Routley. R.,Environmental Philosophy, Monograph Series 2, Dept. of Philosophy, (Research School of Social Science, Australian National University, Canberra, 1980) p.96 and passim; Birch and Cobb. *op. cit.*, Nash, *op. cit.*, Elliot and Gare, *op. cit.*
68. *Ibid.*, p. 273
69. Bookchin *op. cit.*, p. 21
70. *Ibid.*, they comment in a footnote. "The masculine particles are appropriate; so is the resulting one."
71. R. Routley and V. Rautley, *op. cit.*
72. *Ibid.*, p. 112-113
73. Thompson, J. L., "Preservation of Wilderness and the Good Life" in Elliot and Gare, *op. cit,* p. 85.
74. *Ibid.*, p. 126
75. *Ibid.*, p. 99, referring to Mercuse's works Mareuse, II., "Nature and Revolution" in Counter-Revolution and Revolt, *op. cit.*
76. *Ibid.*, p. 97
77. Preston, B.J., "Environmental Ethics; An Ecocentric Approach" (unpublished paper 1982)
78. Bookchin, *op. cit.*, pp. 277-78
79. Birch and Cobb, *op. cit.*, p. 175
80. Tribe, *op. cit,* p. 1338
81. *Ibid.*, p. 1333
82. *Ibid.*, p. 1337
83. *Ibid.*, p. 1338

84. *Ibid.*, p. 1340
85. Leopold, *op. cit.*, p. 238
86. *Ibid.*, p. 240
87. *Ibid.*, p. xviii
88. Bookchin calls for a "direct democracy" which involves not only the freedom to formulate policy by a "re-empowered community" but also involvement in its implementation, *op. cit.*, pp. 336-40.
89. Leopold, *op. cit.*, p. 262
90. Tribe, *op. cit.*, p. 1340
91. Craig, D., "Citizen Participation in Environmental Decision making", *op. cit.*
92. Hardin, "The Tragedy of the Commons" (1968) 162 Science 1243.
93. See Strong, D.H., and E.S. Rosenfield, "Ethics or Expediency: An Environmental Question" 5 Environmental Affairs 255 at 266. They maintain that the more likely way of having an environmental ethic accepted is by way of the concept of enlightened self-interest: "An environmental ethic that is accepted and complied with because it appeals to one's self-interest is not, admittedly, on an altogether sound footding. Such a view continues in part the erroneous concept of one's separateness from nature. The authors believe, however, that an appeal to self-interest is the best if not the only hope for the adoption of an environmental ethic at the present time, when such an ethic is critically needed. Our hope is that ultimately people will recognise and accept the right of other species to exist simply for their own sake and not because people need them." (at 269) For a critique of Hardin's essay and more general discussion of the common theme see O'Riordan and Turner *op. cit.*, pp. 265-321.
94. For an analysis of the possibilities arising from the World Conservation Strategy for the Australian federal jurisdiction, see Wilcox, M., "A National Environmental Law", paper presented at the First National Environmental Law Symposium, Sydney, October 1982. For a critique of the National Conservation Strategy for Australia, see Krone, A. "Managing Conservation : A Strategy for Whom? In (1983) 13 Environmental Law Newsletter 35.
95. World Conservation strategy, chap 11, paras 8 and 9.
96. *Ibid.*, Ch. 11, paras 8-9.
97. Formulated in consultation with David Parner, University of New South Wales, Faculty of Law.
98. "The people have a spiritual relationship with species and the physical features of their environment, expressed through the concept of the dreaming" Ranger Uranum Environmental Inquiry (Second Report 1977 AGPS, Canberra), p.33. Further, "Australian Aborigines in the past, and in the present insofar as traditionally oriented people are concerned had a special view of their natural environment. They were ultimately familiar with everything within it, and the life they led demanded that they shared the same life-essence with all the natural species and elements within that a the Environment. Their natural world was expended to include the natural world conversely, their natural world was humanized, and this was true for the land as such" in Berndt, R M and C.H., The World of the First Australians (Lansdowne Press, 1982), p. 136.
99. See Sax, J. Defending the Environment (Vintage, 1970), Bates, *op. cit.*, p. 212.
100. Stone, C., Should trees have Towards legal Rights for Natural Objects, (Kaufman, 1974), see also Bates *op. cit.*, p. 213.
101. See. *e.g.* EPA Act (N.S.W.) p. 26(c) and Model Provisions, cl. 8, pursuant to s. 117.
102. *E.g.* Native and Historical Objects and Areas Act 1980, Aboriginal Sacred Sites Act 1980 (N.T.) Archaeological and Aboriginal Relics Preservation Act 1972, Historic Buildings Act 1981, Historic Shipwrecks Act 1981 (Vic.) Heritage Act 1977, Historic Houses Act 1980 (N.S.W.); Aboriginal and Historic Relics Preservation Act 1965, South Australian

Heritage Act, 1978 (S.A.); Aboriginal Heritage Act, 1972, Aboriginal Heritage Act (No.2) 1980 (W.A.); Aboriginal Rules Preservation Act 1967 (Qld); Australian Heritage Commission Act 1975, Historic Shipwrecks Act 1976, World Heritage Properties Conservation Act 1983, Aboriginal and Torres Strait Islander (Interim Protection) Act 1984 (Cth).

103. Calvert Cliffs' Co-ordinating Committee to United States Atomic Energy Commission U.S.C.A., DCC 1971 449 F.2d 1109.

104. NEPA Regulations, 1508.27. A summary of the regulation is as follows : The consideration of context means that the significance of an action must be analysed in several contexts such as society as a whole (human, national) the affected region, the affected interests and the locality. Intensity refers to severity of impact; the following should be considered in evaluating intensity; (1) Impacts may be both beneficial and adverse. A significant effect may exist even if the Federal agency believes that on balance the effect will be beneficial (2) The degree to which the proposed action affects public health or safety. (3) Unique characteristics of the geographic area such as proximity to historic or cultural resources, parklands, prime farmlands, wetlands, wild and scenic rivers, or ecologically critical areas. (4) The degree to which the effects on the quality of the human environment are likely to be highly controversial. (5) The degree to which the possible effects on the human environment are highly uncertain or involve unique or unknown risks. (6) The degree to which the action may establish a precedent for publications with significant effects or represents a decision in principle about a future consideration. (7) Whether the action is related to other actions wih individually insignificant but cumulatively significant impacts. (8) The degree to which the action affects items in the National Register of Historic Places or may cause loss or destruction of significant scientific, cultural or historical resources. (9) The degree to which the action may affect species under the Endangered Species Act. (10) Whether the action threatens a violation of Federal, State or local law or requirements imposed for the protection of the environment.

In New South Wales the American phrase "to the fullest extent possible" is also used; see s. III, Environmental Planning and Assessment Act 1979 (N S W) ; see also reg. 56, which has a number of similarities to the American regulation referred to above. For some judicial interpretation of these provisions see Kivi v. Forestry Commission of NSW" (1982) 47 L.G.R.A. 38 and Severn S.C. *v.* Water Resources Comm. (1982) 47 L.G.R.A. 257. See also Farrier, D., "Environmental Assessment in N.S.W:" (1984) I E. &P. L.J. 151.

105. "It is not necessary that everyone in society participate in all decisions. Policy decisions determine the framework/rules which govern managerial or adjudicative environmental decisions. Many of these can be delegated to responsible administrators. It is also unnecessary that every citizen participate in every policy decision. The affected public may vary depending on the nature of the policy decisions. The essential development is that citizens regain the capacity to actively participate in public life". Craig, D., "Democracy and Environmental Planning", *op. cit.*, 31, see also Bookchin, *op. cit.*, p. 337.

106. Environment Canada, Public Consultation Policy (1981).

107. Personal communication; see also Environmental Update (Environment Canada, December 1982). Comprehensive public consultation has also been implemented in a forestry department in Canada—see Public Involvement Handbook (Ministry of Forests, British Columbia, 1981); the Ministry obviously takes a wider view of its "constituency" than resource ministries elsewhere.

108. *For example,* see Beatty, B., Perinotto, T. and Tarlo, K., "Expleding the Jab Myth" 30 chain Reaction (Friends of the Earth Australia, Summer 1982-83), p. 9. It should be noted

that the legal dispute over the Franklin Dam has been resolved. Commonwealth of Australia and Another v. State of Tasmania and Others (1983) 57 A.L.J.R. 450; for implications for environmental law see Bates, G.M., "The Tasmanian Dam Case and its Significance in Environmental Law'' to be published (1984) I E. & P.L.J. No.4.

109. Arnstein, S.R., "A ladder of citizen participation" (1969) 35 Journal of the American Institute of Planners 217. Her ladder comprised 8 rungs; I descending order: Citizen control, Delegated power, Partnership, Placation, Consultation, Informing, Therapy, Manipulation.

110. The Environmental Law Association of New South Wales has forwarded a submission relating to these committees with suggestions for reform to the Minister for Planning and Environment.

111. Personal observation; see also Drupsteen, Th. G., Nederlands Milicurecht in Kort Bestek (Tjeenk-Willink, The Netherlands, 1978), p. 35.

112. Carew-Reid, J., Public Environmental Inquiries (Doctoral thesis, Centre for Environmental and Urban Studies, Macquarie University 1982).

113. *Ibid.*, p. 11

114. *Ibid.*,

115. A.L.R., 28, 1980, p. 257

116. A.L.J.R., 55, 1981, p. 416

117. Environmental legal aid on a federal level enjoyed brief prominence in the early seventies in Australia; *e.g.* the Tasmanian Conservation Trust in the Preceptious Bluff Case; Mineral Holdings (Aust.) Pty Ltd. *v.* Tasmanian Conservation Supreme Court 24/1973. See also Senator Murphy, Ministerial Statement on Legal Aid, Hansard 13 December 1973.

118. For a full review of the Australian situation on standing see Miller, A.S., "Public Interest Group Participation in Decision Making; The Broader Meaning of the Law Reform Commission Proposals" (1979) 10 Fed. L. Rev. 146 Kytou, E. "Locus Standi of Private Individuals seeking a Declaration of Injunction at Common Law" (1982) 13 M.U.L.R.453; Blackshield, A.R., "Alcoa Decision on Standing. How Liberal?" (1981) 6 Legal Service Bulletin 274; The Hon. Mr. Justice Kirby, "Standing: An Australian Overview", paper to First Environmental Law Symposium, Sydney 1982; Fogg, A., "Access and Standing: A Statutory Survey", paper to First National Environmental Law Symposium, Sydney 1982; Bates, G.M., *Environmental Law in Australia* (Butterworths, 1983), pp. 191-223; Bates, G. M. "Protecting Tasmania's Wilderness; Can the Law Help?" (1982) 6 *Legal Service Bulletin* 258; Fowler, R.J. "Environmental Litigation: Standing and the Role of the Courts" paper to Workshop on Industry and Environmental Law, University of Adelaide, 1984 (forthcoming).

119. The phrase "an interested person" was not in the original Bill; see "World Heritage Properties Conservation Act" (1983) 12 *Environmental Law* Newsletter 4.

120. Sax J.L., and Di Mento, J.F., "Environmental Citizen Suits: Three Years Experience under the Michigan Environmental Protection Act" (1974) 4 *Ecology Law Quarterly* 1; see also Haynes, J.K., "Michigan's Environmental Protection Act in its Sixth Year: Substantive Environmental Law from Citizen Suits" (1975) 53 *Journal of Urban Law* 589; Hand, J.P., "Natural Resources and Environmental Law" (1982) 28 *Wayne Law Review* 1025-38.

121. Stone, C., Should Trees Have Standing? Towards Legal Rights for Natural Objects (Kaufimann Inc., Los Altos, 1974). Kirby, *op. cit.* has remarked that Stone's theory "seems unlikely to attract supporters in Australia in view of the conservative approach to reform offered by the High Court".

122. See also Zervos, K., "The Need for an Environmental Defender's Office" in (1983) 12 *Environmental Law Newsletter* 32.

123. See Statement of the Attorney-General with regard to 82-H-7783. "An Act Relating to Environmental Rights", April 21, 1982, Rhode Island.

124. Canadian Environmental Law Association 1973. For an example of a recent Californian proposal for such a Bill of Rights (intended to be embedded in the Californian Constitution), see Carew-Reid, J., "Community involvement: directions for change" (1981) 6 *Legal Service Bulletin* 246.

125. It is recognised that in varying degrees, legislation in Australian states and at the federal level does incorporate some of the elements in the Canadian Environmental Bill of Rights proposal.

126. Lang, R. and Armour, H., The Assessment and Review of Social Impacts (Federal Environment Assessment Review Office, Canada, 1981), p. 70.

5

ENVIRONMENTAL PROBLEM: A Legal-cum-Ethical Solution

I.C. Saxena

Man has to live by nature. In actual practice, however, he yields to his own mores and habits. The standards of living of an individual, a family, a group of persons, a community or a nation depends upon the habits acquired and formed by the unit. The relationship between law and ethics must coexist. Law, doubtless, controls and regulates human conduct in situations of conflict of interest. But for its effective and successful implementation, it must depend upon the will of the people at large. It has been well said that Law is made for man and man is not made for law. This

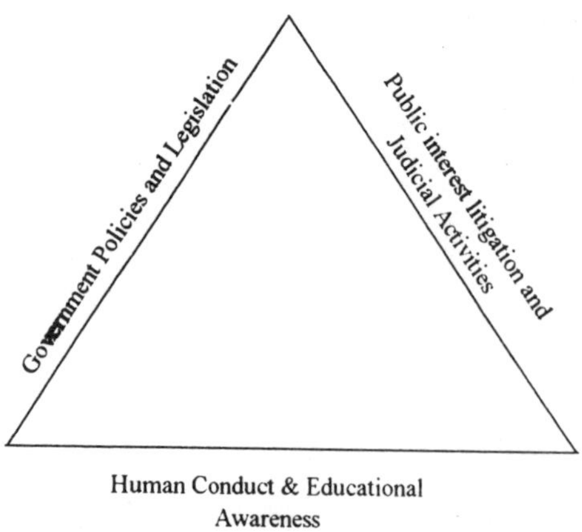

is a democratic process of life. An ethical action springs from the conscience of mankind, while a legal action is sanctioned (imposed) from outside. Ethics even in its perfect and truest form is not a subtitute for law and *vice versa.*

An environmental ethics over-emphasises a code of duties for an individual, ignoring the higher side of human rights. It lacks motivation and makes human action dull. Again there is a difference between ethics and ethical action; the former is theoretical, while the latter abodes in the domain of pragmatism. The important question, however, concerns as to how the ethical part of human conduct can be fortified by other supporting agencies. The answer is simple: through law, education, environmental policies and programmes, and ecological societieis for human welfare etc. The environmental justice is achieved through a triangular amalgam:

After the Declaration of 1972, a succession of legislation followed in India:

(i) The Water (Prevention and Control of Pollution) Act, 1974 (6 of 1974). It was amended by the Water (Prevention and Control of Pollution) Amendment Act, 1988 (Act No. 53 of 1988).

(ii) The Water (Prevention and Control of Pollution) Cess Act, 1977 (Act No. 36 of 1977).

(iii) The Forest (Conservation) Act, 1980. It was amended by the First (Conservation) Amendment Act, 1988 (Act No. 69 of 1988).

(iv) The Air (Prevention and Control of Pollution) Act, 1981 (Act No. 14 of 1981). It was amended by the Air (Prevention and Control of Pollution) Amendment Act, 1987 (Act No. 47 of 1987).

(v) The Environment (Protection) Act, 1986 (Act No. 29 of 1986).

In addition, we learn wildlife protection and avoidance of cruelty to animals act. There are, in addition, constitutional provisions :

Article 21:

No person shall be deprived of his life or personal liberty except according to procedure established by law.

Article 47:

The state shall regard the raising of the level of nutrition and the standard of living of its people and the improvement of public health as among its primary duties and, in particular, the State shall endeavour to bring about prohibition of the consumption except for medicinal purposes of intoxicating drinks and of drugs which are injurious to health.

Article 48-A:

The state shall endeavour to protect and improve the environment and to safeguard the forests and wild life of the country.

Part IV-A
FUNDAMENTAL DUTIES

Article 51-A

It shall be the duty of every citizen of India

* * * *

(a) To protect and improve the natural environment including forests, lakes, rivers and wild life, and to have compassion for living creatures.

Unlike the Consumer Protection Act, 1986, the democratic participation in the environmental legislation is minimal. It is not worthy, however, that Heads of Departments have been made personally liable for their negligence. Also "any person" my notify the authorities of his intention to file a complaint for an alleged environmental offence.

A succession of cases decided by the apex Court and the various High Courts reveals encouraging judicial trends favouring a healthy environment. The fundamental right to life and personal liberty enshrined in Article 21 has been held to include the right to enjoy pollutionless water and air.

A new remedy called the Public Interest Litigation has been invented and applied in Supreme Court and High Court Cases. The strict rules of *locus standi* have been relaxed. A social welfare society, a public spirited individual or a social reformer may initiate a case in public interest on behalf of the destitute, the downtrodden, the disabled, the disadvantaged person, the poor and one who is ignorant of law. Thus the Supreme Court may be moved under Article 32 for the enforcement of the fundamental right of right to life an personal liberty contained under Article 21. This fundamental right includes right to have pollution free air and water. In

L.K. Koolwal v. *The State* (A.I.R. 1988 Raj. 1), the Rajasthan High Court also allowed a writ petition in PIL for keeping the Jaipur city clean.

In *R.R. Delavai* v. *The Indian Overseas Bank,* AIR 1991 (Feb.) Mad. 61, 69, the Madras High Court pointed out briefly the purpose and scope of PIL in the apex court and the High Court. To quote: "Being aware of the limitations of legalism, the Supreme Court in the main and the High Courts to some extent for the last decade and a half did their best to bring law into the service of the power and downtrodden under the banner of Public Interest Litigation. The range is wide enough to cover from bonded labour to prison conditions and from early trial to environment pollution. It is not confined to enforcement of fundamental rights of an individual or a group of persons, but would take in rights of public at large".

A writ petition in public interest litigation will be rejected if it was moved in self-interest, by enmity, animosity, rivalry or mengeance and not in public interest. In cases of PIL, the Supreme Court has suggested/ ordered wide-ranging environmental programmes to be executed by the authorities. School, TV, Radio and Cinema have to play an important role.

Our youths must be taught that forests are our fortunes, jungles are our jewels, water is our wealth, pollutionless air is our priceless art of living. So we live and prosper. Our target of information is not an individual but masses and a sea of humanity. Expert technical advice must also be available to them. May we recommend :

Poor of students we find in a school where planting can be done in summer cool. Even in winter, wearing cloths of Wool Green, green must be the rule!

Our problems pertain to implementation of legislation and orders. Also are the programmes of awareness for the departments and public reform is the last step in the ladder.

6

ENVIRONMENT PROTECTION IN INDIA — Need for Participatory Approach

Dr. Suresh Misra

Environment protection has since the mid 1970's assumed a progressively greater importance in the eyes of the public and has in India now come to be regarded as being as important as world peace, and development. It has been recognised that as a consequence of economic growth and new production methods—but also as a result of consumer behaviour, the environment suffers damage exceeding matters regeneration capability thus endangering the foundations of life. Therefore, environmental planning is needed. Environmental planning may be defined as the control and development of interaction between natural environment and social development or as the regulation of inter-relationship between nature and society to optimise the inter-dependencies between the natural basis of the society and the structure of social activities and production. Environmental planning should be designed to develop interaction between social and natural environment leading to a sustainable development of the society.

The worldwide exploitation of raw materials and destruction of the environment are revealing with increasing urgency that our planet earth is virtually an integrated system. Its natural resources are limited. The overall system of our eco-sphere consists of hierarchically organised sub-system with varying degrees of interchanges and inter-relationship. The human race is obliged to fit itself into the system and place its actions within the general context.

Until recently, it might seem human beings did not have sufficient power to seriously affect the environment for better or worse. It would appear that natural limitations, as opposed to moral limitations would more than suffice to protect the environment from human destruction. However, a re-examination of human history and pre-history from an ecological perspective reveals a long-standing, but changing pattern of anthropogenic environmental destruction, paleolithic hunter gatherers armed with stone topped spears and arrows, traps and not least fire caused local extirpation and in some cases global extinction of other animal species and profoundly altered the character of biotic communities. Neolithic, ancient,medieval and modern agriculturalists caused soil erosion, siltation of surface waters deforestation, salination of both arable lands and fresh waters and desertification. This has now been replaced by the industrial civilization which has polluted the environment with synthetic toxic chemicals and radioactive elements, as well as intensified the kinds of destruction already apparent in the activities of pre-industrial man.

Nowadays nature is called the life supporting and self sustaining system. So a development prospect which is built on the destruction of life supporting and life sustaining system is bound to be counter productive and this is what is happening. This realisation has made us think that we can no longer ignore environment, we can no longer say that environmental problems are the disease of the rich.

Although simple, even obvious, the point that all environmental problems are human problems, in the sence that they are defined by people in terms of their effects on themselves, is not without significance. It means that environmental problems are not acts of gods or plagues visited on us by nature. Generally the situations arise out of our activities, and it is we who designate them problems. Given that we are rational there might be a contradiction here in that we are creating problems for ourselves.

This decade is a critical period for setting environmental policy, as well as the socio-political and scientific agenda, for the twenty-first century. Promoting environmentally sound policies concerning our planets natural resources must become a top priority of national and international agencies and organisations, both Governmental and private. This task is now here more important than in the developing countries. Least able to afford expensive environmental protection measures, the nations of the Third World find themselves under pressure both at home and abroad to trade the protection of irreplaceable natural resources for economic development. Sadly the earths greatest diversity is found in the countries least able to pay to protect it. The destruction of these natural resources, moreover, has dire consequences far beyond the borders of the individual nations.

GLOBAL CONCERNS FOR ENVIRONMENTAL PROBLEMS

Perhaps the global concern for environmental problems can be traced to the seminar on Development and Environment at Founex, Switzerland in 1972 organised by the Secretariat for the United Nation's Confcrence on the Human Environment. The Seminar concluded that environmental problems do not wrongly result from the development process itself but also from the very lack of development. Poor water, inadequate housing and sanitation, malnutrition, disease and natural disaster, were cited as important examples. The term, "pollution of poverty" was later used to described this aspect of the environmental question. Consequently it was suggested that environmental goals provide a new dimension to the development concept itself requiring an integrated approach to environment and development.

There are a number of reasons cited for environmental crises. In a recently released book. *The Third Revolution;* Paul Harrison says that the environmental crisis of the 1970's and 1980's is the outcome of population explosion during the two decades. Environmental impact in any place depends on three factors population, consumption of each person and technology which determines how much space and resources are used and how much waste is produced. His book also focuses on the question of hyper urbanization in the Third World countries. Third World countries which in 1950 had only 39 per cent of urban population had 63 per cent by 1990 and some 85 per cent of the growth in the world urban population in the 1980's occurred in Third World countries. At present there are 23 hyper cities with more than 8 million people and 14 of these are in developed countries where there had been none in 1950. In the Third World, environment had deteriorated as the members living in the cities increased. Bad housing is the most visible problem with typical Third World cities turning into Islands of concrete, steel and glass, surrounded by an ocean of wood, tin and plastic. Urban water needs are still poorly provided for and sanitation is in for worse shape with road gutters, open ditches and canals serving the purpose.

Further in their bid to ape the west, the developing nations have indulged in continued exploitation of the natural resources without any concern for the consequences. Thus developing countries too in the long run will contribute immensely to global environmental pressures and risks. But more importantly the developing countries need to do a bit of soul searching. Industrialization causes immense pressure on land and resulting in destruction of tropical forests for *e.g.* an estimated 30,000 acres of forests are hacked away every day. In the last decade as much as

250 billion tonnes of top soil was eroded and about 50 million acres of productive land rendered barren world wide. This has let not only to environmental problems but also to the creation of a large pool of landless labourers. The beneficiaries are often the large industrial groups and other such powerful lobbies.

THE INDIAN SCENE

In India 40 per cent of our urban and 51 per cent of our rural population fall below the poverty line. In the absence of capital resources, the poor are dependent on the environment for their livelihood. Purity of air and water becomes irrelevant in the absence of good food and shelter. The industrial sector has been pinpointed for being responsible for providing employment to atleast 40 per cent of the total populations. For them the preservation of the environment was not a prime concern resulting in large qualities of waste being released into the atmosphere. Thus atmospheric and river pollution, slack emissions, industrial effluents and sewage disposal are assuming an alarming propositions.

EXTENT OF ENVIRONMENTAL DEGRADATION

Infact the problem of environmental degradation is so acute that on a trip to the hills one's fantasy image of the hills gets shattered. Patches of Green hills turned into ashes, deodar trees axes to half and other debarked tall trees present a haunting sight. Most trees wear a deathly look. The forests are denuding at a faster rate than one could ever imagine. Forest fire is partly to be blamed for deforestation, besides illegal felling. It is estimated that 90 per cent of the forest fires are man made. The uncontrollable fires are no doubt destroying forests and the environment. According to the Modern Forest Fire Control Project (Ministry of Environment and Forest), there were 350 fire incidents in 1984 destroying 15,789.6 hactares and in 1989, 10,797.8 hectares of forests were lost in 510 cases of fire.

There is no doubt that rural and urban economy are intimately connected with forestry. The post independence population explosion and thurst on economic growth in both villages and towns, have made increasing demands on forests for fuelwood, fodder, minor forest produce, industrial raw material and land for income-generating activities such as agriculture, dams and mining. India today has among the world's lowest per capita availability of forest at 0.11 ha. as compared to other developing countries like Thailand with 0.60 ha. and China with 0.13 ha. of forests per person. Let us go a little deeper in the state of India's forests today.

Industrial wood consumption is 28 million cubic meter per annum, but annual forest growth is only 12 million cubic meter. The reminder is made up by depletion of forests beyond their regenerative capacities. Livestock currently requires 932 million tonnes of green and 780 million tonnes of dry fodder annually. Yet only 250 and 414 million tonnes respectively are available. The rest comes from grazing in forest land. Over 90 million livestock graze in the forests, which currently have the ability to sustainably support only 31 million. Over 58 per cent of Indian forests have no or inadequate regeneration capability mainly because of degradation. Consequently the productivity of India's forest is very low averaging 0.7 cubic meter per ha. per year. Fuelwood consumption is estimated at 235 million tonnes per year while annual production is only 90 million tons. Forest yields 40 million ton and the remaining comes from agro-waste or from the forest capital stock.

APPROACHES TO THE SOLUTION OF ENVIRONMENTAL PROBLEMS

This being the state of our environment there is a need to adopt certain specific strategies to protect it. Broad approaches to the solution of environment problems are likely to include one or more of the following elements :

- *(a)* Changes in the attitude and behaviour individuals,
- *(b)* The assessment and control of science and technology,
- *(c)* Specific reforms in society, decision making process,
- *(d)* Radical political-economic changes.

Individual behaviour might be regarded as supplying the fundamental buildings blocks of social processes. The only solution to the environmental crisis is the shared insight of people that they would be happier if they could work together and care for each other.[1] In the end person must be made to feel responsible for the present and future welfare of all mankind.[2] This seems to suggest that the changes in individual attributes will be engineered at the level of society as a whole. It is this sort of cultural change which is a new ethic that is needed, a theology of the earth, a powerful political ideology could emerge from a view of man in nature arising from a convergence of science and religion.[3]

However, if no political, social or cultural awareness in regard to protecting the natural environment is developing in a society and if no value system has been accepted then its the time that calls for a change in the decision making process for bringing about social and economic changes. There are a number of tools, that can be used to bring about social and economic changes. Here we would discuss only one aspet *i.e.*, law as a tool to bring about such changes in the society.

LAW AS A TOOL FOR SOCIAL AND ECONOMIC CHANGE

There is no doubt that law can prove to be a vital tool for bringing about such social and economic changes. Wisely used and effectively employed, it can provide the most peaceful and smooth means of change. There has of late been an enormous increase in the sweep of law. The horizon of law is expanding to cover new areas and there is hardly any field inhuman activity which does not in one way or the other come into contact with law.

Law gives protection to life, liberty and property and provides the means for bringing to book those guilty of violation. Laws lay down norms for specific settlement of disputes and prescribe the procedure. Laws secure basic freedoms and prohibit their infringement. A vital function of law is the surveillance of official action. Legal systems in the modern age also enact and administer welfare programmes and a variety of programmes none of which can be accurately identified with settling disputes between individuals. In the process of assuming manifold functions law has spread its tentacles so wide that whether we like it or not, we cannot escape it at any point of our existence. One of the major fields wherein there has been an interaction between law and social concern has been that of environmental protection.

As described earlier, law gives protection to life, liberty and property and provides means for bringing to book those guilty of violation, then the question is whose life, liberty and property ? It is only man's ? Can man destroy natures life and property ? Do only human being's have a right to life? What will happen if the harmonious man-nature relationship is broken by man and he assumes all the powers to destroy the nature. In such a situation who will protect the rights of the nature? Perhaps it is here that environmental laws are needed to curb these human abuses of nature now more than ever since. Perhaps in India the strategy of environmental protection is a pointer to this fact.

INADEQUACY OF EXISTING LAWS

Environmental protection in India has been on the agenda since the 1960s, yet is was only in 1980s that the seriousness of environmental degradation and the inadequacy of the existing laws to protect environment was realised. Since then a number of steps have been initiated. It was in 1980 that the Government of India set up a committee under the Chairmanship of the Deputy Chairman of the Planning Commission, Shri N.D. Tewari to suggest the administrative and legislature measures that ought to be taken for the protection of the environment. The significance of the Tewari Committee Report lies as much in what it recommended by way of institutional arrangements to tackle environmental problems as in its analysis of major environmental issues confronting the country.

TEWARI COMMITTEE

The Committee laid great emphasis on the need for the proper management of the country's natural resources of land, forest and water in order to conserve the nations ecological base and recommended that a central land commission should be set up as a first step to achieve this goal. It is gratifying to note that this recommendation has since been accepted by the Government and that steps have been taken for its implementation. The Committee also indentified three other areas of concern namely the need to preserve threatened species of flora and fauna and fragile eco-systems from extinction, the need to protect the pollution of fair and land by industrial effluents and wastes and the need to improve the condition of our human settlements. The Committee also stressed that in order to achieve these objectives it would be necessary to improve the level of environmental education in schools and colleges and to enhance the awareness of environmental issues among the people as a whole.

There is no doubt that there are a number of legislations that aim to protect the environment but these laws generally focused on specific types of pollution or on specific categories of hazardous substances. Some major areas of environmental hazards were not covered. There were inadequate linkages in handling matters of industrial and environmental safety, control mechanism to guard against low, insidious build up of hazardous substances especially new chemicals in the environment were weak. Because of a multiplicity of regulatory agencies there was a need for an authority which could assume the lead role in studying, planning and implementing long term requirements of environmental safety and to give direction to and coordinate a system of speedy and adequate response to emergency situations threatening environment. Therefore, an urgent need was felt for the enactment of a general legislation on environmental protection.

ENVIRONMENT PROTECTION ACT, 1986

It is in this context that the enactment of the Environment Protection Act, 1986 is a milestone in environmental protection in India. It had not only become necessary but more so it reflected the awareness and concern of the people and the Government towards environmental protection. The statement of the objects and reasons for the enactment of the Act states that concern over the state of environment has grown the world over since the sixties. The decline in environmental quality has been evidenced by increasing pollution, loss of vegetal cover and biological diversity, excessive concentrations of harmful chemicals in the ambient atmosphere and in food chains; growing risks of environmental accidents and threat to life support systems. Therefore, it was necessary to enact a legislation that would cover these loopholes.

Under the Environment Protection Act, 1986 the Central Government has the power to take all such measures as it deems necessary or expedient for the purpose of protecting and improving the quality of the environment and preventing, controlling and abating environmental pollution. It may appoint authority or authorities with such powers and functions as it deems fit to check environmental pollution. The Act lays down that no person carrying on an industry, operation or process shall discharge or emit or permit to be discharged or emitted any environmental pollutants in excess of such standards as may be prescribed. Further no person shall handle or cause to be handled any hazardous substance except in accordance with such procedure and after employing with such safeguards as may be prescribed. The Act further provides for the setting up of environmental laboratories and punishment for the contravenes of any of the provisions of the Act.

WATER AND AIR (PREVENTION AND CONTROL OF POLLUTION) ACT, 1974

Prior to this Act we had the Water and Air (Prevention and Control of Pollution) Act, 1974, the Indian Forest Act, 1922 and the Forest Conservation Act, 1980 and the Wildlife Act, 1977 and a few more. But in the following discussion we would concentrate only on the above mentioned Acts as these are still very important.

In fact the problem of pollution of rivers and streams assumed a considerable magnitude in recent years as a result of the growth of Industries and the increasing tendency of urbanization. It was, therefore essential to ensure that the domestic and industrial effluents are not allowed to be discharged into the water courses without adequate treatment as such discharges would render the water unsuitable as a source of drinking water as well as for supporting fish life and for use in irrigation. Pollution of rivers and streams also causes increasing damage the country's economy. Similarly with the tendency of the majority of industries to congregate in areas which were already heavily industrialized, the problem of air pollution began to be felt. Studies conducted by various bodies confirmed that the cities of Calcutta, Bombay, Delhi etc. are facing the impact of air pollution on a steadily increasing level.

Therefore, after having considered the relevent local provisions existing in the country the Government came to the conclusion that the existing local provisions were neither adequate nor satisfactory. An urgent need was felt for introducing a comprehensive legislation which would establish unitary agencies in the centre and states to provide for the prevention, abatement and control of pollution. Under the Act of 1974 Boards are to be set up both at the centre and the states. The powers and functions of these boards have been designed. The State Boards would plan a comprehensive programme for the prevention, control or abatement of pollution of streams, wells etc. in the State. A central as well as state laboratories are to be set up.

INDIAN FOREST ACT, 1927

The Indian Forest Act, 1927 consolidates the law relating to forests, transit of forest produce and the duty leviable on timber and other forest produce. Under the Act the State Government may constitute any forest land or waste land which is the property of Government, or over which the Government has proprietary rights, or to the whole or any part of the forest produce of which the Government is entitled, a reserve forest. The State Government may declare any forest land or waste land which is not included in the reserve forest as reserve. It can declare any tree or trees in a protected forest to be reserved. It can also prohibit the quarrying of stone, burning of lime or charcoal. Similarly the Forest (Conservation) Act, 1980 was in recognition of the awareness that deforestation and ecological imbalances as a result of deforestation have become social menace and further deforestation and ecological imbalances should be prevented. Under the Act no state government or authority should make, except with the prior approval of the central government, any order directing that (1) any reserved forest or any portion thereof shall cease to be reserved; (2) any forest land or any portion may be used for non-forest purpose; (3) any forest land may be assigned by way of lease or otherwise to any private person and (4) any forest land or any portion thereof may be cleared of trees which have grown naturally in that land.

WILD LIFE PROTECTION ACT, 1972

Similarly for the protection of wild animals and birds we have the Wild life Protection Act of 1972. Under the Act such officers are to be appointed for the protection of wild life as provided. Restrictions have been placed on the hunting of wild animals. The State governments have been given the power to declare any area to be a Sanctury, a National Park or a Game Reserve.

The number of environmental protection laws in our country are many and very comprehensive. Penalties are provided in the acts. But still we find that environmental degradation is on the increase. It is not enough that we create a structure of legislations. We must also creative a structure of administration to implement the laws as well, we must see that administration in all the relevant departments which are concerned with land and soil, water and forest, and flora and fauna are affected and influenced very deeply by this concern for preservation of environment.

However, in spite of these legislations we are facing a serious threat today. A recent study conducted by the W.H.O. reveals that Delhi, Bombay and Calcutta are badly affected by the problems of air pollution. The levels of air pollution in other Indian cities like Madras, Bangalore and Hyderabad is higher than the safety norms. In other words no Indian city is safe from the menace of air pollution. It is estimated that in Bombay alone motor vehicles of all kinds emit as much as 1,88,000 tons of carbon monoxide and roughly 27,000 tons of SPM. Recently the Ministry of Environment released the data on the pollution levels in the twelve most polluted cities in the country. Delhi tops the chart with 872 tons of pollution load per day, followed by Bombay with 549 tons, Bangalore with 254 tons and Nagpur with 48 tons per day. Problems are more severe in the case of our rivers, forests, and wild life. We have failed in our efforts to save them. Very, recently the World Wild Fund for Nature urged the Indian Government to take tougher measurers to protect the country's wetlands and promote their wise use for the benefit of local populations. According to WWF India, the continuing deterioration of wetlands in the country is a reflection of certain basic flaws and deficiencies in government policy and planning. In fact what is needed today is not a few more legislations but to create an awareness and to involve the people. We have failed in our mission to help create a good environment, though legislative enactments. Therefore, the need is for a mass movement and participatory approach by the people.

CONCLUSION

It has now been realised that nature's resources are finite, and that we have gone about exploiting this nature in a manner which is indeed criminal and is bound to be counter productive. Therefore, we should start thinking more seriously about our environment. So far the concern for environmental protection has been haphazard concern. But now it has to be systematic approach, in fact a wide ranging concern for the protection and preservation of the environment—for our own survival. Just like human beings have rights, nature has also the right to survival. Men do not have the right to destroy nature. Legislative enactments are no doubt necessary and needed to confine man from destroying nature but then laws alone do not bring about reforms. People have to be made aware of the basic fact that they have no business to destroy nature. What is needed is a strong movement that would help create and generate the required spirit to protect the environment.

In fact with the emergence of global industrial human culture, indeed, the human impact on the environment has so increased in force, intensity and ubiquitary that the global eco-system may gradually be degraded to the extent that forms of life presently existing are no longer in a position to adopt to the changed conditions. Therefore, the fear that haunts us today is that people may destroy the environment along with themselves, unless something is urgently done.

REFERENCES

Caldwell, L.K., Environment and Administration : The Politics of Ecology, in Environment, Resources, Pollution and Society (ed.) Weildian, W. Murdoch, Standford, Cambridge, 1971, p.394.

Gary, S., Hartshorn; Key Environmental Issues for Developing Countries, *Journal of International Affairs*, Winter, 1991.

Illich, I.E., 1973, Tools of Convivality, Calder and Boyars, London, 1973, p.50.

John, W., Mellor: Environmental Problems and Poverty, Environment, Vol. 30 No. 9 Nov. 1988.

Khoshoo, T.N., Environmental Concerns and Strategies, Indian Environmental Society, New Delhi, 1984.

Misra, R.P., (ed.) Environmental Ethics : A Dialogue of Cultures. SDF Publication, New Delhi, 1993.

Pirages, D.C., and P.R. Ehrihch; Art II: Social Response to Environmental Imperatives, W.H. Freeman, San Franscisco, 1974, p.64.

Shekhar, Singh, (ed.) Environmental Policy in India, IIPA, May 1984.

7

ENVIRONMENTAL ETHICS AND THE CONSTITUTION OF INDIA

Satish Shastri

"To her fair work did nature link
The human soul that through me ran
And much it grieved my heart to think
What Man has made of man."

The present day increasing tirade against environmental pollution and eco-imbalances proved a growing consciousness about the ecology, economics, energy, employment and equity (Five Es). Most important of these Five Es is the ecology[1] because it deals with basic life supporting systems—land, water, flora, fauna and the atmosphere. Moreover, 'ecology is one of the disciplines consisting of the core of environmental science'. Thus, the environmental management not only includes ecology but also includes energy, land use planning, forestry, population control, sanitation, industrial processes and agriculture, etc. It is abundantly study which includes ecology, physiology, genetics, chemistry, geology, physics, engineering, geography, economics, political science, sociology, psychology, etc. To conclude environmental science is the application of this knowledge to manage the environment.

Air, water, land are the representative samples of natural environment, and geophysical, atmospheric and hydrological systems determines the character of biosphere including biota and mankind of a region. If we try to disturb the nature or natural environment in excess, they disturb and damage us irreparably. Therefore, it is necessary to know how to behave with the components of natural environment. The principles of ethics[2] which guide an individuals as how to behave with the environment is known as environmental ethics. It mainly consists of rules of moral correctness or moral behaviour towards the components of environment *viz.* land, water, air, flora and fauna. In the present paper an attempt has been made to discover and reiterate the environmental ethical rules prevailing in the olden society and how far they are being abided by and recognised by the Indian Constitution.

ENVIRONMENTAL ETHICS IN OLDEN TIMES

Since vedic time the main motto of social life was to have in harmony with the nature. Sages, saints and great teachers of India lived in forests, meditated and express in the form of *Vedas, Upanishads, Smiritis* and *Dharmas.* This literature of olden times preached in one form or the other a worshipful attitudes towards plants, trees, mother earth, sky *aakash,* air *vayu,* water *jal* and animals and to keep a benevolent attitudes towards them. It was regarded a sacred duty to protect them. The Hindu religion enshrined a respect for nature and environmental harmony and conservation. It instructed man to show reverence for the presence of divinity in nature.

A perusal of the Hindu religion, scriptures *Vedas, Upnishads, Smiritis, Puranas, Ramayana, Mahabharata, Geeta,* mythological literatures including stories, social and moral codes and political rules reveals that the following were the general guiding principles to be observed by all in their daily life :

- *(a)* respect nature;
- *(b)* life of living being dependent on various components of nature;
- *(c)* keep harmony with nature;
- *(d)* protect natural environment;
- *(e)* utilise natural resources to satisfy the need of the people;
- *(f)* presence of the divinity of nature in all living and non-living objects;
- *(g)* destruction of nature means destruction of mankind;
- *(h)* All must have compassion for animate objects *e.g.* trees, animals, birds, acquatic life, etc.
- *(i)* Air, water, land, sky, trees, animals are the creation of God and He dwells in all of them. Therefore, to worship them is to worship Him—The creator of the universe;
- *(j)* Man, since one of the creations of the God, has no special

privilege or authority over other creatures; on the other hand has more obligations and duties to protect and improve them;

(k) *Ahimsa Parmo Dharmah* (non-violence) is the *dharma* of the highest order one should be non-violent toward animals, trees, and other micro-organism alike. *Ahimsa* (non-violence) was considered as sin. Therefore, 'not eating of meat in Hinduism is considered both an appropriate conduct and a duty';

(l) Draught, fury of flood and storm desert, heavy rain, burst of clouds, lightening, earthquakes, volcanic eruptions, heavy tides are the violent forms of anger shown by the creator—the God and Goddesses;

(m) Purity of thought and expression and cleanliness of the environment around us should be observed;

(n) All lives, human and non-human including trees, are of equal value and all have same right to existence. It shows that the principle of sancity of life is clearly ingrained in the Hindu religion.

Many verses in *Rigveda* and *Atharvaveda* have been devoted in the praise of Lord *Surya* (Sun), *Vayu Devta* (Lord Air), *Agni Devta* (God Fire), *Varuna Devta* (God of Water), *Prithivi Mata* (Mother Earth), *Vanya Devi* (Goddess of Forest), etc. Therefore, cutting of trees, polluting air, water, land was regarded as sin as they were to be respected and regarded as God and Goddesses. Maintaining them pure was considered to be the duty of everyone. Hindu society did not consider it proper to throw dust on a public path. *Rigveda*[3] *Manusmiriti*[4], *Charak Samhita*[5] have emphasized on the purity of water and healing and medicinal value of the water. Because of these injunctions a system of *Maryada* (code of conduct) developed in the society to keep the water clean and pure.

Similarly, trees and plants have been regarded as indispensable in the life of human being. They have been considered as revered, bestower of good and protector form the evils with a concept of God living in it. Trees and plants are considered as the abode of various God and Goddesses. Though the sense of worship has a background of utility and spiritfulness. *Rigveda* devoted one entire hymn to the praise of healing properties of trees[6]. Following are some of the names of trees associated with the God and Goddess.

Lotus — Laxmi (Goddess of Wealth)

Vat (Banyan)	Brahma (Creator of Universe)
Ashoka	Buddha, Indra
Kadamb	Krishna
Palasa	Brahma, Gandharva
Neem	Sitala, Manasa
Fig	Vishnu, Rudra
Mango	Laxmi, Govardhan
Pipal	Vishnu, Krishna

Thus trees are worshipped as *Vriksa Devta* (Tree Deity) with prayers, offering of water, flower, sweets and encireled by sacred threads. Planting of trees is also regarded as sacred religious duty and work of great virtue. *Matsya Puran* has regarded one tree equal to ten sons. According to *Vaha Purana* 'one who plants one pipal, one neem, one ber, ten flowering plants or creepers, two pomogranases, two oranges and five mango trees will not go to hell[7]'. Therefore, cutting of trees and destruction of flora was considered a sinful act. *Kautiliya*[8] and *Manusmiriti* have prescribed various punishment for destroying trees and plants. *Charak Samhita* has considered the destruction of forests as the most dangerous act for humanity and its welfare.

> The destruction of forests is most dangerous for the nation and for human beings. *Vanaspati* (vegetation) has direct relationship with the well being of the society. Due to the pollution of natural environment and the destruction of *Vanaspati,* many diseases crop up to ruin the nation. Only then *Vanaspati* with medicinal qualities may enhance the nature and cure diseases of human beings.[9]

The above discussions shows that Hindu worship of trees and plants has been partly on utility and partly as a religious duty and mythology. Gradually it because a religious object and object of worship.

ANIMALS, BIRDS AND HINDU WAY OF LIFE

As the above discussion makes it amply clear that Hindu way of life has respect and consideration for natural world including animals and bird. The most important aspect of Hindu Theology is the association accorded to different species with reincarnation and deities and it is believed that Supreme Being has actually gets himself incarnated in the form of various species.[10]

Faith, truth, chastity and the law.

Further, Hindus were advised to treat all other species just like their own children.

'One should look upon deers, camels, monkeys, donkeys, rats, reptiles, birds and flies as though they were their own children, what is that which distinguishes these from those (children)'.[11]

Several Hindu, gods and goddess have animals and birds as their mounts. Some of them associated with Hindicties are as follows :

Lion	Durga
Wild goose	Brahma
Elephant	Indra, Ganesh
Bull	Shiva
Rat	Ganesh
Swan	Saraswati
Eagle	Vishnu
Serpent	Shiva
Fish	Kama
Monkey	Hanuman, Ram
Peacock	Kartikeya, Saraswati
Owl	Laxmi
Crocodile	Ganga
Ass	Sitla
Dog	Bhairava, Dattatrey
Deer	Vayu

Apart from economic importance of animals and birds in Vedic India, they fulfilled significant *ritualistic* and *symbolic* roles in the society. *For example,* cow's milk and other dairy products in religious ceremonies, fasting days and offered as oblations to gods. Looking to the uses and medicinal utility of the cow's milk, urine and dung, cow is sanctified and cow slaughter is treated as highest form of sin.[12] These rituals and sanctity is still maintained and observed today in the daily life of Hindus.

Killing of animals is against basic tenet of Hindu way of life—*Ahimsa* (Non-violence), therefore, deep faith in the doctrine of non-violence it was felt that God's grace can be had by not killing his creatures and killing of mute animals and birds is a sin[13].

By the end of Vedic and Upanishadic period Buddhism and Jainism came into existence. Non-violence, truth, respect and love for other living organism including trees became their basic tenets of their religion. These religions also continued the precepts for environment protection. The Buddhist emperor *Great Asoka* (273-36 B.C.) promoted the planting and preservation of flora and fauna. He prescribed various punishments for the killing of including ants, squirrels, rats, birds and cutting of trees.

ENVIRONMENTAL ETHICS AND THE CONSTITUTION OF INDIA

India has inherited a culture of tolerance, non-violence, equity and compassion for animate objects. In the olden time they were a part of daily life and synthesized with the religion. Religious teachings, social and political norms, and economic policies treated man as a part of nature not as a moulder or superior to it. Air, water, land, animals, plants and human being are the creation of one superior power—The God. Therefore, the fundamental ethics of behaviour with each other was to live in harmony with each other because it was well realised that each one of them is dependent on another and destruction or damage to another is the destruction of self. Each one is complimentary to each other. Therefore, interdependence, cooperative living and close association with other components of environment is the real basis of human life. It became a sacred duty of human being—*homo sapiens* to behave rationally and protect the nature. Wisdom of *Vedas* religious principles of Hindus, and moral doctrine taught the lesson of coexistence between man and his environment through which later on became a part of the daily life of people.

Above-mentioned philosophy of peaceful coexistence with the nature got way in one way or another in Indian constitution. Two articles relating to environment were incorporated in the Indian constitution Articles 48-A[14] and 51-A(g) [15]. Article 48-A is a constitutional pointer to the state to protect and improve the environment and Article 51-A(g) confer a fundamental duty on the citizens of India to protect and improve the environment and have comparison for living creatures. This clearly shows that the Indian Parliament fell in line with old tradition values and conferred on the citizens of India to protect the natural environment including forests, lakes, rivers and compassion for living creatures. The language used in the article clearly indicated the principle of equity, co-existence, reverence of nature and non-violence has been given a legal recognition. The use of the terms 'protect and improve' implies the necessity of the various components of environment for human life and that improvement for human life and that improvement of the natural environment means improvement of the quality of life. Further, protection of the environment implicitly directs us not to cut the trees, keep the water of rivers and lakes, etc. clean and wholesome. This reminiscence us of centuries old 'Chipko movement' of village Kherjarilli of Rajasthan where Amerita Bai, her 4 family members and other 359 persons sacrificed their lives to save trees of the village (popularly know as 'Green Khejris')[16]. Thus, we have a culture where trees are regarded more precious and revered them our lives. The government has also declared the villages of Bishnois in Punjab, Haryana and Rajasthan states as 'reserved areas' and cutting of trees and killing of animals has been declared an offence in those village tarritories. As a result of which if you happen to visit these villages, you can witness deers and other innocuous animals rooming in the village freely and fearlessly.

The term 'to have compassion for living creatures' used in Article 51-A(g) impliedly recognises the principle that all creates are made equal and that animal killing should be prohibited as taught by the principle of non-violence or as the moral code of conduct says 'killing of animals and birds is a sin of highest orders'. Abiding by this philosophy of olden time the Parliament has also passed two Statutes, *viz.* The Wild Life (Protection Act 1972 and cruelty against certain animals 19). It is also in consonance with another ethical principle that unarmed enemy and mute birds and animals should be harmed or attacked. This reminds us a old story of prince Siddharth who saved a swan which was shot at with an arrow by his brother. Same Prince Siddharth became Lord Buddha—a great preacher of non-violence *(Ahimsa)* and harmonious relationship with nature. The object behind this theory compassion for living creatures. Scientifically speaking, animals and birds are the second trophic level of the *food-chain* or foodwebs and help in energy flow. The utility of the animals and their products needs no special description here. It should not also be forgotton that wildlife is the guardian and protection of our forests. Decay of wildlife implies decay of forests. Thus, forests and wildlife are inter-dependent and complementary to each other.

Indian social and moral ethics relating to environment protection and conservation has been accepted by the Indian Courts time and again. Some of the judicial pronouncement upholding old Indian traditions concerning environment are quoted below :

> "Water and rivers have dominated the destiny and fortune of man. Plentiful rivers have brought prosperity to those who lived on their banks.. If Bhagirath brought salvation, Ganga sustains life... ages have rolled up by it and it has remained enternal."[17]
>
> 'In order to arouse amongst the people the consciousness of cleanliness

of environment the Government of India and the governments of the states and of union territories may consider the desirability of organising 'keep the city clean week', 'keep the town clean' and 'keep the villages clean week' ... atleast once a year. During that week the entire city, town and village should be kept as far as possible clean, tidy and free from pollution of land, water and air.'[18]

'Environmental law is based on the realisation of mankind of the dire physical necessity to preserve these invaluable and none too easily replenishable gift of mother nature to man and his grogeny from the reckless wastage and raparious appropriation that common law permits.'[19]

'You must teach your children that the ground beneath their feet is the ashes of our grandfather. So that they will respect the land. Tell your children that the earth is rich with the lives of our kin. Teach your children what we have taught our children. That the earth is our mother. Whatever, befalls the earth befalls the sons of the earth. If man spit upon the ground, they spit upon themselves. ...He is the God of man and his compassion is equal for red and white. This earth is precious to him and to harm the earth is to heap contempt on its creator. ...Contaminate your bed and you will one night suffocate in your own waste.'[20]

'Preservation of the environment and keeping the ecological balance unaffected is a task which not only Government but also every citizen must undertake. It is a social obligation and let us remind every citizen that it is his fundamental duty as enshrined in Art. 51-A(g) of the Constitution.'[21]

Thus, various constitutional provisions and statutes relating to environment have tried to revive and regenerate age old Indian tradition of reverence for nature and not to interfere with nature excessively. It kindless a ray of hope in our hearts that revivals of old environmental ethics would guide mankind to safer, and more peaceful path and retrieve our losses inflicted on nature by our scientific and technological advancements. Therefore, to avoid a major catastrophie or extinction of mankind it is suggested that :

1. We must *live in harmony* with nature. Peaceful coexistence and narmonious relation with nature must be prime motto of our life.
2. Forests, lakes, rivers, animals and birds, all should be treated equally with man because they are complementary to each

other. Damage or destruction of one of them would invite the downfall of the other.

3. *'Ahimsa Paramo Dharmah'* we should follow the cult of non-violence whether we deal with a man, tree or birds and animals. Similarly, we must *have compassion* for all living creatures.
4. *Reverence for nature* and reintegration with nature must be the basis of our code of ethics and value system. Because 'the quality of the environment depends upon the values that we espouse and how we organise our societies.'

Abiding by the above-mentioned principles we can build a hope that humanity will return to consciousness in connection with the biosphere—to the re-enhancement of nature and the implementation of the environmental ethics.

To see a world in a grain of sand,
And heaven in a wild flower,
Hold infinity in the palm of your hand
And eternity in an hour.

William Blake

REFERENCES

1. The term Ecology is derived from Greek world *Olkos* meaning a place to live. Popularly it is known as the study of relationship of an organism or group of organism to their environment. According to Odum it is 'the study of the structure and function of nature.' Odum, E.P., *Fundamentals of Ecology*(1971) Philadelphia W.B. Saunders.
2. Ethics is a system of moral principles or rules of conduct. *Ethics* means the science that 'deals with morals, moral correctness, *Oxford Advanced Learners Distionary* (1989), p.430.
3. *Rigveda,* VII, 42.2
4. *Manusmiriti,* IV, 56.
5. *Charaksmhita, Sutrasthanam* XXVII 213, 215, *Charaksmhita, Vimanusthana* III 6(1).
6. *Rigveda,* X 97.
7. *Varaha Purana,* 172.39.
8. *Kautiliya Arthasastra,* ed. or R. Swasastry, Mysore (1967) Book III Chapter 19, p.78.
9. *Charaksamhita, Vimanasthan,* III 11.
10. *Atharvaved,* XII 1.15.
11. *Srimad Bhaggavatam,* VII 14.9.
12. *Rigveda* X 87.16; *Yajurveda* XIII 47, 49 (No person should kill animals helpful to all and by serving them one should obtain heaven, 47; *Manusmiriti,* V 45 'He who injures innoxious beings with a desire to give himself pleasure, never finds happiness, neither living or dead.'
13. *Yajnavalkyasmiriti, Acaradhyayah* V 180. *Vishnu Purana* III B. 15, *Manusmiriti* V 45.

14. Article 48-A 'The State shall endeavor to protect and improve the environment and to safeguard the forest and wildlife of the country'.
15. Article 51-A(g). It shall be the duty of every citizen of India-to protect and improve the natural environment including forests, lakes, rivers and wildlife and to have compassion for living creatures.
16. The episode took place in 173/A.D.
17. F.K. Hussain v. Union of Intlia, AIR 1990 Ker. 321.
18. M.C. Mehta v. Union of India, AIR 1988 SC 115, 1128.
19. T. Damodhar Rao v. S.O. Municipal Corporation, Hyderabad, AIR 1987 SC 171, 180.
20. Quoted in Shri Sachidanand Pandey v. State of W.B., AIR 1987 SC 1109, 1114.
21. Rural Litigation and Entitlement Kendra v. State of UP, AIR 1987 SC 359, 364.

8

LAW AS A TOOL FOR ENVIRONMENTAL CONSERVATION AND MANAGEMENT IN INDIA

*P.S. Sangal**

Before we take up the role of law as a tool for environmental conservation and management in India, we will first like to give in some detail the constitutional position, as it is well known that laws derive their validity from the constitution.

THE CONSTITUTIONAL POSITION

The Indian Constitution as adopted in 1950 did not deal with the subject of 'protection of environment' as such. However, in 1976, through the Constitution 42nd Amendment Act, environmental protection as such was introduced into the Constitution in the following manner :

In Part IV relating to Directive Principles of State Policy, an Article 48-A was added which is as follows :

> "48-A Protection and improvement of environment and safeguarding of Forests and Wild Life—The State shall endeavour to protect and improve the environment and to safeguard the forests and wild life of the country".

A new Part-IVa was added which introduced in the Constitution of India 'Fundamental Duties'. Article 51A(g) of this part is as follows :

"51A" *Fundamental Duties'*— It shall be the duty of every citizen of India —

* Dr. P. S. Sangal, Dean, Faculty of Law, University of Delhi, Delhi-110 007 (India)

(g) to protect and improve the natural environment including forests, lakes, rivers, and wild life, and to have compassion for living creatures."

These two additions to the Constitution of India make it imperatives for the State to do everything it can to protect and improve the environment which expressly includes here the safeguarding of the forests and wild life of the country.

Besides these Constitutional provisions which expressly provide for environmental protection, in the three lists of the 7th Schedule of the Constitution of India, the following Entries exist which permit the Union of the State or both, to make laws having a bearing directly or indirectly, on environment.

LIST I : UNION LIST

Entry No.

6. Atomic Energy and mineral resource necessary for its production.
14. Entering and agreements with foreign countries and implementing of treaties, agreements and conventions with foreign countries.
24. Shipping and navigation on inland waterways.
25. Maritime shipping and navigation, including shipping and navigation on tidal waters.
29. Airways, regulation and organisation of air traffic and of aerodromes.
52. Industries, the control of which by the Union is declared by Parliament by law to be expedient in the public interest.
53. Regulation and development of oil fields and mineral oil resources.
54. Regulation of mines and mineral development to the extent to which such regulation and development under the control of the Union is declared by Parliament by law to be expedient in the public interest.
56. Regulation and development of inter-State rivers and river valleys.
57. Fishing and fisheries beyond territorial waters.

LIST II : STATE LIST

6. Public health and sanitation; hospitals and dispensaries.
10. Burials and burial grounds; cremations and cremation grounds.
14. Agriculture, including agricultural education and research, protection against pests and prevention of plant diseases.

15. Preservation, protection and improvement of stock and prevention of animal diseases.
17. Water, that is to say, water supplies, irrigation and canals, drainage and embankment, water storage and water power subject to the provisions of Entry 56 of List-I.
18. Land, that is to say, rights in or over land, land tenures including the relation of landlord and tenant and the collection of rents; transfer and alienation of agricultural land, land improvement and agricultural loans; colonization.
21. Fisheries.

LIST III : CONCURRENT LIST

17. Prevention of cruelty to animals.

17A. Forests.

17B. Protection of Wild Animals and Birds.

18. Adulteration of food stuffs and other goods.
19. Drugs and poisons, subject to the provisions of Entry 59 of List I with respeat to opium.
20. Economic and Social Planning.

20A. Population Control and Family Planning.

29. Prevention of the extension from one State to another of infecting or contagious diseases or pests affecting men, animals or plants.
32. Shipping and navigation on inland waterways as regards mechanically propelled vessels,...
36. Factories.
37. Boilers.
38. Archaeological sites and remains other than those declared by or under law made by Parliament to be of national importance.

Under these various powers given to the Union Parliament and the Legislatures to make laws under these Entries in the Constitution as well as the corresponding Entries under the Government of India Act, 1935, quite a number of laws have been framed by the Union and the State Legislatures some of which are given hereunder :

Legislation Relating to Environmental Protection
Selected List of Environment Related Legislation
Enacted by the Union Legislature.

1. Water Pollution

1. The River Boards Act, 1956.
2. The Merchant Shipping (Amendment) Act, 1970.

3. The Water (Prevention and Control of Pollution) Act, 1974.
4. The Water (Prevention and Control of Pollution) Cess Act, 1977.

2. *Air Pollution*
   1. The Indian Boiler Act, 1923.
   2. The Factories Act, 1948.
   3. The Industries (Development and Regulation) Act, 1951.
   4. The Mines and Minerals (Regulation and Development) Act, 1957.
   5. The Air (Prevention and Control of Pollution) Act, 1981.
3. *Radiation*
   1. The Atomic Energy Act, 1962.
4. *Pesticide*
   1. The Insecticides Act, 1968.
   2. The Poison Act, 1919.
5. *Others*
   1. The Wild Life (Protection) Act, 1972.
   2. The Indian Forest Act, 1927.

   2A. The Forest Conservation Act, 1980.

   3. The Indian Fisheries Act, 1897.
   4. The Urban Land (Ceilings and Regulation) Act, 1976.
   5. The Prevention of Food Adulteration Act, 1954.
   6. The Ancient Monuments and Archaeological Sites and Remains Act, 1958.
   7. The Environment (Protection) Act, 1986.
   8. The Public Liability Insurance Act, 1991.

SELECTIVE LIST OF ENVIRONMENT-RELATED LEGISLATION.

Enacted by the State Legislatures

1. *Water Pollution*
   1. Orissa River Pollution Prevention Act, 1953.
   2. Maharashtra Prevention of Water Pollution Act, 1969.
2. *Smoke Control*
   1. The Bengal Smoke Nuisance Act, 1905.
   2. The Gujarat Smoke Nuisance Act, 1963.
   3. The Bombay Smoke Nuisance Act, 1912.
3. *Pest Control*
   1. The A.P. Agricultural Pest and Disease Act, 1919.
   2. The Assam Agricultural Pest and Disease Act, 1954.
   3. The U.P. Agricultural Disease Pests Act, 1954.
   4. The Mysore Destructive Insects and Pests Act, 1917.

5. The Kerala Agricultural Pests and Disease Act, 1958.

4. *Land Utilisation and Land Improvement*
   1. The A.P. Improvement Schemes Act, 1949.
   2. The Acquisition of Land for Flood Control and Prevention of Erosion Act, 1955.
   3. The Bihar Wastelands (Reclamation, Cultivation and Improvement) Act, 1946.
   4. The Delhi Restriction of Uses of Land Act, 1964.

OTHER ATTEMPTS OF LEGAL CONTROL OF POLLUTION

Though the first most comprehensive attempt at prevention and control of water pollution is sought to be made by the Water (Prevention and Control of Pollution) Act, 1974, yet that does not mean that prior to that there was no attempt at legal control of water pollution.

Long standing concern for the purity of water and atmosphere generally is evident from Sections 277 and 278 of the Indian Penal Code, 1960. Section 277 lays down that, whoever, voluntarily corrupts or fouls the water of any public spring or reservoir, so as to render it less fir for the purpose for which it is ordinarily used, shall be punished with imprisonment of either description for a term which may extend to 3 months, or with fine which may extend to 500 rupees, or with both. Section 278 lays down that whoever, voluntarily vitiates the atmosphere in any place so as to make it noxious to the health of the persons in general, dwelling or carrying on business in the neighbourhood or passing along a public way, shall be punished with fine which may extend to 500 rupees.

Almost from the beginning of this century, some of our Municipal and Public Health Acts, particularly those for large cities, on the pattern of United Kingdom's Local Authorities Act, conferred powers on our local bodies for controlling water pollution caused by industrial effluents and for necessary enforcement action against the erring industries. Our Municipal Acts, generally prohibit persons from discharging any pollutant or trade effluent from factories into Municipal drains, except in accordance with the relevant bye-laws. Likewise, no sewage can be discharged into any water course until it has been treated so as not to contaminate the Water. For illustration, Sections 241, 242 and 250 of Delhi Municipal Corporation Act, 1957 could be usefully referred.

> Municipality to draft a plan within six months for removing nuisance. In appeal, Sessions Court reversed the order. The High Court approved of the order of Magistrate. In further appeal, the Supreme Court also affirmed the Magistrate's order.

The Supreme Court in its judgment categorically laid down that where existeid a nuisance in a locality due to open drains, heaps of dirt, pits and excretion by humans for want of lavatories and consequential breeding of mosquitoes, the court could require municipality, under Section 133 of the Criminal Procedure Codc which provides for public nuisance, to abate the nuisance by taking affirmative action on a time bound basis. When such order is made, the municipality cannot take the plea that notwithstanding the public nuisance, financial inability validity exonerated it from statutory liability. The Supreme Court was emphatic in holding that Section 133 Cr.P.C. was categoric although its language snows a discretion resting with the court, because judicial discretion when facts for its exercise are present, has a mandatory import.

The Supreme Court further said that public nuisance because of pollutions being discharged by big factories, to the detriment of the poorer sections, is the challenges to the social justice component of the rule of law. The Supreme Court was quite clear about the fact that a responsible municipal council constituted for the precise purpose of preserving public health cannot run away from the principal duty by pleading financial inability.

RURAL LITIGATION AND ENTITLEMENT KENDRA, DEHRADUN *v.* STATE OF U.P.

Another pace-setter in the field is the Supreme Court judgment in Rural Litigation and Entitlement Kendra, Dehradun *v.* State of U.P.,[1] where the Supreme Court again delivered a historic judgment and held.[2]

"We are clearly of the view that so far as the line-stone quarries classified in category C in the Bhargav Committee Report are concerned which have already been closed down under the directions of the Bhargav Committee should not be allowed to be operated. If the lessees of these lime stone quarries have obtained any stay order from any court permitting them to continue the mining operations, such stay order will stand dissolved and if there are any subsisting leases in respect of any of these lime stone quarries thay shall stand terminated without any liability against the State of Uttar Pradesh. If there are any suits or writ petitions for continuance of expired or unexpired leases in respect of any of these lime stone quarries pending, they will stand dismissed."[3]

Supreme Court on obligation of industry

The Supreme Court of India has lately propounded some principles which can be termed almost revolutionary.

The Supreme Court expressed the view in *M.C. Mehta* v. *Union of India*[4] that an enterprise which is engaged in a hazardous or inherently dangerous industry which poses a potential threat to the heath and safety of the persons working in the factory and residing in the surrounding areas was an absolute and non-delegable duty to the community to ensure that no harm results to anyone on account of the hazardous or inherently dangerous nature of the activity which it has undertaken. The enterprise must be held to be under an obligation to provide that the hazardous or inherently dangerous activity in which it is engaged is conducted with the highest standards of safety and if any harm results on account of such activity, the enterprise must be absolutely liable to compensate for such harm and it should be no answer to the enterprise to say that it had taken all reasonable care and that the harm occurred without any negligence on its part. Since the persons harmed on account of the hazardous or inherently dangerous activity carried on by the enterprise would not be in a position to isolate the process of operation from the hazardous preparation of substance or any other related element that caused the harm, the enterprise must be held strictly liable for causing such harm as a part of the special cost for carrying on the hazardous or inherently dangerous activity. If the enterprise is permitted to carry on a hazardous or inherently dangerous activity for its profits, the law must presume that such permission is conditional on the enterprise absorbing the cost of any accident arising on account of such hazardous or inherently dangerous activity as an appropriate item of its overheads.[5]

Such hazardous or inherently dangerous activity for private profit can be tolerated only on condition that the enterprise engaged in such activity indemnify all those who suffer on account of the carrying on of such activity regardless of whether it is carried on carefully or not. This principle is also sustainable on the ground that the enterprise alone has the resource to discover and guard against hazards or dangers and to provide warning against potential hazards. The Supreme Court, therefore, held[6] that where an enterprise is engaged in a hazardous or inherently dangerous activity and harm occurs to anyone on account of an accident in the operation of such activity resulting, *for example*, in the escape of toxci gas, the enterprise is strictly and absolutely liable to compensate all those who are affected by the accident and such liability is not subject to any of the exceptions which operate *vis-a-vis* the torturous principle of strict liability under the rule in *Rylands* v. *Fletcher*[7].

The Court also pointed out that the measure of compensation in the kind of cases referred to in the preceeding paragraph must be correlated to the magnitude and capacity of the enterprise and the damages awarded must have a deterrent effect.[8] The larger and more prosperous the enterprise, greater must be the amount of compensation payable by it for the harm caused on account of an accident in the carrying on of the hazardous or inherently dangerous activity for the enterprise.[9]

Now it must be clearly understood that the principles so enunciated by the Supreme Court are "Law declared by the Supreme Court" which, according to Article 141 of the Constitution of India "shall be binding on all courts within the Territory of India."

OBLIGATIONS OF OFFICERS OF A COMPANY AS SPELT OUT BY THE SUPREME COURT

While permitting Shriram Foods and Fertilizer Industries to restart its plants for manufacture of caustic chlorine, etc., the Supreme Court gave its permission, subject to certain conditions which were required to be strictly and scrupulously followed by the company. The Court make it clear that if at any time there was violation of any one of more of these conditions, the permission was liable to be withdrawn.

Condition No. (5) of the 11 conditions was as follows[10]:

"(5) The management of Shriram will obtain an undertaking from the Chairman and Managing Director of the Delhi Cloth Mills Ltd. which is the owner of the various units of Shriram as also from the officer or officers, who are in actual management of the caustic chlorine plant that in case there is any escape of chlorine gas resulting in death or injury to the workmen or to the people living in the vicinity, they will be personally resposible for payment of compensation or such death or injury and such undertaking shall be filed in Court within one week from today. "Shriram Industries moved an application as one for clarification though in substance it was an application seeking modification of 3 of these 11 conditions. The aforesaid condition 5 was one of these 3 conditions, modifications of which was sought on the ground that compliance with them would entail operational and practical difficulties.

The contention of Shriram regard to condition 5 was that it was not clear as to who could be described as an officer in actual management of the caustic chlorine plant and that this particular direction required clarifications that the management could obtain the necessary undertaking from such officer.[11]

The Supreme Court observed that in view of the contention which had seriously been pressed on behalf of Shriram in support of their plea that the caustic chlorine plant should be allowed to be reopened as ther was no risk or hazard to the community in the operation of the caustic chlorine plant, there was no reason why the officer or officers who had ultimate control over the affairs of the caustic chlorine plant and/or who were responsible to the management for the efficient operation of the caustic chlorine plant should hesitate to give an undertaking to the Court that in case of death or injury arising on account of escape of chlorine gas, they would be personally responsible.[12] But while making this comment, the Court said that it was not unmindful of the fact that if absolute unlimited liability were to be imposed on any officer or officers in the employment of Shriram for death or injury arising on account of possible escape of chlorine gas, many competent persons would shy away from accepting employment in the company and that would make it difficult for the company to have really competent and professionally qualified persons to manage and operate the caustic chlorine plant.

The Court observed that is would therefore, modify the condition prescribed by it by providing that undertaking should be obtained from the officer who was the 'occupier' of the caustic chlorine plant under the Factories Act, 1948, and/or the officer who was responsible to the management for the actual operation of the caustic chlorine plant as its head, and such undertaking should stipulate that in case there was any escape of chlorine gas resulting in death or injury to the workman or to the people living in the vicinity, the officer concerned would be personally responsible, to the extent of his annual salary with allowances, for payment of compensation for such death or injury but if he showed that such escape of gas took place as a result of an act of God or vis major or sabotage or that he had exercised all due diligence to prevent such escape of gas, he should be entitled to be indemnified by Shriram.[13]

So far as the undertaking to be obtained from the Chairman and Managing Director of Shriram was concerned, it was pointed out by Shriram that DCM Ltd., which was the owner of Shriram, had several units manufacturing different products and each of these units was headed and managed by competent and professionally qualified persons who were responsible for the day to day management of its affairs and the chairman and managing director was not concerned with the day to day functioning of the units and it would not, therefore, be fair and just to require the chairman and managing director to give an undertaking that in case of death or injury resulting on account of escape of chlorine gas, the chairman and managing director would be personally liable to pay compensation. The Court found it difficult to accept this contention of the company.

The Court observed that it did not see any reason why the chairman and/or managing director should not be required to give an undertaking to be personally liable for payment of compensation in case of death or injury resulting on account of escape of chlorine gas, particularly when according to the reports of various expert committees which examine the working of caustic chlorine plant, there was considerable negligence in looking after its safety requirements and in fact considerable repair and renovation with the installation of safety devices had to be carried out at a fairly heavy cost in order to reduce the element of risk or hazard to the community[14]. The Court, however, made it clear that the undertaking to be given by the chairman and/or managing director might provide that no liability would attach to the chairman and/or managing director if he would show that the escape of chlorine gas was due to an act of God or vis major or sabotage. But in all other cases the chairman or managing director should hold himself liable to pay compensation. That alone, according to the Court, would ensure proper and adequate maintenance of safety devices and instruments and operation of the caustic chlorine plant in a manner which would considerably reduce, if not eleminate, risk or hazard to the workmen and to the people living in the vicinity."[15]

CRIMINAL LIABILITY OF AN OFFICER OF A COMPANY

What we have discussed so far is the civil liability of an officer and his company in the case of a company which is guilty of pollution, particularly because of pursuing hazardous process. Liability for compensating the victims is not provided under any of the Pollution Control Laws *i.e.* under the Water (Prevention and Control of Pollution) Act, 1974 of the Air (Prevention and Control of Pollution) Act, 1986. But it has been provided, *inter alia,*[16] in the Supreme Court Judgment of M.C.L. Mehta *(supra),* shall be binding on all courts within the territory of India and, therefore, becomes a part of law of this country under Article 141 of the Constitution of India. But criminal liability is provided under each one of the aforesaid laws.

Chapter VII of the Water Act is titled 'Penalties and Procedure', Section 41(1) of this act says that, whoever, fails to comply with certain named provisions of the Act shall, on conviction, be punishable with imprisonment for a term which may extend to three months or with fine which may extend to Rs. 5,000 or with both and in case the failure continues, with an additional fine which may extend to Rs. 1,000 for every day during which such failure continues after the conviction for the first such failure.

Sub-section (2) of this section says that, whoever, fails to comply with any direction issued by a Court under sub-section (2) of Section 33 shall, on conviction, be punishable with imprisonment for a term which may extend to three months or with fine which may extend to Rs. 5,000 or with both and in case the failure continues, with additional fine which may extend to Rs. 1,000 for every day during which such failure continues after the conviction for the first such failure.

Section 42 of the 1974 Act lays down that, whoever, does certain things specified there, like destroying, pulling down, etc., of any pillar, post, etc., shall be punishable with imprisonment for a term which may extend to three months or with fine which may extent to Rs. 1,000 or with both.

Section 43 provides penalty for contravention of provisions of Section 24 (prohibition on use of stream or well for disposal of polluting matter, etc.) which shall not be less than six months in imprisonment but which may extend to six years and with fine. Section 44 states that, whoever, *contravenes* the provisions of Section 25 (about new outlets) or Section 26 (about existing discharge) shall be punishable with imprisonment for a term which shall not be less than six months but which may extend to six years and with fine.[17]

Section 45 provides for enhanced penalty after previous conviction and it says that if any person, who has been convicted of any offence under Section 24 of Section 25 or Section 26, is again found guilty of an offence involving contravention of the same provision, he shall, on the second, and on every subsequent conviction, be punishable with imprisonment for a term which shall not be less than one year but which may extend to seven years and with fine: provided that for the purpose of this section no cognizance shall be taken of any conviction made more than two years before the commission of the offence which is being punished.

JOINT AND SEVERAL RESPONSIBILITY OF OFFICERS OF A COMPANY

Section 47 of the 1974 Act says that where an offence under this Act has been committed by a company, every person who, at the time of offence was committed was in charge off and was responsible to the company for the conduct of the business of the company as well as the company, shall be deemed to be guilty of the offence and shall be liable to be proceeded against and punished accordingly. Of course, absence of *mens rea* will protect the officer concerned because the *proviso* says that nothing contained in this sub-section shall render any such person liable to any punishment provided in this Act if he proves that the offence was committed without his knowledge or that he exercised all due diligence to prevent the commission of such offence.

However, sub-section (2) of Section 47 makes if clear that notwithstanding anything contained in sub-section (1), where an offence under the Act has been committed by a company and is attributable to any neglect on the part of any director, manager, secretary or other officer of the company, such director or other officer shall also be deemed to be guilty of the offence. This sub-section makes it clear that even if there is no mens rea, the officer will be liable when the offence has been committed due to his neglect also.

There are similar provisions in the other two acts about criminal liability of the officers of companies and under the 1981 Act, as amended in 1987, as well as under the 1986 Act, the punishments and the penalties provided are even higher than those provided under the 1974 Act.[18]

COLLECTIVE RESPONSIBILITY OF BOARD OF DIRECTORS

It should also be noted that the Supreme Court has lately evidenced its keenness about the enforcement of these provisions against the erring officials. The case in print is *UP Pollution Control Board* v *Modi Distillery*.[19] In this case, the Supreme Court observed that on a combined reading of the provisions contained in sub-section (1) and (2) of section 47 of the 1974 Act, their Lordships had no doubt, whatever, that the Chairman, Vice-chairman, Managing Director and Members of the Board of Directors of Modi Industries Ltd., the company, owning the industrial unit Modi Distillery, could be prosecuted as having been in charge of and resposible to the company for the business of the industrial unit, Modi Distillery owned by it, and could be deemed to be guilty of the offence with which they are charged.

The Supreme Court, therefore, allowed the appeal of the UP Pollution Control Board, set aside the judgment and order passed by the Allahabad High Court, and restored the judgment and order passed by the Chief Judicial Magistrate, directing issue of process to the respondents, the chairman, vice-chairman, managing director and members of the Board of Directors of Modi Industries Ltd. The Supreme Court also directed the Chief Judicial Magistrate to proceed with the trial as expeditiously as possible in accordance with law.[20]

TWO RECENT IMPORTANT DEVELOPMENTS

In India, rapid changes are taking place in the field of law. Two of these are almost novel. They are : (1) The enactment of the Public Liability Insurance Act, 1991 which provides, probably for the first time in the world, for all hazardous chemical industries to insure themselves compulsorily to be able to give immediate relief to all the affected parties and (2) the scheme of labelling of environment friendly produces.

(a) The Public Liability Insurance Act, 1991

This legislation can rightly be called a legislative response to Bhopal-type tragedy which occurred in 1984. This Act should be considered as a welcome step as it deals with a very direct fallout of the Bhopal-type tragedy.

The growth of hazardous industries, processes and operations in India has been accompanied by the growing risks from accidents, not only to the workmen employed in the undertakings, but also innocent members of the public who may be in the vicinity. Such accidents lead to death and injury to human beings and other living beings and damage private and public properties. Very often, the majority of the people affected are from the economically weaker sections and suffer great hardships because of delayed relief and compensation. While workers and employees of hazardous installations were protected under separate laws,[21] members of the public were not assured of any relief except through long legal processes. Industrial units seldom had the willingness to readily compensate the victims of accidents and the only remedy available to the victims was to go through prolonged litigation in the courts of law. Some units might not have even the financial resources to provide the minimum relief.

It was felt essential, therefore, to provide for mandatory public liability insurance for installations handling hazardous substances for providing minimum relief to the victims. Such an insurance, apart from safeguarding the interests of the victims of accidents, would also provide cover the enable the industry to discharge its liability in respect of large number of claims arising out of major accidents. If the objective of providing immediate relief is to be achieved, the mandatory public liability insurance should be on the principle of "no fault" liability as it is limited to relief only on a limited scale[22]. However, availability of immediate relief would not prevent the victims to go to courts for claiming larger compensation.[23]

NO FAULT LIABILITY

Section 3 of the Act provides that where death or injury[24] to any person (other than a workmen[25]) or damage to any property has resulted from an accident, the owner[26] shall be liable to give such relicf as is specified in the schedule for such death, injury or damage. This section also provides that in any claim for relief, the claimant shall not be required to plead and establish that the death, injury or damage in respect of which claim has been made was due to any wrongful act, neglect or default or any person. Thus, it lays down no-fault liability. In order to enable the owner to discharge his liability under the Act, every owner is required by Section 4 to take out, before he starts handling[27] any hazardous substance[28], one or more insurance policies providing for contracts or insurance whereby he is insured against liability to give any relief under Section 3. Sub-section (3) of Section 4, however, states that the central government may, by notification, exempt from operation of sub-section (1) any owner, namely, (a) the central government; (b) any state government; (c) any corporation owned or controlled by the central government or a state government or (d) any local authority. Of course, the saving grace is that no such order for exemption should be made in relation to such owner unless a fund has been established and is maintained by the owner in accordance with the rules made in this behalf for meeting any liability which may arise.

Looking to the laudable objective of this law, it is out of place to exempt the government of government-owned or controlled corporations or local authorities. It will be in the fitness of things that the government or its owned or controlled corporations or local authorities should be made amenable to this law and the government should not have the power to exempt them from the operation of the law. It does not make any difference to the victim whether he receives injury from a private party or from a government agency.[29]

Application for claim for relief:

Section 6(1) of the Act provides that an application for claim for relief may be made:

- *(a)* by the person who sustained injury;
- *(b)* by the owner of the property to which the damage has been caused;
- *(c)* where death has resulted from the accident, by all or any of the legal representatives of the deceased; or

(d) by any agent duly authorised by such person or owner of such property or all or any of the legal representatives of the deceased as the case may be.

Sub-section (2) provides that every application under sub-section (1) should be made[30] to the collector and be in such form, containing such particulars and be accompanied by such form, containing such particulars and be accompanied by such documents as may be prescribed. Section 7(1) provides that on receipt of an application under Section 6, the collector shall, after giving notice of the application to the owner and the insurer and after giving the parties (including the insurer) an opportunity of being heard, hold an enquiry[31] into the claim or each of the claims and may make an award determining the amount of relief which appears to him to be just and specifying the person or persons to whom such amount of relief shall be paid.

The collector shall arrange to deliver copies of award to the parties concerned expeditiously and in any case within a period of 15 days from the date of the award.[32] The owner or the insurer, as the case may be, must deposit the entire amount within 30 days of the date of announcement of the award.[33] The collector shall have all the powers of civil courts for the purpose of taking evidence on oath; enforcing the attandance of witnesses; compelling the discovery and production of ducuments and material objects and for such other purposes as may be prescribed. The collector shall be deemed to be civil court for the purpose of Section 195 and Chapter XXVI of the code of Criminal Procedure, 1973.[34]

Where the insurer of the owner, against whom the award is made fails to deposit the amount of such award within 30 days, such amount shall be recoverable from the owner/insurer as arrears of land revenue or of public demand[35]. A claim for relief in respect of death, etc. shall be disposed of as expeditiously as possible[36].

CLAIMS FOR COMPENSATION UNDER OTHER LAWS NOT ORDERED

Section 8 of the Act makes it clear that the right to claim relief under this law in respect of death or injury to any person or damage to any property shall be in addition to any other right to claim compensation in respect thereof under any other law[37] for the time being in force. Of course, the amount of compensation recoverable under any other law shall be reduced by the amount of relief paid under this Act.

PENALTIES FOR VIOLATION UNDER THE ACT

The penalties in case of serious lapses like contravention of any of the provisions of sub-section (1) or sub-sectioin (2) of Section 4, *i.e.* not taking of insurance policies, or failure to comply with any direction issued under Section 12, *i.e.* in regard to prohibition regulation of the handling of any hazardous substance or stoppage of supply of electricity, water, etc. shall be imprisonment for a term which shall not be less than one lakh rupees or with both.[38] For the second or subsequent offence, the punishment provided is imprisonment for a term which shall not be less than two years but which may extend to seven years and with fine which shall not be less than one lakh rupees.[39]

Of course, minor lapses like default in compliance with directions issued under Section 9 or failure to comply with orders issued under sub-section (2) of Section 11 or creating obstruction to any person in discharge of his duties under Section 10 or sub-section (1) or sub-section (3) of section 11, shall be punishable with imprisonment which may extent to three months or with fine which may extend to 10,000 rupees or with both[40].

COMPARABLE THINKING IN THE CONTINENT OF EUROPE

Laws comparable to the present Act will be the laws to be enacted by the Member States under the Council of European Community's Directive on Civil Liability for Damage caused by Waste[41]. This Directive concerns civil liability for damage and injury to the environment caused by waste generated in the course of occupational activity from the moment it arises.

For purposes of this Directive, 'producer' means any natural or legal person whose occupational activities produce waste and/or any one who carried out pre-processing, mixing or other operations resulting in a change in the nature or composition of this waste, until the moment when the damage or injury to the environment is caused. 'Damage' means *(i)* damage resulting from death or physical injury and *(ii)* damage to property. 'Injury to the environment' means a significant and persistent interference in the environment caused by a modification of the physical, chemical or biological conditions of water, soil and/or air insofar as these are not considered to be damaging to property.

Article 3 of the Directive states that the producer of waste shall be liable under civil law for the damage and injury to the environment caused by the waste, irrespective of fault on his part.

Article 4 lays down that the plaintiff may take legal action to obtain:

(a) The prohibition or cessation of the act causing the damage of injury to the environment;
(b) the reimbursement of expenditure arising from measures to prevent the damage or injury to the environment;
(c) the reimbursement of expenditure arising from measurers to compensate for damage to property;
(d) the restoration of the environment to its state immediately prior to the occurrence of injury to the environment or the reimbursement of expenditure incurred in connection with measures taken to this end; and
(e) indemnification for the damage.

Article 14 directs the Member States of the European Community to bring into force, not later than January 1, 1991[42], the laws, regulations and administrative provisions necessary to comply with this directive. Under the same Article, the Member States have further been directed to inform forthwith the Commission about the laws, regulations and administrative provisions which they have enacted.

(b) The Scheme of Labelling of Environment Friendly Products

This novel scheme will be operated on a national basis and provides accredition and labelling for household and other consumer products which meet certain environmental criteria along with quality requirement of the Indian standards for that product.[43] The label shall be known as ECOMARK. Any product which is made, used or disposed of in a way that significantly reduces the harm it would otherwise cause to the environment would be considered as Environment Friendly Product. The objectives of the scheme are as follows :

(i) To provide an incentive for manufactures and importers to reduce adverse environmental impact of products;
(ii) to reward genuine initiatives by companies to reduce adverse environmental impact of their products;
(iii) to assist consumers to become environmentally responsible in their daily lives by providing information to take account of environmental factors in their purchase decisions;
(iv) to encourage citizens to purchase products which have less harmful environmental impacts; and
(v) ultimately to improve the quality of the environment and to encourage the sustainable management of resources.[44]

THE CRITERIA FOR ECOMARK

Environmental criteria[45] for each product category will be notified by the central government and later on shall be translated into Indian Standards by the Bureau of Indian Standards. The criteria shall be for broad environmental levels and aspects, but will be specific at the product level. Products will be examined in terms of the following main environmental impacts :

(a) That they have substantially less potential for pollution than other comparable products in production, usage and disposal;
(b) that they are recycled, recyclable, made from recycled products of biodegradable, where comparable products are not;
(c) that they make significant contribution to saving non-renewable resources, including non-renewable energy resources and natural resources, compared with comparable products;
(d) that the product must contribute to a reduction of the adverse primary criteria which has the highest environmental impact associated with the use of the product and which will be specifically set for each of the product categories.

In determining the primary criteria for a product, the following shall be taken into account :

(a) production process including source of raw-materials;
(b) case of natural resources;
(c) likely impact on the environment;
(d) energy conservation in the production of the product;
(e) effect and extent of waste arising from the production process;
(f) disposal of the product and its container;
(g) utilization of 'waste (and recycled materials);
(h) suitability for recycling of packaging;
(i) biodegradability.[46]

REFERENCES

1. A.I.R. 1985 S.C., 652.
2. *Ibid.*, p.654.
3. The very wide sweep of this order is evident. As a result of this order and the supplementary orders of the Supreme Court, the report is that the Mussoorie Hills are fast returning to their original state of being health resorts from their degraded state of having become

hazardous places for human health.

4. AIR 1987 SC 1086.
5. AIR 1987, SC. 1086.
6. *Ibid.*
7. (1868) L.R. 3 HL 330.
8. This part of the judgment has been criticised on the basis that it is not a good principle to make the quantum of damages depend it is not a good principle to make the quantum to damages depend upon the paying capacity of the agency responsible for the damage, and that deterrence should be achieved through criminal liability.
9. AIR 1987 SC 1086 at p.1100.
10. See *Shriram Foods & Fertilizer Industries* v. *Union of India*, AIR 1987 sc 965 at p.979. This judgment of the Supreme Court can also be called as *M.C. Mehta* v. *Union of India.*
11. See AIR 1987 SC at p.984.
12. *Ibid.*, p.985.
13. *Ibid.*
14. *Ibid.*, p.986.
15. *Ibid.*
16. The cases of compensations for damages caused by negligence of a party are well established. A recent case is *Mukesh Textile Mills (P) Ltd.* v. *Subramanya Sastri*, AIR 1987 Kar.87, in which a person was held liable for damage caused to has neighbours crops by breach of his molasses tank.
17. Sometime back, it was reported in the press that the sub divisional Judicial Magistrate of Patna has convicted the Unit Manager of Bata India Limited, Patna under Sections 41 and 44 of the Water (Prevention and Control of Pollution) Act for discharging effluents of the factory into the Ganga without proper treatment. But keeping in view the fact that the accused had installed a treatment plant and there was nothing on record to show against the previous antecedents, the Court released the Unit Manager, on probation, under Section 360 of the Criminal Procedure Code, on the execution of a bond on Rs. 2,000 for a period of 2 years. He was directed to maintain peace and good conduct during that period. At that time he was General Manager (Environment) and Tannery Advisory in the Company at Calcutta see. The Times of India of Ist March, 1989, under the heading 'Bata Official Convicted for Pollution'.
18. Section 15 of the Environment Protection Act, 1986 is relevant here. It is as follows :

    Penalty for contravention of the provisions of the Act and the Rules, Orders and Directions — (1) Whoever, fails to comply with or contravenes any of the provisions of this Act, or the rules made or orders or directions issued thereunder, shall, in respect of each such failure or contravention, be punishable with imprisonment for a term which may extend to five years or with fine which may extend to one lakh rupees, or with both, and in case the failure or contravention continues, with additional fine which may extend to five thousand rupees for every day during which such failure or contravention continues after the conviction for the first such failure or contravention.

    (2) If the failure or contravention referred to in sub-section (1) continues beyond a period of one year after the date of conviction, the offender shall be punishable with imprisonment for a term which may extend to seven years.
19. (1987) (2) Scale 208.
20. See also P.S. Sangal "Responsibility of Officer under Pollution Control Laws" published in *Corporate Law Adviser*, p. 275, Vol. 1, Issue 5 (May 1989).
21. See, *e.g.* the Workmen's Compensation Act, 1923.
22. The maximum relief under the Act is Rs. 25,000 per person for fatal accidents in addition to re-imbursement for medical expenses, if any, incurred on the victim up to a maximum of Rs. 12,500.

23. This is possible under the law of tort.
24. Injury has been defined in explanation to Section 3 of the Act to include permanent total or permanent partial disability or sickness resulting out of an accident.
25. Under the explanation to Section 3, 'workman' has the meaning assigned to it in the Workmen's Compensation Act, 1923.
26. Under section 2(g) of the Act, "Owner" means a person who has control over handling of any hazardous substance.
27. 'Handling', in relation to any hazardous substance, "means the manufacture, processing, treatment, package, storage, transportation by vehicle, use, collection, destruction, conversion, offering for sale, transfer or the like of such hazardous substance" See 2(c) of the Act.
28. 'Hazardous substance' means any substance or preparation which is defined as hazardous substance under the Environment (Protection) Act, 1986, and exceeding such quantity as may be specified, by notification, by the Central Government; sec. 2(d) of the Act. Under Section 2(e) of the Environment (Protection) Act, 1986, 'hazardous substance' means any substance or preparation which, by reason of its chemical or physico-chemical properties or handling, is liable to cause harm to human beings, other living creatures, plants, micro-organism, property or the environment.
29. Unlike the original Monopolies and Restructive Trade Practices Act, 1969, the Consumer Protection Act, 1986 applies equality to all manufactures, whether governmental or private. Now even MRTP Act has been amended to cover public sector undertakings.
30. No application for relief shall be entertained unless it is made within 5 years of the occurrence of the accident.
31. Subject to the rules, the collector may follow such summary procedure as he thinks fit : sec. 7 (4) of the Act.
32. *Ibid.*, Sec. 7(2).
33. *Ibid.*, Sec. 7(3).
34. *Ibid.*, Sec. 7(5).
35. *Ibid.*, Sec. 7(6).
36. *Ibid.*, Sec. 7(7).
37. This has reference to compensation payable under any other law such as under the law of tort.
38. *Ibid.*, Sec. 14(1).
39. *Ibid.*, Sec. 14(2).
40. *Ibid.*, Sec. 15.
41. Submitted by the Commission on 1 September 1989 (89/C/251/04) published in Official Journal of the European Communities, 4.10.1989.
42. On author's enquiry in March, 1991, he came to know that nothing concrete could emerge by Janaury 1, 1991.
43. Resolution dated 20 February 1991 of the Department of Environment, Forests and Wild Life, Ministry of Environment and Forests, S.R. 85(E), Gazette of India Extra., Pt. II, sec. 3*(i)*, February 21, 1991.
44. *Ibid.*
45. *Ibid.*
46. *Ibid.*

9

GLOBAL CONCERN FOR ENVIRONMENTAL HAZARDS AND REMEDIAL MEASURES

R.G. Padia

During the last twenty-five years one of the basic problems engaging urgent attention has been the deterioration of the environment. Until 1940s, the world centre used to be occupied by most powerful nations which used to exploit the physical and natural resources of their captive colonies. Industrial, scientific and technological development was uneven and limited to a few nations.

After the Second World War, two major developments put in motion a new world order. The first was the establishment of the United Nations and the second the gradual grant of political freedom to a large number of nations in the world. The newly emergent nations, in a bid to attain the level of the developed countries, started exploiting all their available physical and natural resources in all possible ways, unmindful of their side-effects, as also their possible depletion. During this period in many nations the population also rose very rapidly and there was also a natural shift of population to the larger cities in the wake of industrialization which opened new opportunities of employment and opportunity. This brought into focus problems of conservation and protection of environment.

During the earlier centuries when some countries of the North achieved rapid industrialization, they had not faced such enormous environmental problems. But it is indeed a irony that now the developing countries of the world are not in a position to pursue their economic and materialistic policies with the similar relentless disregard of the environmental complications. They have come to realise the grim reality that unprecedented advancement of Science and Technology has also brought in the deleterious effects of ecological imbalance. It has also become clear that in may cases, the natural wealth of a nation is not unlimited and indiscriminate exploitation of the same is liable to generatc not only serious environmental pollution problems but also a risk of depletion of the wealth itself.

The idea that one generation has no moral, legal or equitable right to exploit all the physical and natural wealth of the nation to the detriment of future genereations has now gained ground and so the exploitation of the natural resources has to be judicious. The man has come to realise that ultimately the real object of all development is his right to live in peace, in a safe and secure environment, and this a right which relates to his very existence. This right knows no geographical barriers, since it is a basic human right, an inalienable right available to every human being throughout the world.

There have been a series of international covenants and treaties before the Stockholm Conference of June, 1972, but they did not primarily relate to the environment, and they were negotiated with some other primary object. Some such treaties may be named in this connection, since they did incidently affect the preservation of the global environment.

1. The Nuclear Weapons Tests Ban Treaty of 1963.
2. The treaty for the Prohibition of Nuclear Weapons in Latin America of 1967.
3. The Treaty laying down the Principles Governing Activities of States in the Exploration and Use of Outer Space Including the Moon and Celestial Bodies of 1967.
4. The Treaty on the Non-Proliferation of Nuclear Weapons of 1968.
5. The Treaty on the Prohibition of the Emplacement of Nuclear Weapons on the Seabed and Ocean Floor and Subsoil thereof 1971.

The first major step at the international level directly relating to environment was taken by the United Nations General Assembly in December, 1968 when it decided to convence a conference in 1972 on the Human Environment. In its resolution the General Assembly had specifically noted that the relationship between man and his environment was undergoing profound changes, that the economic development while offering unprecedented opportunities to the man also involved dangers like impairment of the quality of the human environment caused by such factors as air and water pollution, erosion of soil and other forms of soil deterioration, rapidly increasing population and accelerating urbanization.

Among the various decisions, resolutions and recommendation of the Conference was the one which related to "Action Plan" for the protection and enhancement of the environment. It contained three basic ideas :

(a) An "Earthwatch" programme which was devised for indentification of environmental crises. It included evaluation, research and monitoring to collect such data so as to predict important environmental conditions and trends in various parts of the world.

(b) Environmental Management — It included the actual recommendations which were considered desirable or necessary.

(c) Supporting Measures — It included the steps necessary for long range measures, such as, recommendations regarding necessary education, training and public information, organizational arrangements and financial and other forms of assistance.

In its proclamation, the Conference had emphasised that the human race had already acquired a stage where man could transform his environment, and that he had to take prudent care to avoid massive irreversible harm to the earthy environment. The Conference exhorted the states to take all possible steps to prevent pollution of the seas so that hazards to human health and marine life could be minimised; that the discharge of toxic and other substances in the atmosphere and the release of heat in excessive quantities or concentrations should be so controlled as to render them harmless; that science and technology should be applied with identification, avoidance and control of environmental risks; that the states had the responsibility to ensure that their activities of exploitation of their own resources, although an excercise of their own sovereign rights, did not cause damage to the environment of other states; and that the environment must be spared the effects of nuclear weapons and all other means of mass destruction.

Although many states at the Conference insisted on the creation of a specialised Agency of the United Nations relating to human environment, but ultimately, only a Governing Council was formed consisting of 58 members with its own Secretariat to be located at Nairobi, Kenya, a developing country. It may be noted that after the Conference, it is this Governing Council of the United Nations Environmental Programme which acts as a framework in co-ordination of world environment activities. It is this policy making body which is aiding and advising the nations of the world about the environmental hazards and the measures to harmonise their policies consistent with environmental betterment. The Governing Council has also organised several conferences who have made their own suggestions. Thus, Habitat Conference was held in 1976 and it has set out several principles to prevent aggravation of the deteriorating circumstances of people in human settlements, to check uncontrolled urbanisation and rural backwardness.

The basic principles of the Stockholm Conference were reasserted when the tenth anniversary of the conference was celebrated at Nairobi in May, 1982. The Nairobi declaration also adopted a resolution in long-term environmental strategies for achieving "sustainable development to the year 2000 and beyond."

For the last few years new environmental issues have sprung up—the warming of the earth and depletion of ozone layer. According to the leading scientists and environmentalists of the world, there is an excessive emission of carbon dioxide in the atmosphere from the burning of coal, oil, fuels and industrial gases. The warming up of the earth is laible for the melting of the giant glaciers of the Arctic and Antarctic regions which would also raise the level of sea waters, thereby threatening the submerging of the coastal cities of the world. Moreover, in the upper atmosphere, there exists a vast ozone layer which protects the earth from ultra violet rays of the Sun. According to the leading scientists, a hole has been formed in the said layer and the same is gradually widening. The said development has been a matter of deep concern throughout the world. A general view is growing round the world that chlorofloro carbons must be totally eliminated from its consumption. In view of the seriousness of the situation, United Nations Environment Programme gave a slogan "Global Warming Global Warning" for the Annual Environment Day of the year 1989 (*i.e.*, 5th June, 1989). It is suggested that time has come when the Heads of the major military powers of the world must meet without any further delay in order to evolve a satisfactory environmental strategy to meet the possible catastrophe. Earth Summit is planned in 1992 at Rio de Jeneiro, Brazil to deliberate on these and other environmental issues.

It is generally true that in respect of international conferences, conventions and treaties, the real problem is not only to accept in principle certain broad generalisations but reflection of will in translating those resolutions into practice by incorporating them in the municipal laws as also a close and constant vigil by judicial agancies on the acts of the instrumentalities of the State in implementing those laws. It is indeed a matter of pride that deliberations at the Stockholm Conference have been taken note of in all seriousness by Indian Government as well as by the Supreme Court of India. In fact, not only various legislative measures have been devised but the Constitution has also been amended. Thus, by the Constitution (Forty-second Amendment) Act, 1976, Article 48-A has been inserted as one of the Directive Principles according to which the State has to take all necessary measures to protect and improve the environment and to safeguard the forests and wild life of the country.

Similarly, a new Part, IV-A by way of Fundamental Duties has also been added by the same Amendment and Sub-clause (g) of the Article 51-A casts a duty on every citizen of India to protect and improve the natural environment including forests, lakes, river and wild life, and to have compassion for living creatures.

Now some of the more important legislative efforts taken by our country may be alluded to :

(A) THE WILD LIFE (PROTECTION) ACT, 1972

The Act has been passed under the provisions of Article 252 to prevent the rapid decline of wild animals and birds in the country. Poaching of certain animals has been completely prohibited under the Act except for the limited purpose of education or scientific research and scientific management. In respect of certain wild animals, a licence has been made a pre-requisite for their hunting. A provision for licence has also been made for carrying on business in trophy and animal articles.

The Act also provides that the State Government may declare any area to be a sanctuary or as a National Park if it considers that such area is of adequate ecological, faunal, floral, geomorphological, natural or zoological significance for the purpose of protecting, propagating or developing wild life or its environment.

(B) THE WATER (PREVENTION AND CONTROL OF POLLUTION) ACT, 1974

Water being a State subject under Entry 17, the act has been passed by the Parliament under the provisions of Articles 252. Soon after the enactment, the U.P. Legislature has also passed a resolution adopting the Act. The Act has been passed for the prevention and control of water pollution and for taking the requisite steps for maintaining and restoring the wholesomeness of water. On account of large scale discharge of industrial waste into the rivers and streams, the quality of water as well as its utility have been adversely affected. The water of many rivers is no longer fit for even drinking or acquatic life. A general consensus has emerged that rivers and streams should not be used directly as a repository of refuge and rubbish substances.

The Act defines water pollution as such contamination of water or such alteration of physical, chemical or biological properties of water or such discharge of sewage, trade effuents or any other liquid, solid or gaseous substance into water which is likely to render it harmful or which might cause injuries to public health or public saftey, or to the life and health of animals, plants or acquable organisms, or which obstructs the domestic, commercial, industrial or agricultural use of the water. Thus, the definition is very wide and any kind of water pollution in respect of a river or stream can be dealt with under the Act.

The Act makes provisions for the constitution of a Central Board as also of State Boards to take all necessary measures relating to environmental protection and for the prevention and control of water pollution. The State Board may make surveys of any area and of the flow or volume of any river, stream or well. It may also take samples of water from any river, stream or well or sewage or trade effluents for the purpose of making the necessary analysis. A prohibition has been imposed on every person to cause or permit any poisonous, noxious or polluting matter to enter into any river, stream or well. Previous consent of the State Board is required to bring into use any new or altered outlet for the discharge of sewage or trade effluent. The State Board can also take emergency measures where immediate action is required pertaining to any polluting matter. Provisions have been made for the establishment of Central Water Laboratory and State Water Laboratories for testing and analysing the polluted materials. A different Act, namely, The Water (Prevention and Control of Pollution) Cess Act, 1977, has also been passed for the levy and collection of a cess on water consumed by the industries and local authorities, especially as a means to augment the financial resources of the Central Board an the State Boards.

(C) FOREST (CONSERVATION) ACT, 1980

The Act has been passed to prevent deforestation which results in ecological imbalance and environmental deterioration. The Act prevents even the State Governments and any other authority to deserve a forest which is already reserved. The Act also prohibits forest land to be used non-forest purposes, except with the prior approval of the Central Government.

(D) THE AIR (PREVENTION AND CONTROL OF POLLUTION) ACT, 1981

This Act has been passed to provide for the prevention, control and abatement of air pollution. According to its Statement of Objects and Reasons, various pollutants discharged through industrial emission and from certain human activities connected with traffic, heating, use of domestic fuels, and refuge have a detrimental effect not only on the health of the people, but also on animal life, vegetation and property. Air pollution is caused by various private and governmental agencies like industrial plants and power stations, railways and automobiles, researches into peaceful use of nuclear energy, refineries for oils and minerals, mining industries, construction of roads through hilly areas etc. Air pollution also has a tendency to expand itself to all its surrounding areas.

The Act defines air pollutant as any solid, liquid or gaseous substance present in the atmosphere in such degree as may be injurious to human beings and other living creatures, or plants or property or environment itself. The Act adopts the Central Water Board and State Water Boards as the Boards for its own purposes. The Central Board has been entrusted with the functions of improving the quality of air and preventing, controlling and abating air pollution in the country. The Central Board also has the duty to advise the Central Government and to undertake the necessary investigation and research in respect of the problems concerning air pollution.

The State Boards have also been entrusted with various functions, *inter alia,* to inspect industrial plants and the manufacturing processes and also air pollution control areas. They can also prescribe standards of emission of air pollutants into the atmosphere from industrial plants and automobiles. They have the power to take samples of air of emission for the purpose of analysis. The previous consent of the State Board has been made necessary for a person to operate any industrial plant in an air pollution control area. Provision has been made for entry and inspection to ensure that the provisions of the Act are being observed.

(E) THE ENVIRONMENT (PROTECTION) ACT, 1986

The Statement of Objects and Reasons of this Act specially refers to Stockholm Conference and expresses concern about the decline in the environmental quality, increasing pollution, loss of vegetal cover and biological diversity, excessive concentrations of harmful chemicals in the ambient atmosphere, growing risks of environmental accidents and threats of life support systems. While the existing laws relating to environment touch specific aspects, this legislation is general in character.

The Act defines environment as including water, air and the land and inter-relationship existing among them as also between them on the one hand and human beings, other living creatures, plants, micro-organisms and property on the other. The definition is sufficiently wide and rightly transcends the human factor. It may, however, be noted that the Act does not include activities in the Space or Outer Space.

The Act defines environmental pollutant as meaning any solid, liquid or gaseous substance which is or which tends to be injurious to environment. Similarly, the expression 'hazardous substance' has been defined to mean any substance or preparation which on account of its chemical properties is liable to cause harm not only to human beings but also to other living creatures, plants micro-organisms, property or environment.

The Act gives all omnibus powers to the Central Government to take the necessary measures for protecting and improving the quality of the environment, preventing, controlling and abating environmental pollution. The Government has been given the power to lay down standards for emission or discharge of environmental pollutants from any source and for providing the necessary safeguards for the prevention of accidents which might cause environmental pollution. The Government also has the power to regulate or prevent industrial operations in respect of particular areas. The Government has the power to make inspection of any premises, plant, equipment, machinery or any manufacturing process for the purposes of the Act. For determining the nature and extent of environmental pollutants, environmental laboratories can also be established. In case of any environmental pollution, the persons concerned are bound to take the necessary steps to prevent and to mitigate the same and to intimate the said fact to the prescribed authorities.

Now, briefly, some of the judicial pronouncements may be referred to.

In one of the first cases directly causing danger to human health and safety of the inhabitants within a district, *Municipal Council Ratlam* v. *Vardhichand and Others** the Supreme Court rightly upheld the order of the Magistrate passed under Section 133, Cr.P.C., who, in the interests of public health and convenience, had directed the Municipal Council of the district to construct proper drainage system to channalise the flow of dirty water and to take effective steps against the prevention and accumulation

* A.I.R. 1980 S.C. 1622.

of dirty water. In fact, the Supreme Court itself added a few supplementary directives, *inter alia,* asking the Municipal Council to take immediate action to stop the effluents from the Alcohol Plant flowing into the street.

The Supreme Court rightly held that even under the provisions of Section 133 Cr. P.C. the Magistrate had the jurisdiction to direct the necessary affirmative action on the part of the concerned authority on a time bound basis on the correct premise that the judicial process also had an enforcement dimension. The plea of the Municipality about its financial inability was rightly brushed aside as having no juridical basis.

This judgment has cleared the deck for compelling the local authorities throughout the country to discharge their statutory obligations in respect of public health, public safety and public convenience. However, it is surprising that the new horizons of judicial conscience shown by this judgment have not been fully appreciated and cases of similar nature involving similar grievances are not coming to the courts. It would be an over-optimistic view that all the municipalities have completely set their houses in order and there do not remain general grievances of the people concerned.

RURAL LITIGATION AND ENTITLEMENT KENDRA *v.* STATE OF UTTAR PRADESH *

In this case the Court had directed the closure of mining operations through blasting in the Doon Valley. It held that although closure would cause hardship to the persons affected, but it was price that had to be paid for protecting and safeguarding the rights of the people to live in healthy environment with minimal disturbance of ecological balance and without undue affection of air, water and environment. The Court also directed the affected areas to be reclaimed and afforestation and soil conservation programmes to be taken up so as to provide employment opportunities to the affected workers. Subsequently, while delivering detailed reasons in this very case,** the Court observed that the Himalayas are the source of important rivers and they are also responsible for regulating the monsoons and the rainfall in the Indo-gangetic belt. They have been the storehouse of herbs, shrubs, plants and deep forests which help generate congenial conditions for good rains. The court recorded that on account of erratic, irrational and uncontrolled mining operations, the landscape had substantially lost its green cover. Mining operations had to be stopped

---

* A.I.R. 1985 S.C. 652.

** A.I.R. 1987 S.C. 359.

because they led to cutting down of the forest, shaking the natural soil and loosening the rocky structures. The Court expressly referred to the Stockholm Conference and held that with the growth of population and scientific developments, man had started encroaching upon the nature and its assets, the consequences of which were serious. The Court cautioned that the Himalayas and the forest growth on the mountain range should be left uninterfered with, so that there might be sufficient quantity of rain. The top soil might be preserved without being eroded. Afforestation activities should be carried out in the whole valley beyond the hills.

While passing further orders in the same case,* the Court observed that air and water are the most indispensable gifts of Nature for preservation of life. Trees are friends of mankind and they are responsible to purify the air and forests are necessary for human existence and human civilization. It is forests which cause rain and provide timber, fruits, herbs and sports. Forests preserve the soil and act as a reservoir for retaining water which is gradually released in a sustained flow.

In another important pronouncement, M.C. Mehta *v.* Union of India** the Court after express reference to the Acts of 1974 and 1986 as also to Stockholm Conference, directed for the stopping of the working in the tanneries which were discharging effluents in Ganga and which did not set up primary treatment plant for the proper treatment of the waste. The Court held that the financial incapacity of the tanneries to set up primary treatment plants was wholly irrelevant and such tanneries had no right to exist similarly like other industries which also had no right to exist in case they had no financial viability to pay minimum wages to their workers. The Court observed that leather industries consumed large quantities of water for processing of hides and skins into leather and the waste water contained toxic inorganic materials which caused serious loss to acquatic life and polluted ground water resources.

Hon'ble Mr. Justice K.N. Singh, the Ex Chief Justice of India in his own concurring judgment highlighted the importance of river Ganga in the Indian Civilization, culture and life apart from its religious impact on a very large section of the population.

While passing further orders in this very case,*** the Court observed that municipal authorities had the statutory duty to prevent public nuisance caused by the pollution of the river Ganga. The Court issued various directions, *inter alia,* including non-issue of licences for

---

* A.I.R. 1988 S.C. 2187.

** A.I.R. 1988 S.C. 1037.

*** A.I.R. 1988 S.C. 1115.

establishment of new industries unless adequate provisions were made for the treatment of trade effluents. The Court directed that the educational institutions in the country should impart lessons in natural environment including forests, lakes, rivers and wild life and that the subject of natural environment should be included in the text books. The Court also expressed the opinion that the people in general should be made aware of the importance of cleanliness and hazards of pollution. The Court, moreover, also held that the directions issued by it were also applicable to all other municipal corporations and municipalities through the jurisdiction of which the river Ganga flowed. Highlighting the urgency of the problem, the Court observed that the real question was not whether measures for the control of water pollution were necessary, but the real question was whether one could afford to neglect the same. It rightly observed that the importance of controlling pollution was generally not realised until after considerable damage had been done.

In this connection M.C. Mehta *v.* Union of India* may be referred to, which was referred to and decided by a Constitution Bench. The Court held that acting under Article 21 in a public interest litigation, it had a right to award compensation to the victims who had suffered on account of leakage of oleum gas from one of the units of the large corporation. It was held that every industry which was engaged in an inherently hazardous activity, had strict and absolute liability, and the same was not subject to any exception. It was no answer for the Corporation that it had taken all due care and attention and that it was not negligent, and was not liable to pay damages. Moreover, the measure of compensation to be paid by such a Corporation was co related to its magnitude and capacity to pay, and the nature of its liability was by way of social cost it had to bear.

While passing certain orders earlier in this very case,** for restarting a chlorine plant the Division Bench of the Court also suggested for setting up of a High powered Authority for purposes of overseeing the functioning of various other hazardous industries. The Court further observed that in view of the frequency of cases pertaining to environmental pollution and ecological destruction coming to it, it was necessary to have a group of experts to aid and advise the Court to facilitate judicial decisions. It held that the Government should constitute a permanent independent Centre with professionally competent and Public spirited experts to provide the necessary scientific and technological information to the Court. The observations are indeed very important, since they clearly evince the mood

* A.I.R. 1987 S.C. 1086.

** A.I.R. 1987 S.C. 965.

of the Court to be prepared to be saddled with the responsibility to decide such cases in future and not an attempt to evade such important questions of public importance on the ground that they involved disputed questions of fact.

Probally the most important aspect of this case is the observations of the Supreme Court suggesting to the Government of India to set up environmental courts on the regional basis with a right of appeal to the Supreme Court. About five years have passed by since the delivery of the said judgment, but it is unfortunate that the Government has not as yet taken the observations of the Court with the seriousness they deserve.

In Subhash Kumar *v.* State of Bihar,* the Supreme Court speaking through Hon'ble Mr. Justice K.N. Singh (Ex Chief Justice of India) rightly expanded the scope of Article 21, a fundamental right, by holding that the enjoyment of pollution free water and air was included in the right to live guaranteed under Article 21 of the Constitution of India. It was further held that nothing could be permitted to endanger or impair the decent quality of life.

There appears to be only one judgment of the Supreme Court, Shri *Sachidanand Pandey and another v. The State of West Bengal*** which probably does not fully and squarely express the concern of the Court for the preservation of ecological balance. In this case the state authorities allotted four acres plot of land of Zoological Gardens, Calcutta to Taj Group of Hotels on lease, for construction of a five star hotel. Initially, in the judgment, the Supreme Court was very eloquent towards its concern for the environment. It rightly held that industrialization, urbanization, explosion or population, over-exploitation of resources, depletion of traditional sources of energy and raw materials had all contributed to environmental deterioration. There was widespread disappearance all over the world of certain specied of living organisms. Nearly one thousands birds and animal species were facing extinction.

However, the Supreme Court upheld the allotment of land on the specious plea that the object was to encourage tourism and to earn foreign exchange. It is respectfully submitted that this judgment is directly in conflict with the later judgment of the Supreme Court in the case of Bangalore Medical Trust V.B.S. Muddappa.***

This case is a landmark judgment showing great concern of the Court towards town planning and environment. The Court held that the

---

* A.I.R. 1991 S.C. 420.

** A.I.R. 1987 S.C. 1109.

*** 1991 Judgements Today Vol. 3 p. 172.

development authority had no right to divert the space reserved for a park for the construction of even a private hospital. The Court held that free and healthy area in beautiful surroundings was a gift from the people to themselves. Demarcation of an area as a park occupied an important place in social ecology. A local authority could not be permitted in law to raise its revenue at the cost of public welfare. Á park provided benefits to the public at large by way of recreation, enjoyment, ventilation and fresh air and protected the residents from ill-effects of urbanization. It promoted the quality of life by preservation of the character and aesthetic features of the city. In fact, the Court held that the action of the State was in direct conflict with the constitutional mandate to ensure that every state action was inspired by the basic values of individual freedom and dignity towards attainment of a quality of life which made fundamental rights a reality.

It is unfortunate that in this case the earlier Sachidanand's case* was not even referred to. It is respectfully submitted that the two judgments are irreconcilable and had Sachidanand's case been considered, then the present case might have been referred to the larger bench.

In the matter of consciousness about human environment, the Allahabad High Court has not lagged behind. In Arun Kumar *v.* Nagar Mahapalika, Allahabad** a Division Bench judgment which has already been upheld by the Supreme Court, the Hon'ble Mr. Justice R.S. Dhawan held that in the interests of public health, environment and urban planning, the area reserved as park under a Master Plan, must be preserved as park and that grant of leases of open space inside the park by the State Government to various private organisations for purposes including the imparting of education was illegal. In fact, the Court had also directed certain buildings raised inside the parks to be dismantled. The Court had also directed for the phased dismantling of a stadium inside the park which had illegally usurped its vast open space. An important feature of this judgment is that the Court held that the inside environment of a park must also be visible and perceivable from outside and so the high boundary walls of bricks around the park were directed to be scaled down as a respect for the considerations of environment and ecology. The Court further held that it was the common man who was the beneficiary of a planned urban environment and so public places like public streets and public parks were inviolate. They must continue to remain dedicated to the general public, and this dedication could not be abdicted even by the state authorities. The obligation towards the preservation and improvement of the environment

* A.I.R. 1987 S.C. 1109.

** 1987 A.L.J. 1038.

was on both, a citizen as well as the State. The Court further held that a park had a basic structure and the same was inviolate and the usefulness of the institutions inside a park did not render their existence lawful. This case is obviously a forerunner to the later judgment of the Supreme Court in Bangalore Medical Trust.

It may also be pointed out that earlier the same Judge speaking for another Division Bench had held in U.P. Krishak Samaj, Lucknow *v.* Administrator, Nagar Mahapalika, Allahabad,* that even an exhibition or a fair for a limited period of time could not be staged inside a public park and authorities, local or state, were wholly incompetent in law to grant such permission. It would amount to encroachment and illegal occupation of the park.

In the Essential Services and Consumers' Association *v.* Jal Sansthan 1987 A.L.J. 446 spot inspections were made by the Hon'ble Judges of the Allahabad High Court on receiving the complaints of contaminated water. The Court issued various directions to the local authorities including periodic checks by the officials concerned. The judgment, however, makes no reference to the Water (Prevention and Control of Pollution) Act, 1984.

From a close scrutiny of the aforesaid cases concerning environmental protection it would be abundantly clear that they are, in reality, not only an exercise in affirmative field, but the Judges have observed as it they are ligislators. The myth, if there be any, that Indian Supreme Court is traditionally discharging its role in only interpreting laws, is bound to be exploded if a person even casually glances through the judgments delivered by it. And what is more remarkable is that the whole Supreme Court has stood as one single entity in respect of environmental protection. If, to borrow the language of the corporate world, the veil of Indian Judiciary is pierced in respect of environmental case laws, it could easily emerge as Legislature in its true colour.

Some suggestions may be ventured in order to fortify existing laws pertaining to environment. It will be seen that the Environment Protection Act, 1986 defines the environment by referring to, *inter alia,* water and land, but then these are the matters pertaining to State List. It is true that the Statement of Objects and Reasons of the Act refers to the international decisions taken at the Stockholm Conference and the legislation could be regarded as within the provisions of Article 253, yet there is no specific reference to the said Article. Further, the Act prohibits causing of harm not only to human beings but to plants, living creatures, micro-organisms etc. It is not free from doubt whether such a comprehensive piece of

---

* 1986 U.P. Local Bolies and Education Cases, 781.

legislation could withstand the challenge under fundamental rights, specially the right to practise any trade or business. Moreover, the Water Act of 1974, refers to Article 252 for the delegation of legislative authority to Parliament by certain states.

Since the laws in respect of environmental pollution are supposed to be permanent in nature, it would be better to bring about a suitable legislative entry in the Concurrent List in the Constitution in respect of environmental pollution by specially referring to air, water and land pollution in all forms, prevention of hazards to human beings, other living creatures, plants micro-organism and property. The incorporation of the item in the Concurrent List would pave the way in future for the states to make their own laws depending upon their regional requirements.

Secondly, all such laws and legislations pertaining to environmental pollution should be incorporated in the 9th Schedule in view of their urgency, importance and permanence. It must be remembered that 9th Schedule at present already contains more than 100 State Acts relating to only land reforms.

Thirdly, right to pollution free water, air and environment should be incorporated as a distinct fundamental right and it should not be continued to be left as flowing from right to life under Article 21 of the Constitution of India. This will not only highlight the importance of the environment, but it will also make the environment issues free from the vicissitudes of the court's interpretation.

Fourthly, on the pattern of Article 323-A provision should be made for the establishment of Environment Courts, both at central and state levels with one exclusive appeal to the Supreme Court. These courts should be specifically given the powers to constitute fact finding committees and to obtain reports from the experts in their own respective fields.

Moreover, as stated above, there are several laws directly concerned with environmental pollution. It would be in the fitness of things if one comprehensive legislation dealing with various kinds of environmental pollution with the same enforcement agency could be enacted. It would give the appearance of an integrated approach towards the environmental issues of various kinds of pollution and also prevent the use of several repetitive provisions in different acts. Such a law should also incorporate express principles for determination of compensation in case of any deliberate or negligent violation of the Act, as also provisions imposing criminal liability on all the persons concerned including the heads of the departments of the Government as also other officials directly responsible for committing any offence under the Act.

The importance of healthy and pollution free environment cannot be overemphasised in the life of a nation or its citizens. At the same time, we have not reached a stage of industrial, scientific and econonmic development where environmental issues could totally subordinate the equally fundamental object of the State the material well-being of the people and raising their living standards. We have to retrieve millions of people out of their slums and to provide them the necessary means so that they are in a position, comparable to ours, to appreciate global environmental concern. Moreover, these issues should not be permitted by our country to be raised as a pretext to impose trade barriers and deny access of markets to our products in the international comodity. At present, even the most advanced nations tend to create artificial frontiers of protectionism in a bid to prevent entry of foreign goods for promoting their own domestic markets and we must take care to see that environmental issues are not raised in order to provide cover to it. Similarly, every ban should be resisted against our import of new technology and of inputs and raw materials in the name of environmental protection. Import of foreign capital should be considered on the basis of its own relative assessment and our development programmes, and not on the possible environmental impact on account of opening up of new industries.

We must also guard ourselves against the bogey of nuclear environmental holocast. In 1798, Malthus had predicted doom on the basis that population increased on geometrical proportions, whereas, production increased only on arithmetical proportions, and yet the world has survived. After the Second World War, it was seriously debated that in view of possession of nuclear weapons of mass destruction in the hands of Super Powers with conflicting ideologies, the continuance of the world was only a matter of time and, yet we have been able to face the challenges satisfactorily.

Till today we have been successfully able to withstand global pressure into signing nuclear Non-Proliferation Treaty. It would be a sad day if we succumb to consent under the international pressure in the name of preventing environmental pollution. We have already proclaimed as a matter of national policy, peaceful uses of atomic energy to promote our development programmes. I do feel that we must not abandon this policy on the ground that exploitation of atomic energy is likely to contaminate the upper atmosphere. Similarly, we must use all our scientific, and space techniques to detect radio active substances in our atmosphere, notwithstanding the pressure of environmentalists. Our Scientists must be free to explore High Seas in order to discover oil and other mineral wealth lying deep into it, and our efforts must not be thwarted on the supposed ground that we would be upsetting marine ecology and causing disturbance to acquatic life of the sea. We must guard ourselves that political and economic mileage is not extracted from the under developed countries by highlighting environmental issues. As a measure of expression of our sovereignty we must retain freedom of action and the decisions and the discretion should continue to remain ours as to which regulatory and prohibitory measures to adopt to sustain environmental values.

It must be remembered that if the inevitable is to come, if Earth is to sink, our country would not be primarily responsible. Our country could also not prevent it. But I do feel that the scientists world over have the necessary technique and expertise and they would all continue to strive to invent new ones to overcome all the challenges of environmental hazards. Problems concerning global environment are perennial in nature and require long term planning, research and solutions. What is the most urgent need of the hour is to educate the masses and to arouse public consciousness and awareness to enable them to better their own living surrounding. Equilibrium between demands for development and ecological balance is likely to be only a sustained and continuing process and never a final outcome, exactly like equilibrium between production and reproduction.

10

INDIAN FOREST ACT, 1927 (XVI OF 1927)

[21st September, 1927]

An Act to consolidate the law relating to forests, transit of forest produce and the duty leviable on timber and other forest produce

Whereas, it is expedient to consolidate the law relating to forests, the transit of forest produce and the duty leviable on timber and other forest produce; It is hereby enacted as follow :

Chapter I

PRELIMINARY

1. **Short title and extent :**

(1) This Act may be called the Indian Forest Act, 1927.

(2) It extends to the whole of India except of territories which immediately before the 1st November, 1956, were comprised in Part B States.

(3) It applies to the territories which, immediately before the 1st November, 1956, were comprised in the State of Bihar, Bombay, Coorg, Delhi, Madhya Pradesh, Orissa, Punjab, Uttar Pradesh and West Bengal; but the Government of any State may, by notification in the official Gazette, bring this Act into force (In the whole or any specified part of that State in which this Act extends and where it is not in force).

2. **Interpretation clause** : In this Act, unless there is anything repugnant in the subject on context :

(1) "cattle" includes elephants, camels, buffaloes, horses, mares, geldings, ponies, colts, fillies, mules, asses, pigs, rams, ewes, sheep, lambs, goats and kids ;

(2) "forest officer" means any person whom [***], the [State Government] in this behalf, may appoint to carry out all or any of the purpose of this Act or to do anything required by this Act or any rule made thereunder to be done by a Forest Officer ;

(3) "forest offence" means an offence punishable under this Act or under any rule made thereunder ;

"forest produce" includes—

(a) the following whether found in, or brought from, a forest or not, that is to say,
timber, charcoal, caoutchouc, catechu, wool-oil, resin, natural varnish, bark, lac, *mahua* flowers, *mahua* seeds *[kuth],* and myrobolans, and

(b) the following when found in, or brought from, a forest, that is to say, —

(i) trees and leaves, flowers and fruits, and all other parts of produce not hereinbefore mentioned, or trees;

(ii) plants not being trees (including grass, creepers, reeds and moss), and all parts or produce of such plants;

(iii) wild animals and skins, tusks, horns, bones, silk, cocoons, honey and wax, and all other parts of produce of animal, and

(iv) peat, surface soil, rock and minerals (including limestone, laterite, mineral oils, and oil products of mines or quarries);

(4-A) "owner" includes a court of wards in respect of property under the superintendency or charge of such Court;

(5) "river" includes any stream, canal, creek or other channels, natural or artificial ;

(6) "timber" includes tree when they have fallen or have been felled and all wood whether cut up or fashioned or hollowed out for any purpose or not ; and

(7) "tree" includes palms, bamboos, stumps brush-wood and canes.

Unambiguous meaning to be given effect to: It is now well settled that when the words of a statute are clear, plain or unambiguous, *i.e.*, they are reasonably susceptible to only meaning, the courts are bound to give effect to that meaning irrespective of consequences.

By insertion of Sec. 2 (4-A) the word "owner" has been interpreted to include a court of wards in respect of property under its charge.

Amendment: Amendment is in fact a wider term, and it includes abrogation or deletion of a provision in an existing statute. An amendment is not retrospective unless expressly laid down.

Chapter II

OF RESERVED FOREST

3. Power to reserve forest : The [State Government] may constitute any forest-land or waste-land which is the property of Government, or over which the Government has proprietary rights, or to the whole or any part of the forest produce of which the Government is entitled, a reserve forest in the manner hereinafter provided.

4. Notification by State Government :

(1) Whenever, it has been decided to constitute any land, a reserved forest, the [State Government] shall issue a notification in the [Official Gazette]:

(a) declaring that it has been decided to constitute such land a reserved forest;

(b) specifying, as nearly as possible, the situation and limits of such land; and

(c) appointing an officer (hereinafter called "the Forest Settlement officer" to inquire into and determine the existence, nature and extent of any right alléged to exist in favour of any person in or over any land comprised within such limits, or in or over any forest produce, and to deal with the same as provided in this chapter.

Explanation: For the purpose of Cl. *(b),* it shall be sufficient to describe the limit of the forest by roads, rivers, bridges or other well-known or readily intelligible boundaries.

(2) The officer appointed under Cl. *(c)* of sub-section (1) shall ordinarily be a person not holding any forest office except that of Forest Settlement Officer.

(3) Nothing in this section shall prevent the [State Government] from appointing any number of officers not exceeding three, not more, than one of whom shall be a person holding forest office except as aforesaid, to perform the duties of Forest Settlement Officer under this Act.

5. Bar of Accrual of Forest Rights: After the issue of notification under Sec. 4, no right shall be acquired in or over the land comprised in such notification except by succession or under a grant or contract in writing made or entered into by or on behalf of the [Government] or some person in whom such right was vested when the notification was issued; and no fresh clearings for cultivation or for any other purpose shall be made in such land except in accordance with such rules as may be made by the [State Government] in this behalf.

6. Proclamation by Forest Settlement Officer: When a notification has been issued under Sec. 4, the Forest Settlement Officer shall publish in the local vernacular in every town and village in the neighbourhood of the land comprised therein, proclamation :

(a) specifying, as nearly as possible, the situation and limits of the propose forest;
(b) explaining the consequences, which, as hereinafter provided, will ensue on the reservation of such forest; and
(c) fixing a period of not less than three months from the date of such proclamation, and requiring every person claiming any right mentioned in Sec. 4 or Sec. 5 within such period either to present to the Forest Settlement Officer a written notice specifying, or to appear before him and state the nature of such right and the amount and particulars of the compensation (if any) claimed in respect thereof.

7. Inquiry by Forest Settlement Officer : The Forest Settlement Officer shall take down in writing all statements made under Sec.6, and shall at some convenient place inquire into all claims duly preferred under that section, and the existence of any rights mentioned in Sec.4 or Sec.5 and not claimed under Sec.6 so far as the same may be ascertainable from the records of Government and the evidence of any person likely to be acquainted with the same.

8. Powers of Forest Settlement Officer : For the purpose of such inquiry, the Forest Settlement Officer may exercise the following powers that is to say :

(a) power to enter, by himself or any officer authorized by him for the purpose, upon any land, and to survey, demarcate and make a map of the same; and
(b) the powers of a Civil Court in the trial of suits.

9. Extinction of rights : Rights in respect of which no claim has been preferred under Sec.6 and of the existence of which no knowledge has been acquired by inquiry under Sec.7, shall be extinguished unless, before the notification under Sec.20 is published, the person claiming them satisfies the Forest Settlement Officer that he had sufficient cause for not preferring such claim within the period fixed under Sec.6.

10. Treatment of claims relating to practice of shifting cultivation: (1) In the case of a claim relating to the practice of shifting cultivation the Forest Settlement Officer shall record a statement setting forth the particulars of the claim and of any local rule or order under which the practice is allowed or regulated and submit the statement to the [State Government], together with his opinion as to whether the practice should be permitted or prohibited wholly or in part.

(2) On receipt of the statement and opinion, the [State Government], together with his opinion as to whether the practice should be permitted or prohibited wholly or in part.

(3) If such practice is permitted wholly or in part, the Forest Settlement Officer may arrange for its exercise—

(a) by altering the limits of the land under settlement so as to exclude land of sufficient extent, of a suitable kind, and in a locality reasonably convenient for the purposes of the claimants, or

(b) by causing certain portion of the land under settlement to be separately demarcated, and giving permission to the claimants to practice of shifting cultivation therein under such conditions as he may prescribe.

(4) All arrangements made under sub-section (3) shall be subject to the previous sanction of the [State Government].

11. Power to acquire land over which right is claimed :

(1) In the case of a claim to a right in over any land, other than right of way, right of pasture, or a right to forest produce or a watercourse, the Forest Settlement Officer shall pass an order admitting or rejecting the same in whole or in part.

(2) If such claim is admitted in whole or in part, the Forest Settlement Officer shall either :

(i) exclude such land from the limits of the proposed forest; or

(ii) come to an agreement with the owner thereof for the

surrender of his rights; or

(iii) proceed to acquire such land in the manner provided by the Land Acquisition Act, 1894 (1 of 1894).

(3) For the purpose of so acquiring such land, -

(a) the Forest Settlement Officer shall be deemed to be a Collector proceeding under the Land Acquisition Act, 1894 (1 of 1894);

(b) the claimant shall be deemed to be a person interested and appearing before him in pursuance of a notice given under Sec.9 of the Act;

(c) the provisions of the preceding section of that Act shall be deemed to have been complied with; and

(d) the Collector, with the consent of the claimant, or the Court, with the consent of both parties, may award compensation in land, or partly in land and partly in money.

12. Order on claims to rights of pasture or to forest produce : In the case of claim to rights of pasture or to forest produce, the Forest Settlement Officer shall pass an order admitting or rejecting the same in whole or in part.

13. Record to be made by Forest Settlement Officer : The Forest Settlement Officer, when passing any order under Sec. 12, shall record, so far as may be practicable,

(a) the name, father's name, caste, residence and occupation of the person claiming the right; and

(b) the designation, position and area of all fields or groups of fields (if any), and the designation and position of all buildings (if any) in respect of which the exercise of such rights is claimed.

14. Record where he admits claims: If the Forest Settlement Officer admits in whole or in part any claim under Sec. 12 he shall also record the extent to which the claim is so admitted, specifying the number and description of the cattle which the claimant is from time to time entitled to graze in the forest, the season during which such pasture is permitted, the quantity of timber and other forest produce which he is, from time to time, authorised to take or receive, and such other particulars, as the case may require. He shall also record whether the timber or other forest produce obtained by the exercise of the rights claimed may be sold or bartered.

15. Exercise of rights admitted:

(1) After making such record the Forest Settlement Officer shall, to the best of his ability, and having due regard to the maintenance of the reserved forest in respect of which the claim is made, pass such orders as well ensure the continued exercise of the rights so admitted.

(2) For this purpose the Forest Settlement Officer may :

(a) set out some other forest tract of sufficient extent, and in a locality reasonably convenient, for the purpose of such claimants, and record an order conferring upon them a right of pasture or to forest produce (as the case may be) to the extent so admitted; or

(b) so alter the limits of this proposed forest as to exclude forest land of sufficient extent, and in a locality reasonably convenient for the purposes of the claimants; or

(c) record an order continuing to such claimants a right of pasture or to forest produce, as the case may be, to the extent so admitted at such seasons within such portions of the proposed forest, and under such rules, as may be made in this behalf, by the [State Government].

16. Commutation of rights: In case the Forest Settlement Officer finds it impossible, having due regard to the maintenance of the reserved forest, to make such settlement under Sec. 15 as shall ensure the continued exercise of the said rights to the extent so admitted, he shall, subject to such rules as the [State Government] may make in this behalf, commute such rights by the payment to such persons of a sum of money in lieu thereof or by the grant of land or in such other manner as he thinks fit.

17. Appeal from order passed under Sec.11, Sec.12, Sec.15, or Sec. 16: Any person who has made a claim under this Act, or any Forest Officer or other person generally or specially empowered by the [State Government] may, by notification in the [Official Gazette], appoint to hear appeals from such order]:

Provided that the [State Government] may establish a court (hereinafter called the Forest Court) composed of three persons to be appointed by the [State Government], and, when the Forest Court has been so established, all such appeals shall be presented to it.

18. Appeal under Sec. 17:

(1) Every appeal under Section 17, it shall be made by petition in writing, and may be delivered to the Forest Settlement Officer, who shall forward it without delay to the authority competent to hear the same.

(2) If the appeal be to an officer appointed under Sec. 17, it shall be heard in the manner prescribed for the time being for the hearing of appeals in matters relating to land revenue.

(3) If the appeal be to the Forest Court, the Court shall fix a day and a convenient place in the neighbourhood of the proposed forest for hearing the appeal, and shall give notice thereof to the parties, and shall hear such appeal accordingly.

(4) The order passed on the appeal by such officer or Court, or by the majority of the members of such Court, as the case may be, shall, subject only to revision as the [State Government], be final.

19. Pleaders: The [State Government] or any person who has made a claim under the Act, may appoint any person to appear, plead and act on its or his behalf before the Forest Settlement Officer, or the Appellate Officer or Court, in the course of any enquiry or appeal under this Act.

20. Notification declaring forest reserved :

(1) When the following events have occurred, namely :

(a) the period fixed under Sec.6 for preferring claims has elapsed, and all claims, if any, made under that section or Sec.9 have been disposed of by the Forest Settlement Officer;

(b) if any such claims have been made, the period limited by Sec.17 for appealing from the orders passed on such claims has elapsed, and all appeals (if any) presented within such period have been disposed by the Appellate Officer or Court; and

(c) all lands (if any) to be included in the proposed forest, which the Forest Settlement Officer has, under Sec.11, elected to acquire under the Land Acquisition Act, 1894 (1 of 1894), have become vested in the Government under Sec. 16 of that Act,

the [State Government] shall publish a notification in the [Official Gazette] specifying definitely, according to boundary makes erected or otherwise, the limits of the forest which is to be reserved, and declaring the same to be reserved from a date fixed by the notification.

(2) From the date so fixed such forest shall be deemed to be a reserved forest.

21. Publication of translation of such notification in neighbourhood of forest : The Forest Officer shall, before the date fixed by such notification, cause a translation thereof into the local vernacular or be published in every town and village in the neighbourhood outrode of the forest.

22. Power to revise arrangement made under Sec.15 or Sec.18 : The [State Government] may, within five years from the publication of any notification under Sec.20, revise any arrangement made under Sec.15 or Sec.18, and may for this purpose rescind or modify any order made under Sec.15 or Sec.18, and direct that any one of the proceedings, specified in Sec.15 be taken in lieu of any other of such proceedings, or that the rights admitted under Sec.12 be commuted under Sec.16.

23. No right acquired over reserved forest except as here provided : No right of any description shall be acquired in or over a reserved forest except by succession or under a grant or contract in writing made by or on behalf of the [Government] or some person in whom such right was vested when the notification under Sec.20 was issued.

24. Rights not to be alienated without sanction :

(1) Notwithstanding anything contained in Sec.23 no right contained under Cl.(c) of sub-section(2) of Sec.15 shall be alienated by way of grant, sale, lease, mortgage or otherwise without the sanction of the [State Government]:

Provided that, when any such right is appendant to any land or house, it may be sold or otherwise alienated with such land or house.

(2) No timber or other forest produce obtained in exercise of any such right shall be sold or bartered except to such extent as may have been admitted in the order recorded under Sec.14.

25. Power to stop ways and watercourses in reserved forest : The Forest Officer may, with the previous sanction of the [State Government] or of any officer duly authorized by it in this behalf, stop, any public or private way or watercourse in a reserved forest, provided that a substitute for the way or watercourse so stopped, which the [State Government] deems to be reasonably convenient, already exists, or has been provided or constructed by the Forest Officer in lieu thereof.

26. Acts prohibited in such forest :

(1) Any person who :

- *(a)* makes any fresh clearing prohibited by Sect. 5; or
- *(b)* sets fire to a reserved forest, or, in contravention of any rules made by the [State Government] in this behalf, kindles any fire or leaves any fire burning, in such manner as to endanger such a forest; or who in a reserved forest-
- *(c)* kindles, keeps or carries any fire except as such seasons as the Forest Officer may notify in this behalf;
- *(d)* trespasses or pastures cattle, or permits cattle to trespass;
- *(e)* causes any damage by negligence in felling any tree or cutting or dragging any timber;
- *(f)* fells, girdles, lops, taps or burns any tree or strips off the bark or leaves from, or otherwise damages, the same;
- *(g)* quarries stone, burns lime or charcoal, or collects, subjects to any manufacturing process, or removes any forest produce;
- *(h)* clears or breaks up any land for cultivation or any other purpose;
- *(i)* in contravention of any rules made in this behalf by the [State Government] hunts, shoots, fish, poisons water or sets, traps or shares; or
- *(j)* in any area in which the Elephants' Preservation Act, 1879 (VI of 1879), is not in force, kills or catches elephants in contravention of any rules so made; shall be punishable with imprisonment for a term which may extend to six months, or with fine which may extend to five hundred rupees, or with both in addition to such compensation for damage done to the forest as the convicting court may direct to be paid.

(2) Nothing in this section shall be deemed to prohibit :

- *(a)* any act done by permission in writing of the Forest Officer, or under any rule made by [State Government]; or
- *(b)* the exercise of any right continued under Cl.
- *(c)* of sub-section (2) of Sec.15, or created by grant or contract in writing made by or on behalf of the [Government] under Sec.23.

(3) Whenever, fire is caused wilfully or by gross negligence in a reserved forest the [State Government] may (notwithstanding that any penalty has been inflicted under this section) direct that in such forest or any portion thereof the exercise of all rights or pasture or to forest produce shall be suspended for such period as it thinks fit.

27. Power to declare forest no longer reserved :

(1) The [State Government] may, [* * *] by notification, in the [Official Gazette], direct that, from a date fixed by such notification, any forest or any portion thereof reserved under this Act shall cease to be reserved forest.

(2) From the date so fixed such forest or portion shall cease to be reserved; but the rights (if any) which have been extinguished therein shall not revive in consequence of such cessation.

Chapter III

OF VILLAGE FORESTS

28. Formation of village forests :

(1) The [State Government] may assign to any village community the rights of Government to or over any land has been constituted a reserved forest, and may cancel such assignment. All forest so assigned shall be called village forests.

(2) The [State Government] may make rules for regulating the management of village forests, prescribing the conditions under which the community to which any such assignment is made may be provided with timber or other forest produce or pasture, and their duties for the protection and improvement of such forest.

(3) All the provisions of this Act relating to reserved forests shall (so far as they are not inconsistent with the rules so made) apply to village forests.

Chapter IV

OF PROTECTED FORESTS

29. Protected forests :

(1) The [State Government] may, by notification in the [Official

Gazette] declare the provisions of this chapter applicable to any forest-land or waste-land which is not included in a reserved forest, but which is the property of Government, or over which the Government has proprietary rights, or to the whole or any part of the forest produce of which the Government is entitled.

(2) The forest-land and waste-land comprised in any such notification shall be called a "protected forest".

(3) No such notification shall be made unless the nature and extent of the rights of Government and of private persons in or over the forest-land or waste-land comprised therein have been inquired into and recorded at a survey or settlement, or in such other manner as the [State Government] thinks sufficient. Every such record shall be presumed to be correct until the contrary is proved:

Provided that if, in the case of any forest-land or waste-land, the [State Government] thinks that such enquiry and record are necessary but that they will occupy such length of time as in the meantime to endanger the rights of Government, the [State Government] may, pending such inquiry and record, declare such land to be a protected forest, but so as not to abridge or affect rights of individuals or communities.

Minor's private forest—State on termination of lease, not entitled to its produce :

The need to continue the lease for a few private forests was perhaps not felt. On the termination of the lease the private property reverted to the owners. However, so far as the plaintiff's forests were concerned they continued under the State's management, since he was a minor. But on that account the State was not "entitled" to the forest produce from such private forests. Therefore, the notification issued under Sec.29 could have no application to such private forests.

30. Power to issue notification reserving trees, etc :

The [State Government] may, by notification in the [Official Gazette],-

(a) declare any trees or clause of trees in a protected forest to be reserved from a date fixed by the notification;

(b) declare that any portion of such forest specified in the notification shall be closed for such term, not exceeding

thirty years as the [State Government] thinks fit, and that the rights of private persons, if any, over such portion shall be suspended during such term provided that the remainder of such forest be sufficient and in a locality reasonably convenient, for the due exercise of the rights suspended in the portion so closed; or

(c) prohibit, from a date fixed as aforesaid, the quarrying of stone or the burning of lime or charcoal, or the collection or subjection to any manufacturing process, or removal of, any forest produce in any such forest, and the breaking up or clearing for cultivation for buildings for herding cattle or any other purpose of any land in any such forest.

31. Publication or translation of such notification in neighbourhood : The Collector shall cause a translation into the local vernacular of every notification issued under Sec.30 to be affixed in a conspicuous place in every town and village in the neighbourhood of the forest comprised in the notification.

32. Power to make rules for protected forests: The [State Government] may make rules to regulate the following matters, namely:

(a) the cutting, sawing, conversion and removal of trees and timber, and the collection, manufacture and removal of forest produce, from protected forests;

(b) the granting of licences to inhabitants of towns and villages in the vicinity of protected forests to take trees, timber or other forest produce for their own use, and the production and return of such licences by such persons;

(c) the granting of licences to persons felling or removing trees or timber or other forest produce from such forests for the purposes of trade, and the production and return of such licences by such persons;

(d) the payments, if any, to be made by the person mentioned in Cls.(b) and (c) for permission to cut such trees, or to collect and remove such timber or other forest produce;

(e) the other payments, if any, to be made by them in respect of such trees, timber and produce, and the places where such payment shall be made;

(f) the examination of forest produce passing out of such forests;

(g) the clearing and breaking up of land for cultivation or other purposes in such forest;

(h) the protection from fire or timber lying in such forests and trees reserved under Sec.30; and

(i) the cutting of grass and pasturing of cattle in such forests;

(j) hunting, shooting, fishing, poisoning water and setting traps or snares in such forest, and the killing or catching of elephants in such forests in areas in which the Elephants' Preservation Act, 1879 (VI of 1879) is not in force;

(k) the protection and management of any portion of a forest closed under Sec.30; and

(l) the exercise of rights referred to in Sec.29.

33. Penalties for acts in contravention of notification under Sec. 30 or for rules under Sec. 32 :

(1) Any person commits any of following offences, namely :

(a) felles, girdles, lops, taps or burns any tree reserved under Sec.30 or strips of the barks or leaves from or otherwise damages, any such trees;

(b) contrary to any prohibition under Sec.30, quarries any stone or burns any lime or charcoal, or collects, subjects to any manufacturing process, or removes, any forest produce;

(c) contrary to any prohibition under Sec.30, breaks up or clears for cultivation or any other purpose any land in any protected forest;

(d) sets fire to such forest, or kindles a fire without taking all reasonable precaution to prevent its spreading to any tree reserved under Sec.30, whether standing, fallen or felled, or to any closed portion of such forest;

(e) leaves burning any fire kindled by him in the vicinity of any such trees or closed portion;

(f) fells any trees or drags any timber so as to damage any trees reserved as aforesaid;

(g) permits cattle to damage any such tree; and

(h) infringes any rule made under Sec.32;

shall be punishable with imprisonment for a term which may extend to six months or with fine which may extend to five hundred rupees, or with both.

(2) Whenever, fire is caused wilfully or by gross negligence in a protected forest, the [State Government] may, notwithstanding that any penalty has been inflicted under

this section, direct that in such forest or any portion thereof the exercise of pasture or to forest produce shall be suspended for such period as it thinks fit.

34. Nothing in this chapter to prohibit acts done in certain cases: Nothing in this chapter shall be deemed to prohibit any act done with the permission in writing of the Forest Officer, or in accordance with rules made under Sec.32, or except as regards any portion, of a forest closed under Sec.30, or as regards any rights the exercise of which has been suspended under Sec.33, in the exercise of any right recorded under Sec.29.

Chapter V

OF THE CONTROL OVER FORESTS AND LANDS NOT BEING THE PROPERTY OF GOVERNMENT

35. Protection of forests for special purposes:

(1) The [State Government] may, by notification in the [official Gazette], regulate or prohibit in any forest or waste land :

(a) the breaking up or clearing of land for cultivation;

(b) the pasturing of cattle; or

(c) the firing or clearing of the vegetation;

when such regulation or prohibition appears necessary for any of the following purposes;

(i) for protection against storms, winds, rolling stones; floods and avalanches;

(ii) for the preservation of the soil on the ridges and slopes and in the valleys or hilly tracts, the prevention of landslips or of the formation of ravines and torrents, or the protection of land against erosion or the deposit thereon of sand, stones or gravel;

(iii) for the maintenance of a water supply in springs, rivers and tanks;

(iv) for the protection of roads, bridges, railways and other lines of communication;

(v) for the preservation of public health.

(2) The [State Government] may, for any, such purpose, construct at its own expense, in or upon any forest or waste land, such as it thinks fit.

(3) No notification shall be made under sub-section (1) nor shall any work be begun under sub-section (2) until after the issue of a notice to the owner of such forest or land calling on him to show cause, within a reasonable period to be specified in such notice, why such notification shall not be made or work constructed, as the case may be and until his objections, if any, and any evidence he may produce in support of the same, have been heard by an officer duly appointed in that behalf and have been considered by the [State Government].

36. Power to assume management of forests :

(1) In case of neglect of or willful disobedience to any regulation or prohibition under Sec.35, or if the purposes of any work to be constructed under that section so require, the [State Government] may, after notice in writing to the owner to such forest of land and after considering his objections, if any, place the same under the control of a forest officer, and may declare that all or any of the provisions of this Act relating to reserved forests shall apply to such forest or land.

(2) The net profits, if any, arising from the management of such forest or land shall be paid to the said owner.

37. Expropriation of forests in certain cases :

(1) In any case under this chapter in which the [State Government] considers that, in lieu of placing the forest or land under the control of a Forest Officer the same should be acquired for public purposes, the [State Government] may proceed to acquire it in the manner provided by the Land Acquisition Act, 1894 (1 of 1894).

(2) The owner of any forest or land comprised in any notification under Sec.35 may, at any time not less than three or more than twelve years from the date thereof, require that such forest or land shall be acquired for public purposes, and the [State Government] shall acquire such forest of land accordingly.

38. Protection of forests at request of owners :

(1) The owner of any land or there be more than one owner thereof, the owners of shares therein amounting in the aggregate to at

least two-thirds thereof may, with a view to the formation or conservation of forests thereon, represent in writing to the Collector their desire—

(a) that such land be managed on their behalf by the Forest Officer as a reserved or a protected forest on such terms as may be mutually agreed upon; or

(b) that all or any of the provision of the Act be applied to such land.

(2) In either case, [State Government] may, by notification in the [Official Gazette], apply to such land and such provisions of this Act as it thinks suitable to the circumstance thereof and as may be desired by the applicants.

Chapter VI

OF THE DUTY ON TIMBER AND OTHER FOREST PRODUCE

39. Power to impose duty on timber and other forest produce:

(1) The [Central Government] may levy a duty in such manner, at such places and at such rates as it may declare by notification in the [Official Gazette] on all timber or other forest produce—

(a) which is produced in [the territories to which this Act extends] and in respect of which [the Government] has any right;

(b) which is brought from any place outside [the territories to which this Act extends].

(2) In every case in which such duty is directed to be levied *ad valorem*, the [Central Government] may fix by like notification the value on which such duty shall be assessed.

(3) All duties on timber or other forest-produce which, at the time when this Act comes into force in any territory, are levied therein under the authority of the [State Government] shall be deemed to be and to have been duly levid under the provision of this Act.

(4) Notwithstanding anything in this section, the [State Government] may, until provision to the contrary is made by the [Parliament] continue to levy any duty which was lawfully levying before the commencement of [Constitution] under this section as then in force:

Provided that nothing in this sub-section authorized the levy of any duty which as between timber or other forest produce of the locality outside the [State] discriminates in favour of the former, or which, in the case of the timber or other forest produce of localities outside the [State] discriminates between timber or other forest produce of one locality and similar or other forest produce of another locality].

40. Limit not to apply to purchase money or royalty: Nothing in this Chapter shall be deemed to limit the amount, if any, chargeable as purchase money or royalty on any timber or other forest produce, although the same is levid on such timber or produce while in transit, in the same manner as duty is levid.

Chapter VII

OF THE CONTROL OF TIMBER AND OTHER FOREST PRODUCE IN TRANSIT

41. Power to make rules to regulate transit of forest produce:

(1) The control of all rivers and their banks as regards the floating of timber as well as the control of all timber and other forest produce in transit by land or water, is vested in the [State Government], and it may make rules or regulate the transit of all timber and other forest produce.

(2) In particular and without prejudice to the generality of the foregoing power, such rules may—

(a) prescribe the routes by which alone timber or other forest produce may be imported, exported or moved into, from or within [the State];

(b) prohibit the import or export or moving of such timber or other produce without a pass from an officer duly authorized to issue the same, or otherwise than in accordance with the conditions of such pass;

(c) provide for the issue, production and return of such passes and or the payment of fees therefor;

(d) provide for the stoppage, reporting, examination and marking of timber or other forest produce in transit in respect of which there is reason to believe that any money is payable to [the Government] on account of the price thereof, or on account of any duty, fee, royalty or charge due thereon, or to which it is desirable for the purpose of this Act to affix a mark;

(e) provide for the establishment and regulation of depots to

which such timber or other produce shall be taken by those in charge of it for examination, or for the payment of such money, or in order that such marks may be affixed to it; and the conditions under which such timber or other produce shall be brought to, stored at and removed from such depots;

(*f*) prohibit the closing up or obstructing of the channel or blanks of any river used for the transit of timber or other forest produce, and the throwing of grass, brushwood, or leaves into any such river or any act which may cause such river to be closed or obstructed;

(*g*) provide for the prevention or removal of any obstruction of the channel or banks of any such river, and for recovering the cost of such provision or removal from the person whose acts of negligence necessitated the same;

(*h*) prohibit absolutely or subject to conditions, within specified local limits, the establishment of saw-pits, the converting, cutting, burning, concealing or marking of timber, the altering or effacing of any marks of the same, or the possession or carrying of marking hammers or other implements used for marking timber;

(*i*) regulate the use of property marks of timber, and the registration of such marks; prescribe the time for which such registration shall hold good; limit the number of such marks that may be registered by any one person, and provide for the levy of fees for such registration.

(3) The [State Government] may direct that any rule made under this section shall not apply to any specified class of timber or other forest produce or to any specified local area.

41A. Powers of Central Government as to movements of timber across customs frontiers: Notwithstanding anything in Sec.41, the Central Government may make rules to prescribe the route by which alone timber or other forest produce may be imported, exported or moved into or [from the territories to which this Act extends] across any customs frontier as defined by the Central Government, and any rules made under Sec.41 shall have effect subject to the rules made under this section.].

42. Penalty for breach of rules made under Sec. 41:

(1) The [State Government] may be such rules prescribe as penalties for the contravention thereof imprisonment for a term which

may extend to six months, or fine which may extend to five hundred rupees, or both.

(2) Such rules may provide that penalties which are double of those mentioned in sub-section (1) may be inflicted in cases where the offence is committed after sunset and before sunrise or after preparation for resistance of lawful authority, or where the offender has been previously convicted of a like offence.

43. Government and Forest Officer not liable for damage to forest produce at depot: The [Government] shall not be responsible for any loss or damage which may occur in respect of any timber or other forest produce while at a depot established under a rule made under Sec.41, or while detained elsewhere for the purposes of this Act; and no Forest Officer shall be responsible for any such loss or damage, unless he causes such loss or damage negligently, maliciously or fraudulently.

44. All persons bound to aid in case of accident at depot: In case of any accident or emergency involving danger to any property at any such depot, every person employed at such depot, whether by the [Government] or by any private persons, shall render assistance to any Forest Officer or Police Officer demanding his aid in averting such danger or securing such property from damage or loss.

Chapter VIII

OF THE COLLECTION OF DRIFT AND STRANDED TIMBER

45. Certain kinds of timber to be deemed property of Government until title thereto proved, may be collected accordingly:

(1) All timber found a drift beached, stranded or sunk; all wood or timber bearing marks which have not been registered in accordance with the rules made under Sec.41, or on which the marks have been obliterated, altered or defaced by fire or otherwise, and in such areas as the [State Government] directs all unmarked wood and timber, shall be deemed to be the property of Government, unless and until any person established his right and title thereto, as provided in this chapter.

(2) Such timber may be collected by any Forest Officer or other person entitled to collect the same by virtue of any rule made under Sec. 51 and may be brought to any depot which the Forest Officer may notify as a depot for the reception of drift timber.

(3) The [State Government] may, by notification in the [Official Gazette], exempt any class of timber from the provisions of this section.

46. Notice to claimants of drift timber: Public notice shall from time to time be given by the Forest Officer of timber collected under Sec.45. Such notice shall contain a description of the timber and shall require any person claiming the same to present to such officer within a period not less than two months from the date of such notice, a written statement of such claim.

47. Procedure on claim preferred to such timber :

(1) When any such statement is presented as aforesaid, the Forest Officer may, after making such inquiry, as he thinks fit, either reject the claim after recording his reasons for so doing, or deliver the timber to the claimant.

(2) If such timber is claimed by more than one person, the Forest Officer may either deliver the same to any of such person whom he deems entitled thereto, or may refer the claimants to the Civil Court, and retain the timber pending the receipt of an order from any such Court for its disposal.

(3) Any person whose claim has been rejected under this section may, within three months from the date of such rejection, institute a suit to recover possession of the timber claimed by him; but no person shall recover any compensation or costs against the [Government], or against any Forest Officer, on account of such rejection, or the detention or removal of any timber or the delivery thereof to any other person under this section.

(4) No such timber shall be subject to process of any civil, criminal or revenue court until it has been delivered, or a suit has been brought, as provided in this section.

48. Disposal of unclaimed timber: If no such statement is presented as aforesaid, or if the claimant omits to prepare his claim in the manner and within the period fixed by the notice issued under Sec.46, or on such claim having been so preferred by him and having been rejected, omits to institute a suit to recover possession of such timber within the further period fixed by Sec.47, the ownership of such timber shall vest in the Government or when such timber has been delivered to another person under Sec.47 in such other person free from all encumbrances not created by him.

49. Government and its officers not liable for damage to such timbers : [Government] shall not be responsible for any loss or damage which may occur in respect of any timber collected under Sec.45 and no Forest Officer shall be responsible for any such loss or damage, unless he causes such loss or damage negligently, maliciously or fraudulently.

50. Payments to be made by claimant before timber is delivered to him : No person shall be entitled to recover possession of any timber collected or delivered as aforesaid until he has paid to the Forest Officer or other person entitled to receive it such sum on account thereof as may be due under any rule made under Sec.51.

51. Power to make rules and prescribe penalties :

(1) The [State Government] may make rules to regulate the following matters, namely:

(a) the salving, collection and disposal of all timber mentioned in Sec.45;

(b) the use and registration of boats used in salving and collecting timber;

(c) the amounts to be paid for salving, collecting, moving storing disposing of such timber, and

(d) the use and registration of hammers and other instruments to be used for making such timber.

(2) The [State Government] may prescribe, as penalties for the contravention of any rules made under this section, imprisonment for a term which may extend to six months, or fine which may extend to five hundred rupees, or both.

Chapter IX

PENALTIES AND PROCEDURE

52. Seizure of property liable to confiscation:

(1) When there is reason to believe that a forest offence has been committed in respect of any forest produce, such produce, together with all tools, boats, carts or cattle used in committing any such offence, may be seized by any forest officer or police officer.

(2) Every officer seizing any property under this section shall place on such property a mark indicating that the same has been so seized, and shall, as soon as may be, make a report of such seizure to the Magistrate having jurisdiction to try the offence on account

of which the seizure has been made :

Provided that, when the forest produce with respect to which such offence is believed to have been committed is the property of Government and the offender is unknown, it shall be sufficient if the officer makes, as soon as may bc, a report of the circumstances to his official superior.

53. Power to release property seized under Sec. 52: Any Forest Officer of a rank not inferior to that of a Ranger who, or whose subordinate has seized any tools, boats, carts, or cattle under Sec.52, may release the same on the execution by the owner thereof of a bond for the production of the property so released, if and when so required, before the Magistrate having jurisdiction to try the offence on account of which the seizure has been made.

54. Procedure thereupon : Upon the receipt of any such report, the Magistrate shall, with all convenient despatch, take such measures as may be necessary for the arrest and trial of the offender and the disposal of the property according to law.

55. Forest produce, tools, etc. when liable to confiscation :

(1) All timber or forest produce which is not the property of Government and in respect of which a forest offence has been committed, and all tool, boats, carts and cattle used in committing any forest offence, shall be liable to confiscation.

(2) Such confiscation may be in addition to any other punishment prescribed for such offence.

56. Disposal, on conclusion of trial for forest offence, of produce, in respect of which it was committed : When the trial of any forest offence is concluded, any forest-produce in respect of which such offence has been committed shall, if it is the property of Government or has been confiscated, be taken charge of by a Forest Officer, and, in any other case, may be disposed of in such manner as the Court may direct.

57. Procedure when offender not known, or cannot be found: When the offenders is not known or cannot be found, the Magistrate may, if he finds that an offence has been committed, order the property in respect of which the offence has been committed to be confiscated and taken charge of by the Forest Officer, or to be made over to the person whom the Magistrate deems to be entitled to the same:

Provided that no such order shall be made until the expiration of one month from the date of seizing such property, or without hearing the person, if any, claiming any right thereto, and the evidence, if any, which he may produce in support of his claim.

58. Procedure as to perishable property seized under Sec.52: The Magistrate may, notwithstanding anything herein before contained; direct the sale of any property seized under Sec.52 and subject to speedy and natural decay, and may deal with the proceeds as he would have dealt with such property if it had not been sold.

59. Appeal from orders under Sec.55, Sec.56 or Sec.57: The officer who made the seizure under Sec.52, or any of his official superiors, or any person claiming to be interested in the property so seized, may within one month from the date of any order passed under Sec.55, Sec.56 or Sec.57, appeal therefrom the Court to which orders made, by such Magistrate are ordinarily appealable, and the order passed on such appeal shall be final.

60. Property when to vest in Government: When an order for the confiscation of any property has been passed under Sec.55 or Sec.57, as the case may be, and the period limited by Sec.59 for an appeal from such order has elapsed, and no such appeal has been preferred, or when on such an appeal being preferred, the Appellate Court confirms such order in respect of the whole or a portion of such property, such property or such portion thereof, as the case may be, shall vest in the Government free from all encumbrances.

61. Saving of power to release property seized: Nothing herein before contained shall be deemed to prevent any officer empowered in this behalfby the [State Government] from directing at any time the immediate release of any property seized under Sec.52.

62. Punishment for wrongful seizure: Any Forest Officer or Police Officer who vexatiously and unnecessarily seizes any property on pretence of seizing property liable to confiscation under the Act shall be punishable with imprisonment for a term which may extend to six months, or with fine which may extend to five hundred rupees or with both.

63. Penalty for counterfeiting or defacing marks on trees and timber and for altering boundary marks: Whoever, with intent to cause damage or injury to the public or to any person, or to cause wrongful gain as defined in the Indian Penal Code (XLV of 1860) :

(a) knowingly counterfeits upon any timber or standing tree a mark used by forest officer to indicate that such timber of tree is the property of the Government or of some person, or that it may lawfully be cut or removed by some person; or

(b) alters, defaces or obliterates any such mark placed on a tree

or timber by or under the authority of a forest officer; or

(c) alters, moves, destroys or defaces any boundary-mark of any forest or waste land to which the provisions of this Act are applied;

shall be punishable with imprisonment for term which may extend to two years, or with fine, or with both.

64. Power to arrest without warrant :

(1) Any forest officer or police officer may, without orders from a Magistrate and without a warrant arrest any person against whom a reasonable suspicion exists of his having been concerned in any forest-offence punishable with imprisonment for one month or upwards.

(2) Every officer making an arrest under this section shall, without unnecessary delay and subject to the provisions of this Act as to release on bond, take or send the persons arrested before the Magistrate having jurisdiction in the case, or to the officer-in-charge of the nearest police station.

(3) Nothing in this section shall be deemed to authorize such arrest for any act which is offence under Chapter IV unless such act has been prohibited under Cl. *(c)* of Sec.30.

65. Power to release on a bond a person arrested : Any forest officer of a rank not inferior to that of a Ranger, who, or whose subordinate has arrested any person under the provisions of Sec.61 may release such person on his executing a bond to appear, if and when so required, before the Magistrate having jurisdiction in the case, or before the officer-in-charge of the nearest police station.

66. Power to prevent commission of offence : Every forest officer and police officer shall prevent, and may interfere for the purpose of preventing the commission of any forest-offence.

67. Power to try offences summarily : The District Magistrate or any Magistrate of the first class specially empowered in this behalf by the [State Government] may try summarily, under the Code of Criminal Procedure, 1898 (V of 1898), any forest-offence punishable with imprisonment for a term not exceeding six months, or fine not exceeding five hundred rupees, or both.

68. Power to compound offence: The [State Government] may be notification in the [official Gazette], empower a forest officer—

(a) to accept from any person against whom a reasonable

suspicion exists that he has committed by forest-offence, other than an offence specified in Sec.62 or Sec.63, a sum of money by way of compensation for the offence which such person is suspected to have committed, and

(b) when any property has been seized as liable to confiscation to release the same on payment of the value thereof as estimated by such officer.

(2) On the payment of such sum of money, or such value, or both, as the case may be, to such officer, the suspected person, if in custody, shall be discharged, the property, if any, seized shall be released, and no further proceedings shall be taken against such person or property.

(3) A forest officer shall not be empowered under this section unless he is a forest officer or a rank not inferior to that of a Ranger and is in receipt of a monthly salary amounting to at least one hundred rupees, and the sum of money accepted as compensation under Cl. *(a)* of sub-section (1) shall in no case exceed the sum of fifty rupees.

69. Presumption that forest-produce belongs to Government : When in any proceedings taken under this Act, or in consequence of anything done under this Act, a question arises as to whether any forest-produce is the property of the Government, such producc shall be presumed to be the property of the Government, until the contrary is proved.

Chapter X

CATTLE TRESPASS

70. Cattle Trespass Act, 1871, to apply : Cattle trespassing in a reserved forest or in any portion of the protected forest which has been lawfully closed to grazing shall be deemed to be cattle doing damage to a public plantation within the meaning of Sec.11 of the Cattle Trespass Act, 1871 (1 of 1871), and may be seized and impounded as such by any forest officer or police officer.

71. Power to alter fines fixed under that Act : The [State Government] may, by notification in the [Official Gazette], direct that in lieu of the lines fixed under Sec.12 of the Cattle Trespass Act, 1871 (1 of 1871), there shall be levied for each head of cattle impounded under Sec.70 of this Act, such fines as it thinks fit, but not exceeding the following, that is to say, -

For each elephant	..	Ten rupees.
For each buffalo or camel	...	Two rupees.
For each horse, mare, gelding, pony, colt, filly, mule, bull, bullock, cow or heifer	...	One rupee
For each calf, ass, pig, ram, ewe, sheep, lamb, goat or kid...	...	Fifty paise

Chapter XI

OF FOREST OFFICERS

72. State Government may invest Forest Officers with certain powers:

(1) The [State Government] may invest any Forest Officer with all or any of the following powers, that is to say,
   - (a) power to enter upon any land and to survey, demarcate and make a map of the same;
   - (b) the powers of a Civil Court to compel the attendance of witnesses and the production of documents and material objects;
   - (c) power to issue a search-warrant under the Code of Criminal Procedure, 1898 (V of 1898); or
   - (d) power to hold an inquiry into forest offences, and, in the course of such inquiry, to receive and record evidence.

(2) Any evidence recorded under Cl. (d) of sub-section (1) shall be admissible in any subsequent trial before a Magistrate, provided that it has been taken in the presence of the accused person.

73. Forest Officers deemed to be public servants: All Forest Officers shall be deemed to be public servants within the meaning of the Indian Penal Code (XLV of 1860).

74. Indemnity for acts done in good faith : No suit shall lie against any public servant for anything done by him in good faith under this Act.

75. Forest Officers not to trade : Except with the permission in writing of the [State Government] no Forest Officer, shall as principal or agent, trade in timber or other forest-produce, or be or become interested in any lease of any forest or in any contract for working any forest, whether in or outside [the territories to which this Act extends].

Chapter XII

SUBSIDIARY RULES

76. Additional powers to make rules :
The [State Government] may make rules :

- *(a)* to prescribe and limit the powers and duties of any Forest Officer under this Act;
- *(b)* to regulate the rewards to be paid to officers and informers out of the proceeds of fines and confiscation under this Act;
- *(c)* for the preservation, reproduction and disposal of trees and timber belonging to the Government, but grown on lands belonging to or in the occupation of private persons; and
- *(d)* generally, to carry out the provisions of this Act.

77. Penalties for breach of rules : Any person contravening any rule under this Act, for the contravention of which no special penalty is provided, shall be punishable with imprisonment for a term which may extend to one month, or fine which may extend to five hundred rupees, or both.

78. Rules when to have force of law : All rules made by the [State Government] under this Act shall be published in the [Official Gazette], and shall thereupon, so far as they are consistent with this Act, have effect as if enacted therein.

Chapter XIII

MISCELLANEOUS

79. Persons bound to assist forest officer and police officer:

(1) Every person who exercises any right in a reserved or protected forest or who is permitted to take any forest produce from, or to cut and remove timber or to pasture cattle in, such forest, and every person who is employed by any such person in such forest, and every person in any village contiguous to such forest who is employed by the [Government], or who receives emoluments from the [Government] for the services to be performed to the community, shall be bound to furnish without unnecessary delay to the nearest forest officer or police officer any information he

may possess respecting the commission of, or intention to commit, any forest offence, and shall forthwith take steps, whether so required by any forest officer or police officer or not,

(a) to extinguish any forest fire in such forest of which he has knowledge or information;

(b) to prevent by any lawful means in his power any fire in the vicinity of such forest of which he has knowledge or information from spreading to such forests, and shall assist any forest officer or police officer demanding his aid

(c) in preventing the commission in such forest of any forest offence; and

(d) when there is reason to believe that any such offence has been committed in such forest, in discovering and arresting the offender.

(2) Any person who, being bound so to do, without lawful excuse (the burden of proving which shall lie upon such person) fails :

(a) to furnish without unnecessary delay to the nearest forest officer or police officer any information required by sub-section (1);

(b) to take steps as required by sub-section (1) to extinguish any forest fire in a reserved or protected forest;

(c) to prevent, as required by sub-section (1), any fire in the vicinity of such forest from spreading to such forest; or

(d) to assist any forest officer or police officer demanding his aid in preventing the commission in such forest of any forest offence, or when there is reason to believe that any such offence has been committed in such forest, in discovering and arresting the offenders,

shall be punishable with imprisonment for a term which may extend to one month, or with fine which may extend to two hundred rupees, or with both.

80. Management of forests the joint property of Government and other persons :

(1) If the Government and any person be jointly interested in any forest or waste-land, or in whole or any part of the produce thereof, the [State Government] may either

(a) undertake the management of such forest, waste land or produce accounting to such person for his interest in the same; or

(b) issue such regulations for the management of the forest, wasteland or produce by the person so jointly interested as it deems necessary for the management thereof and the interests of all parties therein.

(2) When the [State Government] undertakes under Cl. (a) of sub-section (1) the management of any forest, waste land or produce, it may, by notification in the [Official Gazette], declare that any of the provisions contained in Chapters II and IV shall apply to such forest, waste land or produce, and thereupon such provisions shall apply accordingly.

81. Failure to perform service for which a share in the produce of Government forest is enjoyed : If any person be entitled to a share in the produce of any forest which is the property of Government or over which the Government has proprietary rights or to any part of the forest produce of which the Government is entitled, upon the condition of duly performing any service connected with such forest, such share shall be liable to confiscation in the event of the fact being established to the satisfaction of the [State Government] that such service is no longer so performed :

Provided that no such share shall be confiscated until the person entitled thereto, and the evidence, if any, which he may produce in proof of the due performance of such service, have been by an officer duly appointed in that behalf by the [State Government].

82. Recovery of money due to Government : All money payable to the Government under this Act, or under any rules made under this Act, or on Account of the price of any forest-produce, or expenses incurred in the execution of this Act in respect of such produce, may, if not paid when due, be recovered under the law for the time being in force as if it were an arrear of land revenue.

83. Lien on forest-produce for such money :

(1) When any such money is payable for or in respect of any forest produce, the amount thereof shall be deemed to be a first charge on such produce, and such produce may be taken possession of by a Forest Officer until such amount has been paid.

(2) If such amount is not paid when due, the forest officer may sell such produce by public auction, and the proceeds of the sale shall be applied first in discharge of such amount.

(3) The surplus, if any, if not claimed within two months from the date of sale by the person entitled thereto, shall be forfeited to [Government].

84. Land acquired under this Act to be deemed to be needed for a public purpose under the Land Acquisition Act, 1894: Whenever, it appears to the [State Government] that any land is required for any of the purposes of this Act, such land shall be deemed to be needed for a public purpose within the meaning of Sec.4 of the Land Acquisition Act, 1894 (1 of 1894).

85. Recovery of penalties due under bond : When any person, in accordance with any provision of this Act, or in compliance with any rule made thereunder, binds himself by any bond or instrument to perform any duty or act of covenants by any bond or instrument that he, or that he and his servants and agents will abstain from any act, the whole sum mentioned in such bond of instrument as the amount to be paid in case of a breach of the conditions thereof may, notwithstanding anything in Sec.74 of the Indian Contract Act, 1872 (IX of 1872), be recovered from him in case of such breach as if it were an arrest of land revenue.

85. A. Saving for rights of Central Government : Nothing in this Act shall authorize a Government of any State to make any order or do anything in relation to any property not vested in that State or otherwise prejudice any rights of the Central Government or the Government of any other State without the consent of the Government.]

86. Repeals: *[Repealed by Sec. 2 and Schedule of the Repealing and Amending Act. 1948 (2 of 1948].*

THE SCHEDULE : *[Repealed by Sec.2 and Schedule of the Repealing and Amending Act, 1948 (2 of 1948).]*

THE FOREST (CONSERVATION) ACT, 1980
(No. 69 of 1980)

[27th December, 1980]

An Act to provide for the conservation of forest and for matters connected therewith or ancillary or incidental thereto

Be it enacted by Parliament in the Thirty-first year of the Republic of India as follows:

1. Short title, extent and commencement :

(1) This Act may be called the Forest (Conservation) Act, 1980.
(2) It extends to the whole of India except the State of Jammu and Kashmir.
(3) It shall be deemed to have come into force on the 25th day of October, 1980.

2. Restriction on the preservation of forests or use of forest land for non-forest purpose : Notwithstanding anything contained in any other law for the time being in force in a State, no State Government or other authority shall make, except with the prior approval of the Central Government, any order directing :

(i) that any reserved forest (within the meaning of the expression "reserved forest" in any law for the time being in force in that State) or any portion thereof, shall cease to be reserved ;
(ii) that any forest land or any portion thereof may be used for any non-forest purpose ;
(iii) that any forest land or any portion thereof may be assigned by way of lease or otherwise to any private person or to any authority, corporation, agency or any other organisation so owned, managed or controlled by Government ;
(iv) that any forest land or any portion thereof may be cleared or trees which have grown naturally in that land or portion, for the purpose of using it for re-afforestation.

Explanation : For the purpose of this section "non-forest purpose" means the breaking up or clearing of any forest land or portion thereof for:

(a) the cultivation of tea, coffee, spices, rubber, palms, oil-bearing plants, horticultural crops or medicinal plants ;
(b) any purpose other than re-afforestation,

but does not include any work relating or ancillary to conservation, development and management of forest and wild life, namely, the establishment of check-posts, firelines, wireless communications and construction of fencing, bridges and culverts, dams, water holes, trench marks, boundary marks, pipelines or other like purposes.

3. Constitution of Advisory Committee : The Central Government may constitute a Committee consisting of such number of persons as it may deem fit to advise that Government with regard to :

(i) the grant of approval under Sec. 2 ; and
(ii) any other matter connected with the conservation of forests which may be referred to it by the Central Government.

3-A. Penalty for contravention of the provisions of the Act : Whoever, contravenes or abets the contravention of any of the provisions of Sec. 2, shall be punishable with simple imprisonment for a period which may extend to fifteen days.

3-B. Offences by authorities and Government departments:

(1) Where any offence under this Act has been committed :

(a) by any department of Government, the head of the department; or

(b) by an authority, every person, who, at the time the offence was committed, was directly in charge of, and was responsible to, the authority for the conduct shall be deemed to be guilty of the offence and shall be liable to be guilty of the offence and shall be liable to be proceeded against and punished accordingly ;

Provided that nothing contained in this sub-section shall render the head of the department or any person referred to in Cl. (b), liable to any punishment if he proves that the offence was committed without his knowledge or that he exercised all due diligence to prevent the commission of such offence.

(2) Notwithstanding anything contained in sub-section (1), where an offence punishable under the Act has been committed by a department of Government or any authority referred to in Cl.(b) of sub-section (1) and it is proved that the offence has been committed with the consent or connivance of, or is attributable to any neglect on the part of, any person other than the persons referred to in Cl. *(b)* of Section (1), such officer or persons shall also be deemed to be guilty of that offence and shall be liable to be proceeded against and punished accordingly.

4. Power to make rules:

(1) The Central Government may, by notification in the Official Gazette, make rules for carrying out the provisions of this Act.

(2) Every rule made under this Act shall be laid, as soon as may be, after is it made, before each House of Parliament, while it is in session, for a total period of thirty days which may be comprised in one session or in two or more successive sessions and if, before the expiry of the session immediately following the session or the successive sessions aforesaid, both Houses agree in making any modification in the rule or both Houses agree that the rule should not be made, the rule shall thereafter have effect only in such modified form or be of no effect, as the case may be ; so, however, that any such modification or annulment shall be without

prejudice to the validity of anything previously done under that rule.

5. Repeal and saving:

(1) The Forest (Conservation) Ordinance, 1980, is hereby repealed.

(2) Notwithstanding such repeal, anything done or any action taken under the provisions of the said Ordinance shall be deemed to have been done or taken under this corresponding provisions of this Act.

11

THE WATER (PREVENTION AND CONTROL OF POLLUTION) ACT, 1974
(ACT NO. 6 OF 1974)

(23rd March 1974)

An Act to provide the prevention and control of water pollution and the maintaining or restoring of wholesomeness of water, for the establishment, with a view to carrying out the purposes aforesaid, of boards for the prevention and control of water pollution, for conferring on and assigning to such boards powers and functions relating thereto and for matters connected therewith.

Whereas, it is expedient to provide for the prevention and control of water pollution and the maintaining or restoring of wholesomeness of water, for the establishment, with a view to carrying out the purposes aforesaid, of boards for the prevention and control of water pollution and for conferring on and assigning to such Boards powers and functions relating thereto :

And whereas Parliament has no power to make laws for the states with respect to any of the matters aforesaid except as provided in Articles 249 and 250 of the Constitution ;

And whereas in pursuance of clause (1) of Article 252 of the Constitution resolutions have been passed by all the Houses of the Legislatures of the States of Assam, Bihar, Gujarat, Haryana, Himachal Pradesh, Jammu and Kashmir, Karnataka, Kerala, Madhya Pradesh, Rajasthan, Tripura and West Bengal to the effect that the matters aforesaid should be regulated in those states by Parliament by laws ;

Be it enacted by Parliament in the Twenty-fifth Year of the Republic of India as follows :

Chapter I

PRELIMINARY

1. Short title, application and commencement

(1) This Act may be called the Water (Prevention and Control of Pollution) Act, 1974.

(2) It applies in the first instance to the whole of the States of Assam, Bihar, Gujarat, Haryana, Himachal Pradesh, Jammu and Kashmir, Karnataka, Kerala, Madhya Pradesh, Rajasthan, Tripura and West Bengal and the Union Territories; and it shall apply to such other State which adopts this Act by resolution passed in that behalf under clause (1) of Article [252] of the Constitution.

(3) It shall come into force, at once in the States of Assam, Bihar, Gujarat, Haryana, Himachal Pradesh, Jammu and Kashmir, Karnataka, Kerala, Madhya Pradesh, Rajasthan, Tripura and West Bengal and in the Unions Territories, and in any other State which adopts this Act under clause (1) of Article 252 of the Constitution on the date of such adoption and any reference in this Act to the commencement of this Act, shall, in relation to any State or Union Territory, mean the date on which this Act comes into force in such State or Union Territory.

2. Definitions

In this Act, unless the context otherwise requires,-

(a) "Board" means the Central Board or a State Board ;

(b) "Central Board" means the Central Pollution Control Board constituted under Section 3 ;

(c) "member" means a member of a Board and includes the chairman thereof ;

(d) "occupier" in relation to any factory or premises means the person who has control over the affairs of the factory or the premises, and includes, in relation to any substance, the person in possession of the substance ;

(dd) "outlet" includes any conduit pipe or channel, open or closed, carrying sewage or trade effluent or any other holding arrangement which causes, or is likely to cause, pollution ;

(e) "pollution" means such contamination of water or such alteration of the physical, chemical or biological properties

of water of such discharge of any sewage or trade effluent or of any other liquid, gaseous or solid substance into water (whether directly or indirectly) as may, or is likely to create a nuisance or render such water harmful or injurious to public health or safety, or to domestic, commercial, industrial agricultural or other legitimate uses, or to the life and health of animals or of acquatic organisms ;

(f) "prescribed" means prescribed by rules made under this Act by the Central Government or, as the case may be, the State Government;

(g) "sewage effluent" means effluent from any sewerage system or sewage disposal works and includes sullage from open drains ;

(gg) "sewer" means any conduit pipe or channel, open or closed, carrying sewage or trade effluent ;

(h) "State Board" means a State Pollution Control Board constituted under Section 4 ;

(i) "State Government" in relation to a Union Territory means the Administrator thereof appointed under Article 239 of the Constitution ;

(j) "stream" includes—

(i) river;

(ii) water course (whether flowing or for the time being) ;

(iii) Inland water (whether natural or artificial);

(iv) subterranean waters;

(v) sea or tidal waters to such extent or, as the case may be, such point as the State Government may, by notification in the Official Gazette, specify in this behalf ;

(k) "trade effluent" includes any liquid, gaseous or solid substance which is discharged from any premises used for carrying on any [industry, operation or process or treatment and disposal system] other than domestic sewage.

Chapter II

THE CENTRAL AND STATE BOARDS FOR PREVENTION AND CONTROL OF WATER POLLUTION

3. Constitution of Central Board

(1) The Central Government shall, with effect from such date (being a date not later than six months of the commencement of this Act

in the States of Assam, Bihar, Gujarat, Haryana, Himachal Pradesh, Jammu & Kashmir, Karnataka, Madhya Pradesh, Rajasthan, Tripura and West Bengal and in the Union Territories) as it may, by notification in the Official Gazette, appoint, constitute a Central Board to be called the [Central Pollution on Control Board] to exercise the powers conferred on and perform the functions assigned to that Board under this Act.

(2) The Central Board shall consist of the following members, namely :

(a) a full-time chairman, being a person having special knowledge or practical experience in respect of [matters relating to environmental protection] or a person having knowledge and experience in administering institutions dealing with the matters aforesaid, to be nominated by the Central Government;

(b) [Such number of officials, not exceeding five] to be nominated by the Central Government to represent that Government ;

(c) such member of persons, not exceeding five, to be nominated by the Central Government, from amongst the members of the State Boards, of whom not exceeding two shall be from those referred to in clause *(c)* of sub-section (2) of Section 4;

(d) such number of non-officials, not exceeding three to be nominated by the Central Government, to represent the interests of agriculture, fishery or industry or trade or an other interest which, in the opinion of the Central Government, ought to be represented ;

(e) Two persons to represent the companies or corporations owned controlled or managed by the Central Government, to be nominated by that Government ;

(f) a full-time member-secretary, possessing qualifications, knowledge and experience of scientific, engineering or management aspects of pollution control, to be appointed by the Central Government.]

(3) The Central Board shall be a body corporate with the name aforesaid having perpetual succession and a common seal with power, subject to the provisions of this Act, to acquire, hold and dispose of property and to contract, and may, by aforesaid name, sue or be sued.

4. Constitution of State Boards

(1) The State Government shall, with effect from such date as it may, by notification in the Official Gazette, appoint, constitute a

[State Pollution Control Board] under such name may be specified in the notification, to exercise the powers conferred on and perform the functions assigned to that Board under this Act.

(2) A State Board shall consist of the following members namely :

(a) a chairman, being a person having special knowledge or practice experience in respect of [matter relating to environmental protection] or a person having knowledge and experience in administering institutions dealing with the matters aforesaid, to be nominated by the State Government; [Provided that the chairman may be either whole-time or part-time as the State Government may think fit ;]

(b) [such number of official, not exceeding five], to be nominated by the State Government to represent that Government ;

(c) [such number of persons, not exceeding five,] to be nominated by the State Government from amongst the members of the local authorities functioning within the State ;

(d) [such number of non-official, not exceeding three], to be nominated by the State Government to represent the interests of agriculture, fishery or industry or trade or any other interest which, in the opinion of the State Government, ought to be represented ;

(e) two persons to represent the companies or corporations owned, controlled or managed by the State Government, to be nominated by that Government ;

(f) a full-time member-secretary possessing qualifications, knowledge and experience of scientific, engineering or management aspects of pollution control, to be appointed by the State Government].

(3) Every State Board shall be a body corporate with the name specified by the State Government in the notification under sub-section (1), having perpetual succession and a common seal with power, subject to the provisions of this Act, to acquire, hold and dispose of property and to contract, and may, by the said name, sue or be sued.

(4) Notwithstanding anything contained in this section, no State Board shall be constituted for a Union Territory and in relation to a Union Territory, the Central Board shall exercise the powers and perform the functions of a state for that Union Territory provided that in relation to any Union Territory the Central Board delegate all or any of its powers and functions under this sub-section to such person or body of persons as the Central

Government may specify.

5. Terms and conditions of service of members

(1) Save as otherwise provided by or under this Act, a member of a Board, other than a member-secretary, shall hold office for a time of three years from the date of his nomination

Provided that a member shall, notwithstanding the expiration of its term, continue to hold office until his successor enters upon his office.

(2) The term of office of a member of a Board nominated under clause *(b)* or clause *(e)* of sub-section (2) of Section 3 or clause *(b)* or clause *(e)* of sub-section (2) of Section 4 shall come to an end as soon as he ceases to hold the office under the Central Government or the State Government or, as the case may be, the company or corporation owned, controlled or managed by the Central Government or the State Government, by virtue of which he was nominated.

(3) The Central Government or as the case may be, the State Government may, if it thinks fit, remove any member of a Board before the expiry of his terms of office, after giving him reasonable opportunity of showing cause against the same.

(4) A member of a Board, other than the member-secretary, may at any time resign his office by writing under his hand addressed:-

(a) in the case of the chairman, to the Central Government or as the case may be the State Government ; and

(b) in any other case to the chairman of the Board.

and the seat of the chairman or such other member shall thereupon become vacant.

(5) A member of a Board, other than the member-secretary, shall be deemed to have vacated his seat if he is absent without reason, sufficient in the opinion of the Board, from three consecutive meetings of the Board, or where he is nominated under clause *(c)* or clause *(e)* of sub-section (2) of Section 3, or under clause *(c)* or clause *(c)* of Section 4, if he ceases to be, a member of the State Board or the local authority or, as the case may be, of the company or corporation owned, controlled or managed by the Central Government of the State Government and such vacation of seat shall, in either case, take effect from such date as the Central Government or, as he case may be, the State Government may, by notification in the Official Gazette, specify.

(6) A casual vacancy in a Board shall be filled by a fresh nomination

and the person nominated to fill the vacancy shall hold office only for the remainder of the term for which the member in whose place he was nominated.

(7) A member of a Board [shall be eligible for renomination].

(8) The other terms and conditions of service of member of a Board other than the Chairman and member-secretary, shall be such as may be prescribed.

(9) The other terms and conditions of service of the chairman shall be as may be prescribed.

The member who fails to attend three consecutive meetings of the Board without sufficient cause, shall be-deemed to have vacated his seat for good. A member nominated to fill in a casual vacancy shall continue to hold office only for the remaining term of his predecessor.

6. Disqualifications

(1) No person shall be a member of a Board, who :

(a) is, or at any time has been adjudged insolvent or has suspended payment of his debts or has compounded with his creditors, or

(b) is of unsound mind and stands so declared by a competent court, or

(c) is, or has been, convicted of an offence which, in the opinion of the Central Government or, as the case may be, of the State Government, involves moral turpitude, or

(d) is, or at any time has been, convicted of an offence under this Act, or

(e) has directly or indirectly by himself or by any partner, any share or interest in any firm or company carrying on the business of manufacture, sale or hire of machinery, plant, equipment, apparatus or fittings for the treatment of a sewage or under effluents, or

(f) is a director or a secretary, manager or other salaried officer or employee of any company or firm having any contract with the Board, or with the Government constituting the Board, or with a local authority in the State, or with a company or corporation owned, controlled or managed by the Government, for the carrying out of sewerage schemes or for the installation of plants for the treatment of sewage or trade effluents, or

(g) has so abused, in the opinion of the Central Government or as the case may be, of the State Government, his position as a members, as to render his continuance on the Board

detrimental to the interest of the general public.

(2) No order of removal shall be made by the Central Government or the State Government, as the case may be, under this section unless the member concerned has been given a reasonable opportunity of showing cause against the same.

(3) Notwithstanding anything contained in sub-sections (1) and (7) of Section 5, a member who has been removed under this section shall not be eligible for renomination as a member.

7. Vacation of seats by members

If a member of a Board becomes subject to any of the disqualifications specified in section 6, his seat shall become vacant.

8. Meetings of Board

A Board shall meet at least once in every three months and shall observe such rules of procedure in regard to the transaction of business at its meetings as may be prescribed :

Provided that if the opinion of the chairman, any business of an urgent nature is to be transacted, he may convene a meeting of the Board at such time as he thinks fit for the aforesaid purpose.

9. Constitution of committees

(1) A Board may constitute as many committees consisting wholly of members or wholly of other persons or partly of members and partly of other persons, and for such purpose or purposes as it may think fit.

(2) A committee constituted under this section shall meet at such time and such place, and shall observe such rules of procedure in regard to the transaction of business at its meetings, as may be prescribed.

(3) The members of a committee (other than the members of the Board) shall be paid such fees and allowances, for attending its meetings and for attending to any other work of the Board as may be prescribed.

10. Temporary association of persons with Board for particular purposes

(1) A Board may associate with itself in such manner, and for such purposes, as may be prescribed any person whose assistance or advice it may desire to obtain in performing any of its functions under this Act.

(2) A person associated with the Board under sub-section (1) for any purpose shall have a right to take part in the discussions of the Board relevant to that purpose, but shall not have a right to vote

at a meeting of the Board, and shall not be a member for any other purpose.

(3) A person associated with the Board under sub-section (1) for any purpose shall be paid fees and allowances, for attending its meetings and for attending to any other work of the Board, as may be prescribed.

11. Vacancy in Board not to invalidate acts or proceedings

No act or proceeding of a Board or any committee thereof shall be called in question on the ground merely of the existence of any vacancy in or any defect in the constitution of, the Board or such committee, as the case may be.

11A. Delegation of powers to Chairman

The Chairman of Boards shall exercise such powers and perform such duties as may be prescribed or as may, from time to time, be delegated to him by the Board.

12. Member-secretary and officers and other employees of Board

(1) The terms and conditions of service of the member-secretary shall be such as may be prescribed.

(2) The member-secretary shall exercise such powers and perform such duties as may be prescribed or as may, from time to time, be delegated to him by the Board or its chairman.

(3) Subject to such rules as may by the Central Government or, as the case may be, the State Government in this behalf, a Board may appoint such officers and employees as it considers necessary for the efficient performance of its functions.

(3A) The method of recruitment and the terms and conditions of service (including the scales of pay) of the officers (other than the member-secretary) and other employees of the Central Board or a State Board shall be such may be determined by regulations made by the Central Board, or, as the case may be, by the State Board :

Provided that no regulation made under this sub-section shall take effect unless :

(a) in the case of a regulation made by the Central Board, it is approved by the Central Government ; and

(b) in the case of a regulation made by a State Board, it is approved by the State Government.

(3B) The Board may, by general or special order and subject to such conditions and limitations, if any, as may be specified in the order, delegate to any officer of the Board such of its powers and functions under this Act as it may deem necessary.

(4) Subject to such conditions as may be prescribed, a Board may from time to time appoint any qualified person to be a consulting engineer to the Board and pay him such salaries and allowances and subject him to such other terms and conditions of service as it thinks fit.

Chapter III

JOINT BOARDS

13. Constitution of Joint Boards

(1) Not withstanding any thing contained in this Act, an agreement may be entered into :

(a) by two or more governments of contignuous sates, or

(b) by the Central Government (in respect of one or more Union Territories) and one or more Government of States continuous to such Union Territory of Union Territories.

to be in force for such period and to be subject to renewal for such further period, if any, as may be specified in the agreement to provide for the constitution of a Joint Boards :

(i) in a case referred to in clause *(a)*, for all the participating states, and

(ii) in a case referred to in clause *(b)*, for the participating Union Territory of Union Territories and the State or States.

(2) An agreement under this section may :

(a) provide, in a case referred to in clause *(a)* of sub-section (1), for the apportionment between the participating States and in a case referred to in clause *(b)* of that sub-section, for the apportionments between the Central Governments, of the expenditure in connection with the Joint Board ;

(b) determine, in a case referred to in clause *(a)* of sub-section (1) which of the participating State Governments and in a case referred to in clause *(b)* of that sub-section, whether the Central Government or the participating State Government (if there or more than one participating State, also which of the participating State Governments) shall exercise and perform the several powers and functions of the State Government under this Act and the references in this Act to

the Government shall be constructed accordingly ;

(c) provide for consultation, in case referred to in clause (a) of sub-section (1) between the participating State governments and in a case referred to in clause *(b)* of that sub-section, between the Central governments or State governments either generally or with reference to particular matters arising under this Act ;

(d) make such incidental and ancillary provisions, not inconsistent with this Act, as may be deemed necessary or expedient for giving effect to the agreement.

(3) An agreement under this section shall be published, in a case referred to in a clause *(a)* of sub-section (1), in official Gazette of the participating states and in a case referred to in clause *(b)* of that sub-section in the Official Gazette of the participating Union Territory or Union Territories and the participating State of States.

14. Composition of Joint Boards

(1) A joint Board constituted in pursuance of an agreement entered into under clause (a) of sub-section (1) of Section 13 shall 13 consist of the following members namely :

(a) a full-time chairman, being a person having special knowledge or practical experiences in respect of [matters relating to environmental protection] or a person having knowledge and experience in administering institutions dealing with the matters aforesaid, to be nominated by the Central Government;

(b) two officials from each of the participating states to be nominated by the concerned participating State Government to represent that Government ;

(c) one person to be nominated by each of the participating State Government from amongst the members of the local authorities functioning within the State concerned ;

(d) one non-official to be nominated by each of the participating State governments to represent the interests of agriculture, fishery or industry or trade in the State concerned or any other interest which, in the opinion of the participating State Government, is to be represented ;

(e) two persons to be nominated by the Central Government to represent the companies or corporations owned, controlled or managed by the participating State governments ;

[*(f)* a full-time member-secretary possessing qualifications, knowledge and experience of scientific, engineering or management aspects of pollution control, to be appointed by the Central Government].

(2) A Joint Board constituted in pursuance of an agreement entered into under clause *(b)* of sub-section (1) of Section 13 shall consist of the following namely :

(a) a full time chairman, being a person having special knowledge or practical experience in respect of [matters relating to environmental protection,] or a person having knowledge and experience in administering institution dealing with the matters aforesaid, to be nominated by the Central Government;

(b) two officials to be nominated by the Central Government from the participating Union Territory or each of the participating Union Territories, as the case may be, and two officials to be nominated, from the participating State or each of the participating states as the case may be, by the concerned participating State Government ;

(c) one person to be nominated by the Central Government from amongst the members of the local authorities functioning within the participating Union Territories of each of the participating Union Territories, as the case may be, and one person to be nominated, from amongst the members of the local authorities functioning within the participating State or each of the participating states, as the case may be, by the concerned participating State Government ;

(d) one non-official to be nominated by the Central Government and one person to be nominated by the participating State Government or State governments to represent the interests of agriculture, fishery or industry or trade in the Union Territory or in each of the Union Territories or the State or in each of the states, as the case may be, or any other interest which in the opinion of the Central Government or as the case may be of the State Government is to be represented ;

(e) two persons to be nominated by the Central Government to represent the companies or corporations owned, controlled or managed by the Central Government and situated in the participating Union territories and two persons to be nominated by the Central Government represent the companies or corporations owned controlled or managed by the participating State Governments;

(f) a full-time member-secretary possessing qualifications,

knowledge and experience of scientific, engineering or management aspects of pollution control, to be appointed by the Central Government.

(3) When a Joint Board is constituted in pursuance of an agreement under clause *(b)* of sub-section (1) of Section 13, the provisions of sub-section (4) of Section 4 shall cease to apply in relation to the Union Territory for which the Joint Board is constituted.

(4) Subject to the provisions of sub-section (3), the provisions of sub-section (3) of Section 4 and Sections 5 to 12 (inclusive) shall apply in relation to the Joint Board and its member-secretary as they apply in relation to a State Board and its member-secretary.

(5) Any reference in this Act to the State Board shall, unless the context otherwise requires, be construed as including a Joint Board.

15. Special provision relating to giving of directions

Notwithstanding anything contained in this Act where any Joint Board is constituted under Section 13 :

(a) the Government of the State of which the Joint Board is constituted shall be competent to give any direction under this Act only in cases where such direction relates to a matter within the exclusive territorial jurisdiction of the State ;

(b) The Central Government alone shall be competent to give any direction under this Act where such direction relates to a matter within the territorial jurisdiction of two or more states or pertaining to a Union Territory.

Chapter IV

POWERS AND FUNCTION OF BOARDS

16. (1) Subject to the provisions of this Act, the main function of the Central Board shall be to promote cleanliness of streams and wells in different areas of the states.

(2) In particular and without prejudice to the generality of the foregoing function, the Central Board may perform all or any of the following functions, namely :

(a) advise the Central Government on any matter concerning the prevention and control of water pollution.

(b) co-ordinate the activities of the State Boards and resolve disputes among them ;

(c) provide technical assistance and guidance to the State Boards, carry out and sponsor investigations and research relating to

problems of water pollution and prevention, control or abatement of water pollution ;

(d) plan and organise the training of persons engaged or to be engaged in programmes for the prevention, control or abatement of water pollution on such terms and conditions as the Central Board may specify ;

(e) organise through mass media a comprehensive programme regarding the prevention and control of water pollution ;

(ee) perform such of the functions of any State Board as may be specified in an order made under sub-section (2) of Section-18.

(f) collect, compile and publish technical and statistical data relating to water pollution and the measures devised for its effective prevention and control and prepare manuals, codes or guides relating to treatment and disposal of sewage and trade effluents and disseminate information connected therewith ;

(g) lay down, modify or annul, in consultation with the State Government concerned, the standards for a stream or well :

Provided that different standards may be laid down for the same stream or well or for different steams of wells, having regard to the quality of water, flow characteristics of the stream or well and the nature of the use of the water in such streams or well or streams or wells;

(h) plan and cause to be executed a nation wide programme for the prevention, control or abatement of water pollution;

(i) perform such other functions as may be prescribed.

(3) The Board may establish or recognise a laboratory or laboratories to enable the Board to perform its functions under this section efficiently, including the analysis of samples of water from any stream of well or of samples of any sewage or trade effluents.

17. Functions of State Boards

(1) Subject to the provisions of this Act, the functions of State Board shall be :

(a) to plan a comprehensive programme for the prevention, control or abatement of pollution of streams and wells in the State and to secure the execution thereof ;

(b) to advise the State Government on any matter concerning the prevention, control or abetment of water pollution ;

(c) to collect and disseminate information relating to water pollution and the prevention, control or abatement thereof ;

(*d*) to encourage, conduct and participate in investigations and research relating to problems of water pollution and prevention control or abatement of water pollution;

(*e*) to collaborate with the Central Board in organising the training of persons engaged or to be engaged in programme relating to prevention, control or abatement of water pollution and to organise mass education programmes relating thereto;

(*f*) inspect sewage or trade effluents and to review plans, specifications or other data relating to plants set up for the treatment of water, works for the purification thereof and the system for the disposal of sewage or trade effluents or in connection with the grant of any consent as required by this Act ;

(*g*) to lay down, modify or annul effluent standards for the sewage and trade effluents and for the quality of receiving waters (not being water in an inter-State stream) resulting from the discharge of effluents and classify waters of the State ;

(*h*) to evolve economical and reliable methods of treatment of sewage and trade effluents, having regard to the peculiar conditions of soils, climate and water resources of different regions and more especially the prevailing flow characteristics of water in streams and wells which render it impossible to attain even the minimum degree of dilution ;

(*i*) to evolve methods of utilisation of sewage and suitable trade effluents in agriculture ;

(*j*) to evolve efficient methods of disposal of sewage and trade effluents on land, as are necessary on account of the predominant conditions of scant stream flows that do not provide for major part of the year the minimum degree of dilution ;

(l) to make, vary or revoke any order :

(*i*) for the prevention, control or abatement of discharge of waste into streams or wells ;

(*ii*) requiring any person concerned to construct new systems for the disposal of sewage and trade effluents or to modify, alter or extend any such existing system or to adopt such remedial measures as are necessary to prevent, control or abate water pollution ;

(*m*) to lay down effluent standards to be complied with by persons while causing discharge of sewage or sullage or both and to lay down, modify or annul effluent standards for the sewage and trade effluents ;

(n) to advise the State Government with respect to the location of any industry the carrying on of which is likely to pollute a stream or well ;

(o) to perform such other functions as may be prescribed or as may, from time to time, be entrusted to it by the Central Board of the State Government.

(2) The Board may establish or recognise a laboratory or laboratories to enable the Board to perform its functions under this section efficiently, including the analysis of samples of water from any stream or well or of samples of any sewage or trade effluents.

18. Powers to give directions

(1) In the performance of its functions under this Act :

(a) the Central Board shall be bound by such directions in writing as the Central Government may give to it ; and

(b) every State Board shall be bound by such directions in writing as the Central Board or the State Government may give to it:

Provided that where a direction given by the State Government is inconsistent with the direction given by the Central Board, the matter shall be referred to the Central Government for its decision.

(2) Where the Central Government is of the opinion that any State Board has defaulted in complying with any directions given by the Central Board under sub-section (1) and as a result of such default a grave emergency has arisen and it is necessary or expedient so to do in the public interest, it may, by order, direct the Central Board to perform any of the functions of the State Board in relation to such area, for such period and for such purposes, as may be specified in the order.

(3) Where the Central Board performs any of the functions of the State Board in pursuance of a direction under sub-section (2), the expenses, if any, incurred by the Central Board with respect to the performance of such functions may, if the State Board is empowered to recover such expenses, be recovered by the Central Board with interest (at such reasonable rate as the Central Government may, by order, fix) from the date when a demand for such expenses is made until it is paid from the person or persons concerned as arrears of land revenue or of public demand.

(4) For the removal of doubts, it is hereby declared that any

directions to perform the functions of any State Board given under sub-section (2) in respect of any area would not preclude the State Board from performing such functions in any other area in the State or any of its other functions in that area.

Chapter V

PREVENTION AND CONTROL OF WATER POLLUTION

19. Power of State Government to restrict the application of the Act to certain areas

(1) Notwithstanding anything contained in this Act, if the State Government, after consultation with, or on the recommendation of the State Board, is of the opinion that the provision of this Act need not apply to the entire State, it may, by notification in the Official Gazette, restrict the application of this Act to such area or areas as may be declared therein as water pollution, and control area or areas and thereupon the provisions of this Act shall apply only to such area of areas.

(2) Each water pollution, prevention and control area may be declared either by reference to a map by reference to the line of any watershed or the boundary of any district or partly by one method and partly by another.

(3) The State Government may, by notification in the Official Gazette:

(a) alter any water pollution, prevention and control area whether by way of extension or reduction; or

(b) define a new water pollution, prevention and control area in which may be merged one or more water pollution, prevention and control areas, or any part of parts thereof.

20. Power to obtain information

(1) For the purpose of enabling a State Board to perform the functions conferred on it by or under this Act the State Board or any officer empowered by it in that behalf, may make surveys of any area and gauge and keep records of the flow or volume and other characteristics of any stream or well in such area, and may take steps for the measurement and recording of the rainfall in such area or any part thereof and for the installation and maintenance for those purposes of gauges or other apparatus and works connected therewith and carry out stream surveys and may take such other steps as may be necessary in order to obtain information required for the purposes aforesaid.

(2) A State Board may give directions requiring any person who in its opinion is abstracting water from any such stream or well in the area in quantities which are substantial in relation to the flow or volume of that stream or well or is discharging sewage or trade effluent into any such stream or well, to give such information as to the abstraction or the discharge at such times and in such form as may be specified in the directions.

(3) Without prejudice to the provisions of sub-section (2), a State Board may, with a view to preventing or controlling pollution of water give directions requiring any person incharge of any establishment where any [industry, operation or treatment and disposal system] is carried on, to furnish to it information regarding the construction, installation, or operation of such establishment or of any disposal system or of any extension or addition thereto in such establishment and such other particulars as may be prescribed.

21. Power to take samples of effluents and procedure to be followed in connection therewith

(1) A State Board or any officer empowered by it in this behalf shall have power to take for the purpose of analysis samples of water from any stream or well or samples of any sewage or trade effluent which is passing from any plant or vessel or from or over any place into any such stream or well.

(2) The result of any analysis of a sample of any sewage or trade effluent taken under sub-section (1) shall not be admissible in evidence in any legal proceeding unless the provisions of sub-sections (3), (4) and (5) are complied with.

(3) Subject to the provisions of sub-sections (4) and (5), when a sample (composite or otherwise as may be warranted by the process used) of any sewage or trade effluent is taken for analysis under sub-section (1), the person taking the sample shall :

(a) serve on the person in charge of or having control over, the plant or vessel or in occupation of the place (which person is hereinafter referred to as the occupier) or any agent of such occupier, a notice, then and there in such form as may be prescribed of his intention to have it so analysed ;

(b) in the presence of the occupier or his agent, divide the sample into two parts ;

(c) cause each part to be placed in a container which shall be marked and sealed and shall also be signed both by the person

taking the sample and the occupier or his agent ;

(d) send one container forthwith :

(i) in a case where such sample is taken from any area situated in a Union Territory, to the laboratory established or recognised by the Central Board under Section 16; and

(ii) in any other case, to the laboratory established or recognised by the State Board under Section 17 ;

(e) on the request of the occupier of his agent, send the second container :

(i) in a case where such sample is taken from any area situated in Union Territory, to the laboratory established or specified under sub-section (1) of Section 51; and

(ii) in any other case, to the laboratory established or specified under sub-section (1) of Section 52.

(4) When a sample of any sewage or trade effluent is taken for analysis under sub-section (1) and the person taking the sample serves on the occupier of his agent, a notice under clause (a) of sub-section (3) and the occupier of his agent, willfully absents himself, then;

(a) the sample so taken shall be placed in a container which shall be marked and sealed and shall also be signed by the person taking the sample and the same shall be sent forthwith by such person for analysis to the laboratory referred to in sub-clause (i) or sub-clause (ii), as the case may be, of clause (e) of sub-section (3) and such person shall inform the Government analyst appointed under sub-section (1) or sub-section (2), as the case may be, of Section 53, in writing about the wilful absence or the occupier of his agent :

(b) the cost incurred in getting such sample analysed shall be payable by the occupier of his agent and in case of default of such payment, the same shall be recoverable from the occupier of his agent, as the case may be, as an arrear of land revenue or of public demand :

Provided that no such recovery shall be made unless the occupier or, as the case may be, his agent has been given a reasonable opportunity of being heard in the matter.

(5) When a sample of any sewage or trade of effluent is taken for analysis under sub-section (1) and the person taking the sample serves on the occupier of his agent a notice under clause *(a)* of sub-section (3) and the occupier or his agent who is present at the time of taking the sample does not make a request for dividing

the sample into parts as provided in clause *(b)* of sub-section (3), then, sample so taken shall be placed in a container which shall be marked and sealed and shall also be signed by the person taking the sample and the same shall be sent forthwith by such person for analysis to the laboratory referred to in sub-clause *(i),* or sub-clause *(ii),* as the case may be, of clause *(d)* of sub-section (3).

22. Reports of the result of analysis on samples taken under Section 21

(1) Where a sample of any sewage or trade effluent has been sent for analysis to the laboratory established or recognised by the Central Board or, as the case may be, the State Board, the concerned Board analyst appointed under sub-section (3) of Section 53 shall analyse the sample and submit a report in the prescribed form of the result of such analysis in triplicate to the Central Board or the State Board, as the case may be.

(2) On receipt of the report under sub-section (1) one copy of the report shall be sent by the Central Board or the State Board, as the case may be to the occupier of his agent referred to in Section 21, another copy shall be preserved for production before the court in case any legal proceedings are taken against him and the other copy shall be kept by the concerned Board.

(3) Where a sample has been sent for analysis under clause (e) of sub-section (3) or sub-section (4) or sub-section (4) of Section 21 to any laboratory mentioned therein, the Government analyst referred to in that sub-section shall analyse the sample and submit a report in the prescribed form of the result of the analysis in triplicate to the Central Board or, as the case may be, the State Board which shall comply with the provisions of sub-section (2).

(4) If there is any inconsistency or discrepancy between, or variation in the results of the analysis carried out by the laboratory established or recognised by the Central Board of the State Board, as the case may be, that of the laboratory established or specified under Section 51 or Section 52, as the case may be, the report of the latter shall prevail.

(5) Any cost incurred in getting any sample analysed at the request of the occupier or his agent shall be payable by such occupier of his agent and in case of default the same shall be recoverable from him as arrears of land revenue or of public demand.

23. Power of entry and inspection

(1) Subject to the provisions of this section, any person empowered by a State Board in this behalf shall have a right at any time to enter with such assistance as he considers necessary, any place:

(a) for the purpose of performing any of the functions of the Board entrusted to him ;

(b) for the purpose of determining whether and if so in what manner, any such functions are to be performed or whether any provisions of this Act or the rules made thereunder or any notice, order, direction or authorisation served, made, given, or granted under this Act is being or has been complied with;

(c) for the purpose of examining any plant, record, register, document or any other material object or for conducting a search of any place in which he has reason to believe that an offence under this Act or the rules made thereunder has been or is being or in about to committed and for seizing any such plant, record, register, document or other material object, if he has reason to believe that if may furnish evidence of the commission of an offence punishable under this Act or the rules made thereunder :

Provided that the right to enter under this sub-section for the inspection of a well shall be exercised only at reasonable hours in a case where such well is situated in any premises used for residential purposes and the water thereof is used exclusively for domestic purposes.

(2) The provisions of the Code of Criminal Procedure, 1973, (2 of 1974) or, in relation to the State of Jammu and Kashmir, the provisions of any corresponding law in force in that State, shall, so far as may be, apply to any search of seizure under this section as they, apply to any search to seizure made under the authority of a warrant issued under [Section 94] of the said Code, or as the case may be, under the corresponding provisions of the said law.

Explanation — For the purposes of this section, "place" includes vessel.

24. Prohibition on use of stream or well for disposal of polluting matter etc.

(1) Subject to the provisions of the section :

(a) no person shall knowingly cause or permit any poisonous, noxious or polluting matter determined in accordance with such standards as may be laid down by the State Board to

enter (whether directly or indirectly) into any [stream or well or sewer or on land] ; or

(b) no person shall knowingly cause or permit to enter into any stream any other matter which may tend, either directly or in combination with similar matters, to impede the proper flow of the water of the stream in a manner leading or likely to lead to a substantial aggravation of pollution due to other causes or of its consequences.

(2) A person shall not be guilty of an offence under sub-section (1), by reason only of having done or caused to be done any of the following acts, namely :

(a) constructing, improving or maintaining in or across on the bank or bed of any stream any building, bridge, weir, dam, sluice dock, pier, drain or sewer or other permanent works which he has a right to construct, improve or maintain ;

(b) depositing any materials on the bank or in the bed of any stream for the purpose of reclaiming land or for supporting, repairing or protecting the bank or bed of such stream provided such materials are not capable of polluting such stream ;

(c) putting into any stream any sand or gravel or other natural deposit which has flowed from or been deposited by the current of such stream ;

(d) causing or permitting, with the consent of the State Board, the deposit accumulated in a well, pond or reservoir to enter into any stream ;

(3) The State Government may, after consultation with, or on the recommendation of the State Board, exempt, by notification in the Official Gazette, any person from the operation of sub-section (1) subject of such conditions, if any, as may be specified in the notification and any condition so specified may by a like notification be altered, varied or amended.

25. Restrictions on new outlets and new discharges

(1) Subject to the provisions of this section, no person shall, without the previous consent of the State Board :

(a) establish or take any steps to establish any industry, operation or process, or any treatment and disposal system or any extension or addition thereto, which is likely to discharge sewage or trade effluent into a stream or well or sewer or on land (such discharge being hereafter in this section referred

to as discharge of sewage);

or

(b) bring into use any new or altered outlet for the discharge of sewage;

or

(c) begin to make any new discharge of sewage :

Provided that a person in the process of taking any steps to establish any industry, operation or process immediately before the commencement of the Water (Prevention and Control of Pollution) Amendment Act, 1988, for which no consent was necessary prior to such commencement, may continue to do so for a period of three months from such commencement or, if he has made an application for such consent, within the said period of three months from such commencement or, if he has made an application for such consent, within the said period of three months, till the disposal of such application.

(2) An application for consent of the State Board under sub-section (1) shall be made in such form, contain such particulars and shall be accompanied by such fees as may be prescribed.

(3) The State Board may make such inquiry as it may deem fit in respect of the application for consent referred to in sub-section (1) and in making any such inquiry shall follow such procedure as may be prescribed.

(4) The State Board may :

(a) grant its consent refered to in sub-section (1) subject to such conditions as it may impose, being

(i) in cases referred to in clauses *(a)* and *(b)* of sub-section (1) of Section 25, conditions as to the point of discharge of sewage or as to the use of that outlet or any other outlet for discharge of sewage ;

(ii) in the case of a new discharge, conditions as to the nature and composition, temperature, volume or rate of discharge of the effluent from the land or premises from which the discharge or new discharge is to be made ; and

(iii) that the consent will be valid only for such period as may be specified in the order,

and any such conditions imposed shall be binding on any person establishing or taking any steps to establish any industry, operation or process, or treatment and disposal system or extension or addition thereto, or using the new or altered outlet, or discharging the effluent from the land or premises aforesaid; or

(b) refuse such consent for reasons to be recorded in writing.

(5) Where, without the consent of the State Board, any industry, operation or process, or any treatment and disposal system or any extension or addition thereto, is established, or any steps for such establishment have been taken or a new or altered outlet is brought into use for the discharge of sewage or a new discharge of sewage is made, the State Board may serve on the person who has established or taken steps to establish any industry, operation or process, or any treatment and disposal system or any extension or addition thereto, or using the outlet, or making the discharge, as the case may be, a notice imposing any such conditions as it might have imposed on an application for its consent in respect of such establishment, such outlet or discharge.

(6) Every State Board shall maintain a register containing particulars of the conditions imposed under this section and so much of the register as relates to any outlet, or to any effluent, from any land or premises shall be open to inspection at all reasonable hours by any person interested in, or affected by such outlet, land or premises, as the case may be, or by any person authorised by him in this behalf and the conditions so contained in such register shall be conclusive proof that the consent was granted subject to such conditions.

(7) The consent referred to in sub-section (1) shall, unless given or refused earlier, be deemed to have been given unconditionally on the expiry of a period of four months of the making of an application in this behalf complete in all respects to the State Board.

(8) For the purposes of this section and Section 27 and 30;

(a) the expression "new or altered outlet" means any outlet which is wholly or partly constructed on or after the commencement of this Act or which (whether so constructed or not) is substantially altered after such commencement:

(b) he expression "new discharge" means a discharge which is not, as respects the nature and composition, temperature, volume, and rate of discharge of the effluent substantially a continuation of a discharge made within the preceding twelve months (whether by the same or a different outlet), so however, that a discharge which is in other respects a continuation of previous discharge made as aforesaid shall not be deemed to be a new discharge by reason of any reduction of the temperature of volume of rate of discharge of the affluent as compared with the previous discharge.

26. Provision regarding existing discharge of sewage or trade effluent.

Where immediately before the commencement of this Act any person was discharging any sewage or trade effluent into a [stream or well or sewer or on land the provisions of Section 25 shall, so far as may be apply in relation to such person as they apply in relation to the person referred to in that section to the modification that the application for consent to be made under sub-section (2) of that section shall be made on or before such date as may be specified by the State Government by notification this behalf in the Official Gazette.

27. Refusal or with drawal of consent by State Board.

(1) A State Board shall not grant its consent under sub-section (4) of Section 25 for the establishment of any industry, operation or process, or treatment and disposal system or extension of addition thereto, or to the bringing into use of a new or altered outlet unless the industry, operation or process, or treatment and disposal system or extension or addition thereto, or the outlet is so established as to comply with any conditions imposed by the Board to enable it to exercise its rights to take samples of the effluent.

(2) A State Board may from time to time review—

(a) any condition imposed under section 25 or section 26 and may serve on the person to whom a consent under Section 25 or Section 26 is granted a notice making any reasonable variation of or revoking any such condition :

(b) the refusal of any consent referred to in sub-section (1) of Section 25 or Section 26 or the grant of such consent without any condition, and may make such orders as it deems fit.]

(3) Any condition imposed under Section 25 or Section 26 shall be subject to any verification made under sub-section (2) and shall continue in force until revoked under that sub-section.

28. Appeals

(1) Any person aggrieved by an order made by the State Board under Section 25, Section 26 or Section 27 may, within thirty days from the date on which the order is communicated to him, prefer an appeal to such authority (hereinafter referred to as the appellate authority) as the State Government may think fit to constitute :

Provided that the appellate authority may entertain the appeal after the expiry of the said period of thirty days if such authority is satisfied that the appellant was prevented by sufficient cause from filing the appeal in time.

(2) An appellate authority shall consist of a single person or three persons, as the State Government may think fit, to be appointed by that Government.

(3) The form and manner in which an appeal may be preferred under sub-section (1), the fees payable for such appeal and the procedure to be followed by the appellate authority shall be such as may be prescribed.

(4) On receipt of an appeal preferred under sub-section (1), the appellate authority shall, after giving the appellant and the State Board an opportunity of being heard, dispose of the appeal as expeditiously as possible.

(5) If the appellate authority determines that any condition imposed, of the variation of any condition, as the case may be, was unreasonable, then :

(a) where the appeal is in respect of the unreasonableness of any condition imposed, such authority may direct either that the condition shall be treated as anulled or that there shall be substituted for it such condition as appears to it to be reasonable ;

(b) where the appeal is in respect of the unreasonableness of any variation of a condition, such authority may direct either that the condition shall be treated as continuing in force unvaried or that it shall be varied in such manner as appears to it to be reasonable.

29. Revision

(1) The State Government may at any time either of its own motion or an application made to it in this behalf, call for the records of any case where an order has been made by the State Board under Section 25, Section 26 or Section 27 for the purpose of satisfying itself as to be legality or propriety of any such order and may pass such order in relation thereto as it may think fit :

Provided that the State Government shall not pass any order under this sub-section without affording the State Board and the person who may be effected by such order a reasonable opportunity of being heard in the matter.

(2) The State Government shall not revise any order made under Section 25, Section 26, or Section 27 where as appeal against that order lies to the appellate authority, but has not been preferred or where an appeal has been preferred such appeal is pending before the appellate authority.

30. Power of State Board to carry out certain works

(1) Where under this Act, any conditions have been imposed on any person while granting consent under Section 25 or Section 26 and such condition require such person to execute any work in connection therewith and such work has not been executed within such time as may be specified in this behalf, the State Board may serve on the person concerned a notice requiring him within such time (not being less than thirty days) as may be specified in the notice to execute the work specified therein.

(2) If the person concerned fails to execute the work as required in the notice referred to in sub-section (1), then, after the expiration of the time specified in the said notice, the State Board may itself execute or cause to be executed such work.

(3) All expenses incurred by the State Board for the execution of the aforesaid work, together with interest, at such rate as the State Government may, by order, fix, from the date when a demand for the expenses is made until it is paid, may be recovered by that Board from the person concerned, as arrears of land revenue, or of public demand.

31. Furnishing of information to State Board and other agencies in certain cases

(1) If at any place where any industry, operation or process, or any treatment and disposal system or any extension or addition thereto is being carried on. due to accident or other unforeseen act or event, any poisonous, noxious or polluting matter is being discharged, or is likely to be discharged into a stream or well or sewer or on land and, as a result of such discharge, the water in any stream or well is being polluted, or is likely to be polluted, than the person incharge of such place shall forthwith intimate the occurrence of such accident, act or event to the State Board and such other authorities or agencies as may be prescribed.

(2) Where any local authority operates any sewerage system or sewage works, the provisions of sub-section (1) shall apply to such local authority as they apply in relation to the person incharge of the place where any industry or trade is being carried on.

32. Emergency measures in case of pollution of stream or well

(1) Where it appears to the State Board that any poisonous, noxious or polluting matter is present in [any stream or well or on lands] by reason of the discharge of such matter in such stream or well or has entered into that stream or well due to any accident or other

unforeseen act or event, and if the Board is of opinion that it is necessary or expedient to take immediate action, it may for reasons to be recorded in writing, carry out such operations as it may consider necessary for all or any of the following purposes, that is to say :

(a) removing that matter from [stream or well or on land] and disposing it of in such manner as the Board considers appropriate ;

(b) remedying or mitigating any pollution caused by its presence in the stream of well ;

(c) issuing orders immediately restraining or prohibiting the person concerned from discharging any poisonous, noxious or polluting matter into the [stream or well or on land] or from making insanitary use of the stream or well.

(2) The power conferred by sub-section (1) does not include the power to construct any works of a temporary character which are removed on or before the completion of the operations.

33. Power of Board to make application to courts for restraining apprehended pollution of water in streams or wells

(1) Where it is apprehended by a Board that the water in any Stream or well is likely to be polluted by reason of the disposal or likely disposal of any matter in such stream or well or in any sewer or on any land, or otherwise, the Board may make an application to a court, not inferior to that of a Metropolitan Magistrate or a Judicial Magistrate of the first class, for restraining the person who is likely to cause such pollution from so causing.

(2) On receipt of an application under sub-section (1) the court may make such order as it deems fit.

(3) Where under sub-section (2) the court makes an order restraining any person from polluting the water in any stream or well, it may in that order :

(i) direct the person who is likely to cause or has caused the pollution of the water in the stream or well, to desist from taking such action as is likely to cause pollution or, as the case may be to remove from such stream or well, such matter, and

(ii) authorise the Board, if the direction under clause (1) (being a direction for the removal of any matter from such stream or well) is not complied with by the person to whom such direction is issued to undertake the removal and disposal of the matter in such manner as may be specified by the court.

(4) All expenses incurred by the Board in removing any matter

in pursuance of the authorisation under clause (ii) of sub-section (3) or in disposal of any such matter may be defrayed out of any money obtained by the Board from such disposal and any balance outstanding shall be recoverable from the person concerned as arrears of land revenue or of public demand.

33A. Power to give directions

Notwithstanding anything contained in any other law, but subject to the provisions of this Act, and to any directions that the Central Government may give in this behalf, a Board may, in the exercise of its powers and performance of its functions under this Act, issue any directions in writing to any person, officer or authority, and such person, officer or authority shall be bound to comply with such directions.

Explanation : For the avoidance of doubts, it is hereby declared that the power to issue directions under this section incudes the power to direct:

(a) the closure, prohibition or regulation of any industry, operation or process ; or

(b) the stoppage or regulation of supply of electricity, water or any other service.

Chapter VI

FUNDS, ACCOUNTS AND AUDIT

34. Contributions by Central Government

The Central Government may, after due appropriation made by Parliament by law in this behalf, make in each financial year such contributions to the Central Board as it may think necessary to enable the Board to perform its functions under this Act.

35. Contributions by State Government

The State Government may, after due appropriation made by the Legislature of the State by law in this behalf, make in each financial year such contributions to the State Board as it may think necessary to enable that Board to perform its functions under this Act.

36. Funds of Central Board

(1) The Central Board shall have its own fund and all sums which may, from time to time, be paid to it by the Central Government and all other receipts (by way of gifts, grants, donations, benefactions fees or otherwise) of that Board shall be carried to the fund of the Board and all payments by the Board shall be made therefrom.

(2) The Central Board may expend such sums as it thinks fit for performing its functions under this Act, and, where any law for the time being in force relating to the prevention, control or abatement of air pollution provides for the performance of any function under such law by the Central Board, also for performing its functions under such law and such sums shall be treated as expenditure payable out of the fund of that Board.

37. Fund of State Board

(1) The State Board shall have its own fund, and the sums which may, from time to time, be paid to it by State Government and all other receipts (by way of gifts, grants, donation, benefactions fees or otherwise) of that Board shall be carried to the fund of the Board and all payments by the Board shall be made therefrom.

(2) The State Board may expend such sum as it thinks fit for performing its functions under this Act, and, where any law for the time being in force relating to the prevention, control or abatement of air pollution provides for the performance of any functions under such law by the State Board, also for performing its functions under such law and such sums shall be treated as expenditure payable out of the fund of that Board.

37A. Borrowing powers of Boards

A Board may, with the consent of, or in accordance with, the terms of any general or special authority given to it by the Central Government or, as the case may be, the State Government, borrow money from any source by way of loans or issue of bonds, debentures or such other instruments, as it may deem fit, for the performance of all or any of its functions under this Act.

38. Budget

The Central Board or, as the case may be, the State Board shall during each financial year, prepare, in such form and at such time as may be prescribed, a budget in respect of the financial year next ensuing showing the estimated receipt and expenditure copies thereof shall be forwarded to the Central Government or, as the case may be, the State Government.

39. Annual Report

(1) The Central Board shall, during each financial year, prepare, in such form as may be prescribed, an annual report giving full account of its activities under this Act during the previous financial year and copies thereof shall be forwarded to the Central Government within four months from the last date of the previous financial year and that Government shall cause every

such report to be laid before both Houses of Parliament within nine months from the last date of the previous financial year and that Government shall cause every such report to be laid before the State Legislature within a period of nine months from the last date of the previous financial year.

(2) Every State Board shall, during each financial year, prepare, in such form as may be prescribed, an annual report giving full account of its activities under the Act during the previous financial year and copies thereof shall be forwarded to the State Government within four months from the last date of the previous financial year and that Government shall cause every such report to be laid before the State Legislature within a period of nine months from the last date of the previous year.

40. Accounts and audit

(1) Every Board shall maintain proper accounts and other relevant records and prepare an annual statement of account in such form as may be prescribed by the Central Government or, as the case may be, the State Government.

(2) The accounts of the Board shall be audited by an auditor duly qualified to act as an auditor of companies under Section 226 of the Companies Act, 1956 (1 of 1956).

(3) The said auditor shall be appointed by the Central Government or, as the case may be, the State Government on the advice of the Comptroller and Auditor General of India.

(4) Every auditor appointed to audit the accounts of the Board under this Act shall have the right to demand the production of books, accounts connected vouchers and other documents and papers and to inspect any of the offices of the Board.

(5) Every such auditor shall send a copy of his report together with an audited copy of the accounts to the Central Government or, as the case may be, the State Government.

(6) The Central Government shall, as soon as may be after the receipt of the audit report under sub-section (5), cause the same to be laid before both Houses of Parliament.

(7) The State Government shall, as soon as may be after the receipt of the audit report under sub-section (5), cause the same to be laid before the State Legislature.

Chapter VII

PENALTIES AND PROCEDURE

41. Failure to comply with directions under sub-section (2) or sub-section (3) of Section 20 or orders issued under clause (e) of sub-section (1) of Section 32 or directions issued under sub-section (2) of Section 33 or Section 33A

(1) Whoever fails to comply with any direction given under sub-section (2) of sub-section (3) of Section 20 within such time as may be specified in the direction shall, on conviction, be punishable with imprisonment for a term which may extend to three months or with fine which may extend to ten thousand rupees or with both and in case the failure continues, with an additional fine which may extend to five thousand rupees for every day during which such failure continues after the conviction for the first such failure.

(2) Whoever, fails to comply with any order issued under clause (c) of sub-section (1) of Section 32 or any direction issued by a court under sub-section (2) of Section 33 or any direction issued under Section 33A shall, in respect of each such failure and on conviction, be punishable with imprisonment for a term which shall not be less than one year and six months but which may extend to six years and with fine, and in case the failure continues, with an additional fine which may extend to five thousand rupees for every day during which such failure continues after the conviction for the first such failure.

(3) If the failure referred to in sub-section (2) continues beyond a period of one year after the date of conviction, the offender shall, on conviction, be punishable with imprisonment for a term which shall not be less than two years but which may extend to seven years and with fine.

42. Penalty for certain acts

(1) Whoever :

(a) destroys, pulls down, removes, injures or defaces any pillar, post or stake fixed in the ground or any notice or other matter put up, inscribed or placed, by or under the authority of the Board, or

(b) obstructs any person acting under the orders or directions of the Board from exercising his powers and performing his functions under this Act, or

(c) damages any works or property belonging to the Board, or

(d) fails to furnish to any officer or other employee of the Board any information required by him for the purpose of this Act, or

(e) fails to intimate the occurrence of any accident or other unforeseen act or even under Section 31 to the Board and other authorities or agencies as required by that section, or

(f) in giving any information which he is required to give under this Act, knowingly or willfully makes a statement which is false in any material particular, or

(g) for the purpose of obtaining any consent under Section 25 of Section 26, knowingly or willfully makes a statement which is false in any material particular,

shall be punishable with imprisonment for a term which may extend to three months or with fine which may extend to [ten thousand rupees] or with both.

(2) Where for the grant of consent in pursuance of the provisions of Section 25 or Section 26 the use of a matter or gauge or other measure or monitoring device is required and such device is used for the purposes of those provisions, any person who knowingly or willfully alters or interferes with that device so as to prevent it from monitoring or measuring correctly shall be punishable with imprisonment for a term which may extend to three months or fine which may extend to one thousand rupees or with both.

43. Penalty for contravention of provisions of Section 24

Whoever, contravenes the provisions of Section 24 shall be punishable with imprisonment for a term which shall not be less than [one year and six months] but which may extend to six years and with fine.

44. Penalty for contravention of Section 25 or Section 26

Whoever, contravenes the provisions of Section 25 of Section 26 shall be punishable with imprisonment for a term which shall not be less than [one year and six months] but which may extend to six years and with fine.

45. Enhanced penalty after previous conviction

If any person who has been convicted of any offence under section 24 of Section 25 or Section 26 is again found guilty of an offence involving a contravention of the same provision, he shall, on the second and on every subsequent conviction, be punishable with imprisonment for a term which shall not be less than [two years] but which may extend to seven years and with fine:

Provided that for the purpose of this section no cognizance shall be taken of any conviction made more than two years before the commission of the offence which is being punished.

45A. Penalty for contravention of certain provisions of the Act

Whoever, contravenes any of the provisions of this Act or fails to comply with any order or direction given under this Act, for which no penalty has been elsewhere provided in this Act, shall be punishable with imprisonment which may extend to three months or with fine which may extend to ten thousand rupees or with both, and in the case of a continuing contravention or failure, with an additional fine which may extend to five thousand rupees for every day during which such contravention or failure continues after conviction for the first such contravention or failure.

46. Publication of names of offenders

If any person convicted of an offence under this Act commits a like offence afterwards it shall be lawful for the court before which the second or subsequent conviction takes place to cause the offender's name and place of residence, the offence and the penalty imposed to be published at the offender's expense in such newspapers or in such other manner as the court may direct and the expenses of such publication shall be deemed to be part of the cost attending the conviction and shall be recoverable in the same manner as a fine.

47. Offence by companies

(1) Where an offence under this Act has been committed by a company, every person who at the time the offence was committed was in charge of, and was responsible to the company for the conduct of, the business of the company, as well as the company, shall be deemed to be guilty of the offence and shall be liable to be proceed against and punished accordingly:

Provided that nothing contained in this sub-section shall render any such person liable to any punishment provided in this Act if he proves that the offence was committed without his knowledge or that he exercised all due diligence to prevent the commission of such offence.

(2) Notwithstanding anything contained in sub-section (1), where an offence under this Act has been committed by a company and it is proved that the offence has been committed with the consent or connivance of, or is attributable to any neglect on the part of, any director, manager, secretary or other officer shall also be deemed to be guilty of that offence and shall be liable to be proceeded against and punished accordingly.

Explanation : For the purposes of this section,-

(a) "company" means any body corporate, and includes a firm or other association of individuals ; and

(b) "director" in relation to a firm means a partner in the firm.

48. Offences by Government Departments

Where an offence under this Act has been committed by any Department of Government, the Head of the Department shall be deemed to be guilty of the offence and shall be liable to be proceed against and punished accordingly :

Provided that nothing contained in this section shall render such Head of the Department liable to any punishment if he proves that the offence was committed without his knowledge or that he exercised all due diligence to prevent the commission of such offence.

49. Cognizance of offence

(1) No court shall take cognizance of any offence under this Act except on a complaint made by :

(a) a Board or any officer authorised in this behalf by it ; or

(b) any person who has given notice of not less than sixty days, in the manner prescribed, of the alleged offence and of his intention to make a complaint, to the Board or officer authorised as aforesaid,

and no court inferior to that of a Metropolitan Magistrate or a Judicial Magistrate of the first class shall try any offence punishable under this Act." (1) No court shall take congnizance of any offence under this Act except on a complaint made by, or with the previous sanction in writing of the State Board, and no court inferior to that of a Metropolitan Magistrate or a Judicial Magistrate of the first class shall try any offence punishable under this Act.

(2) Where a complaint has been made under clause (b) of sub-section (1), the Board shall, on demand by such person, make available the relevant reports in its possession to that person:

Provided that the Board may refuse to make any such report available to such person if the same is, in its opinion, against the public interests."

(3) Notwithstanding anything contained in section 29 of the Code of Criminal Procedure, 1973 (2 of 1974) it shall be lawful for any Judicial Magistrate of the first class or for any Metropolitan Magistrate to pass a sentence of imprisonment for a term exceeding two years or of fine exceeding two thousand rupees on any person convicted of an offence punishable under this Act.

50. Members, officers and servants of Boards to be public servants

All members, officers and servants of a Board when acting or purporting to act in pursuance of any of the provisions of this Act and the rules made thereunder shall be deemed to be public servants within the meaning of Section 21 (45 of 1860) of the Indian Penal Code.

Chapter VIII

MISCELLANEOUS

51. Central Water Laboratory :

(1) The Central Government may, by notification in the Official Gazette,

(a) establish a Central Water Laboratory; or

(b) specify any laboratory of institute as a Central Water Laboratory, to carry out the functions entrusted to the Central Water Laboratory under this Act.

(2) The Central Government may, after consultation with the Central Board, makes rules prescribing—

(a) the functions of the Central Water Laboratory;

(b) the procedures for the submission to the said laboratory of samples of water or of sewage or trade effluent for analysis or tests, the form of the laboratory's report thereon and the fees payable in respect of such report;

(c) such other matters as may be necessary or expedient to enable that laboratory to carry out its functions.

52. State Water Laboratory

(1) The State Government may, by notification in the official Gazette :

(a) establish a State Water Laboratory; or

(b) specify any laboratory or institute as a State Water Laboratory, to carry out the functions entrusted to the State Water Laboratory under this Act.

(2) The State Government may, after consultation with the State Board, make rules prescribing :

(a) the functions of the State Water Laboratory ;

(b) the procedure for the submission to the said laboratory of samples of water or of sewage or trade effluent for analysis or tests, the form of the laboratory's report thereupon and the fees payable in respect of such report ;

(c) such other matters as may be necessary or expedient to enable that laboratory to carry out its functions.

53. Analysis

(1) The Central Government may, by notification in the Official Gazette, appoint such persons as it thinks fit and having the prescribed qualifications to be Government analysts for the

purpose of analysis of samples of water or of sewage or trade effluent sent for analysis to any laboratory established or specified under sub-section (1) of Section 51.

(2) The State Government may, by notification in the Official Gazette, appoint such persons as it thinks fit and having the prescribed qualifications to by Government analysts for the purpose of analysis of samples of water of sewage or trade effluent sent for analysis to any laboratory establishment or specified under sub-section (1) of Section 52.

(3) Without prejudice to the provisions of sub-section (3) of Section 12, the Central Board or, as the case may be, the State Board may, by notification in the Official Gazette, and the approval of the Central Government or the State Government, as the case may be, appoint such persons as it thinks fit and having the prescribed qualifications to be Board analysts for the purpose of analysis of samples of water or of sewage or trade effluent sent for analysis to any laboratory established or recognised under Section 16, or, as the case may be, under Section 17.

54. Reports of analysts

Any documents purporting to be a report signed by a Government analyst or as the case may be, a Board analyst may be used as evidence of the facts stated there in any proceedings under this Act.

55. Local authorities to assist

All local authorities shall render such help and assistance and furnish such information to be the Board as it may require for the discharge of its functions, and shall make available to the Board for inspection and examination such records, maps plans and other documents as may be necessary for the discharge of its functions.

56. Compulsory acquisition of lands for the State Board

Any land require by a State Board for the efficient performance of its functions under this Act shall be deemed to be needed for a public purpose and such land shall be acquired for the State Board under the provisions of the Land Acquisition Act, 1894 (1 of 1894), or under any other corresponding law for the time being in force.

57. Returns and reports

The Central Board shall furnish to the Central Government, and a State Board shall furnish to the State Government and to the Central Board such reports, returns, statistics, account and other information with respect to its funds or activities as that Government, or as the case may be, the Central Board may, from time to time, require.

58. Bar of jurisdiction

No civil court shall have jurisdiction to entertain any suit or proceeding in respect of any matter which an appellate authority constituted under this Act is empowered by or under this Act to determine, and no injunction shall be granted by any court or other authority in respect of any action taken in pursuance of any power conferred by or under this Act.

59. Protection of action taken in good faith

No suit or other proceedings shall lie against the Government or any officer of Government or any member or officer of a Board in respect of anything which is in good faith done or intended to be done in persuance of this Act or the rules made thereunder.

60. Overriding effect

The provisions of this Act shall have effect notwithstanding anything inconsistent therewith contained in any enactment other than this Act.

61. Power of Central Government to supersede the Central Board and Joint Boards :

(1) If at any time the Central Government is of opinion :

(a) that the Central Board or any Joint Board has persistently made default in the performance of the functions imposed on it by or under this Act; or

(b) that circumstances exist which render it necessary in the public interest so to do,

the Central Government may, by notification in the Official Gazette, supersede the Central Board or such Joint Board, as the case may be, for such period, not exceeding one year, as may be specified in the notification:

Provided that before issuing a notification under this sub-section for the reasons mentioned in clause (a) the Central Government shall give a reasonable opportunity to the Central Board or such Joint Board as the case may be, to show cause why it should not be superseded and shall consider the explanations and objections, if any, of the Central Board or such Joint Board, as the case may be.

(2) Upon the publication of a notification under sub-section (1) superseding the Central Board or any Joint Board :

(a) all the members shall, as from the date of supersession vacate their offices as such ;

(b) all the powers, functions and duties which may, be or under this Act, be exercised, performed or discharged by the Central Board or such Joint Board shall, until the Central Board or the Joint Board, as the case may be is reconstituted under sub-section (3) be exercised, performed or discharged by such person or persons as the Central Government may

direct ;

(c) all property owned or controlled by the Central Board or such Joint Board shall until the Central Board or the Joint-Board, as the case may be, is reconstituted under sub-section (3) vest in the Central Government.

(3) On the expiration of the period of supersession specified in the notification issued under sub-section (1), the Central Government may :

(a) extend the period of supersession for such further term, not exceeding six months, as it may consider necessary; or

(b) reconstitute the Central Board or the Joint Board, as the case may be, by fresh nomination or appointment : as the case may be, and in such case any person who vacated his office under clause *(a)* of sub-section (2) shall not be deemed disqualified for nomination or appointment:

Provided that the Central Government may at any time before the expiration of the period of supersession, whether originally specified under sub-section (1) or as extended under this sub-section, take action under clause *(b)* of this sub-section.

The State Boards can also be superseded by the State Governments concerned as in the case of Central Board and Joint Boards.

62. Power of State Government to supersede State Board

(1) If at any time the State Government is of opinion :

(a) that the state Board has persistently made default in the performance of the functions imposed on it by or under this Act; or

(b) that circumstances exist which render it necessary in the public interest so to do,

the State Government may, by notification in the Official Gazette, supersede the State Board for such period, not exceeding one year, as may be specified in the notification:

Provided that before issuing a notification under this sub-section for the reasons mentioned in clause *(a)*, the State Government shall give a reasonable opportunity to the State Board to show cause why it should not be superseded and shall consider the explanations and objections,if any, of the State Board.

(2) Upon the publication of a notification under sub-section (1) superseding the State Board, the provisions of sub-section (2) and (3) of Section 61 shall apply in relation to the supersession of the State Board as they apply in relation to be supersession of the Central Board or a Joint Board by the Central Government.

63. Power of Central Government to make rules :

(1) The Central Government may, simultaneously with the constitution of the Central Board, make rules in respect of the matters specified in sub-section (2):

Provided that when the Central Board has been constituted, no such rule shall be made, varied, amended or repealed without consulting the Board.

(2) In particular, and without prejudice to the generality of the foregoing power, such rules may provide for all of any of the following matter, namely :

(a) the terms and conditions of service of the members (other than the chairman and member-secretary) of the Central Board under sub-section (8) of Section 5 ;

(b) the intervals and the time and place at which meetings of the Central Board or of any committee thereof constituted under this Act, shall be held and the procedure to be followed at such meetings, including the quorum necessary for the transaction of business under Section 8, and under sub-section (2) of Section 9 ;

(c) the fees and allowances to be paid to such members of a committee of the Central Board as are not members of the Board under sub-section (3) of Section 9 ;

(d) the manner in which and the purposes for which person may be associated with the Central Board under sub-section (1) of Section 10 and the fees and allowances payable to such persons ;

(e) the terms and conditions of service of the chairman and the member-secretary of Central Board under sub-section (9) of Section 5 and under sub-section (1) of Section 12 ;

(f) conditions subject to which a person may be appointed as a consulting engineer to the Central Board under sub-section (4) of Section 12 ;

(g) the powers and duties to be exercised and performed by the chairman and the member-secretary of the Central Board ;

(h) the form of the report of the Central Board analyst under sub-section (1) of Section 22 ;

(k) the form of the report of the Government analyst under sub-section (3) of Section 22 ;

(I) the form in which and the time within which the budget of the Central Board may be prepared and forwarded to the Central Government under Section 38 ;

(II) the form in which the annual report of the Central Board may be prepared under Section 39 ;

(m) the form in which the accounts of the Central Board may be maintained under Section 40 ;

(mm) the manner in which notice of intention to make a complaint shall be given to the Central Board or officer authorised by it under Section 49 ;

(n) any other matter relating to the Central Board, including the powers and functions of that Board in relation to Union Territories ;

(o) any other matter which has to be, or may be, prescribed.

(3) Every rule made by the Central Government under this Act shall be laid, as soon as may be after it is made, before each House of Parliament while it is in session for a total period of thirty days which may be comprised in one session or in two or more successive sessions, and if, [before the expiry of the session immediately following the session or the successive sessions aforesaid], both Houses agree in making any modification in the rule or both Houses agree that the rule should not be made, the rule shall thereafter have effect only in such modified form or be of no effect, as the case may be; so, however, that any such modification or annulment shall be without prejudice to the validity of anything previously done under that rule.

64. Powers of State Government to make rules

(1) The State Government may, simultaneously with the constitution of the State Board, make rules to carry out the purposes of this Act in respect of matters not falling within the purview of Section 63 :

Provided that when the State Board has been constituted no such rule shall be made, varied, amended or repealed without consulting that Board.

(2) In particular, and without prejudice to the generality of the forgoing power, such rules may provide for all of any of the following matters, namely :

(a) the terms and conditions of service of the members (other than the chairman and the member-secretary) of the State Board under sub-section (8) of Section 5 ;

(b) the time and place of meetings of the State Board or any committee of that Board constituted under this Act and the procedure to be followed at such meeting, including the quorum necessary for the transaction of business under Section 8 and under sub-section (2) of Section 9 ;

(c) the fees and allowances to be paid to such members of a committee of the State Board as are not members of the Board under sub-section (3) of Section 9 ;

(d) the manner in which and the purposes for which persons may be associated with the State Board under sub-section (1) of Section 10 [and the fees and allowances payable to such persons ;

(e) the terms and conditions of service of the chairman and the member-secretary of the State Board under sub-section (9) of Section 5 and under sub-section (1) of Section 12 ;

(f) the conditions subject to which a person may be appointed as a consulting engineer to the State Board under sub-section (4) of Section 12 ;

(g) the powers and duties to be exercised and discharged by the chairman and the member-secretary of the State Board ;

(h) the form of the notice referred to in Section 21 ;

(i) the form of the report of the State Board analyst under sub-section (1) of Section 22 ;

(j) the form of the report of the Government analyst under sub-section (3) of Section 22 ;

(k) the form of application for the consent of the State Board under sub-section (2) of Section 25, and the particulars it may contain ;

(l) the manner in which inquiry under sub-section (3) of Section 25 may be made in respect of an application for obtaining consent of the State Board and the matters to be taken into account in granting or refusing such consent;

(m) the form and manner in which appeals may be filed, the fees payable in respect of such appeals and the procedure to be followed by the appellate authority in disposing of the appeals under sub-section (3) of Section 28;

(n) the form in which and the time within which the budget of the State Board may be prepared and forwarded to the State Government under Section 381

(nn) the form in which annual report of the State Board may be prepared under Section 39;

(o) the form in which the accounts of the State Board may be maintained under sub-section (1) of Section 40;

(oo) the manner in which notice of intention to make a complaint shall be given to the State Board or officer authorised by it under Section 499;

(p) any other matter which has to be, or may be, prescribed.

12

THE AIR (PREVENTION AND CONTROL OF POLLUTION) ACT, 1981 (No. 14 of 1981)

[29th March 1981]

An Act to provide for the prevention, control and abatement of air pollution, for the establishment, with a view to carrying out the aforesaid purposes, of Boards, for conferring on and assigning to such boards powers and functions relating thereto and for matters connected therewith.

Whereas decisions were taken at the United Nations Conference on the Human Environment held in Stockholm in June 1972, in which India participated, to take appropriate steps for the preservation of the natural resources of the earth which, among other things, include the preservation of the quality of air and control of air pollution;

And, whereas, it is considered necessary to implement the decisions aforesaid insofar as they relate to the preservation of the quality of air and control of air pollution;

Be it enacted by Parliament in the Thirty-second Year of the Republic of India as follows :

Chapter I

PRELIMINARY

1. Short title, extent and commencement

(1) This Act may be called the Air (Prevention and Control of Pollution) Act, 1981.

(2) It extends to the whole of India.

(3) It shall come into force on such date as the Central Government may, by notification in the Official Gazette, appoint.

2. Definitions

In this Act, unless the context otherwise requires,-

(a) "air pollutant" means any solid, liquid or gaseous substance [including noise] present in the atmosphere in such concentration as may be or tend to be injurious to human beings or other living creatures or plants or property or environment;

(b) "air pollution" means the presence in the atmosphere of any air-pollutant;

(c) "approved appliance" means any equipment or gadget used for the burning of any combustible material or for generating or consuming any fume, gas or particulate matter and approved by the State Board for the purpose of this Act;

(d) "approved fuel" means any fuel approved by the State Board for the purposes of this Act;

(e) "automobile" means any vehicle powered either by internal combustion engine or by any method of generating power to drive such vehicle by burning fuel;

(f) "Board" means the Central Board or a State Board;

(g) "Central Board" means the [Central Board for the prevention and Control of Water Pollution] constituted under Section 3 of the Water (Prevention and Control of Pollution) Act, 1974 (6 of 1974);

(h) "chimney" includes any structure with an opening or outlet from or through which any air pollutant may be emitted;

(i) "control equipment" means any apparatus, device, equipment or system to control the quality and manner of emission of any air pollution and includes any device used for securing the efficient operation of any industrial plant;

(j) "emission" means any solid or liquid or gaseous substance coming out of any chimney, duct or flue or any other outlet;

(k) "industrial plant" means any plant used for any industrial or trade purposes and emitting any air pollutant into the atmosphere;

(l) "member" means a member of the Central Board or a State Board, as the case may be, and includes the Chairman thereof;

(m) "occupier", in relation to any factory or premises, means the person who has control over the affairs of the factory or the premises, and includes, in relation to any substance, the person in possession of the substance;

(*n*) "prescribed" means prescribed by rules and made under this Act by the Central Government or, as the case may be, the State Government;

(*o*) "State Board" means—

(*i*) in relation to a State in which the Water (Prevention and Control of Pollution) Act, 1974 (6 of 1974), is in force and the State Government has constituted for that State a [State Board for the Prevention and Control of Water Pollution] under Section 4 of that Act, the said State Board; and

(*ii*) in relation to any other State, the State Board for the Prevention and Control of Air Pollution constituted by the State Government under Section 5 of this Act.

Chapter II

CENTRAL AND STATE BOARDS FOR THE PREVENTION AND CONTROL OF AIR POLLUTION

3. Central Board for the Prevention and Control of Air Pollution

The Central Board for the Prevention and Control of Water Pollution constituted under Section 3 of the Water (Prevention and Control of Pollution) Act, 1974 (6 of 1974), shall, without prejudice to the exercise and performance of its powers and functions under that Act, exercise the powers and perform the functions of the Central Board for the Prevention and Control of Air Pollution under this Act.

4. State Boards for the Prevention and Control of Water Pollution to be State Boards for the Prevention and Control of Air Pollution

In any State in which the Water (Prevention and Control of Pollution) Act, 1974 (6 of 1974), is in force and the State Government has constituted for that State a State Board for the Prevention and Control of Water Pollution under Section 4 of that Act, such State Board shall be deemed to be the State Board for the Prevention and Control of Air Pollution constituted under Section 5 of this Act and accordingly that State Board for the Prevention and Control of Water Pollution shall, without prejudice to the exercise and performance of its powers and functions under that Act, exercise the powers and perform the functions of the State Board for the Prevention and Control of Air Pollution under this Act.

5. Constitution of State Boards

(1) In any State in which the Water (Prevention and Control of Pollution) Act, 1974 (6 of 1974), is not in force, or that Act is in force but the State Government has not constituted a [State Board for the Prevention and Control of Water Pollution] under that Act, the State Government shall, with effect from such date as it may, by notification in the Official Gazette, appoint, constitute a State Board for the Prevention and Control of Air Pollution under such name as may be specified in the notification, to exercise the powers conferred on, and perform the functions assigned to, that Board under this Act.

(2) A State Board constituted under this Act shall consist of the following members, namely :

(a) a Chairman, being a person having special knowledge or practical experience in respect of matters relating to environmental protection, to be nominated by the State Government :

Provided that the Chairman may be either whole-time or part-time as the State Government may think fit;

(b) such number of officials, not exceeding five, as the State Government may think fit, to be nominated by the State Government to represent that Government;

(c) such number of persons, not exceeding five, as the State Government may think fit, to be nominated by the State Government from amongst the members of the local authorities functioning within the State;

(d) such number of non-officials, not exceeding three, as the State Government may think fit, to be nominated by the State Government to represent the interests of agriculture, fishery or industry or trade or labour or any other interest, which, in the opinion of that Government, ought to be represented;

(e) two persons to represent the companies or corporations owned, controlled or managed by the State Government, to be nominated by that Government;

(f) a full-time member-secretary having such qualifications knowledge and experience of scientific, engineering or management aspects of pollution control as may be prescribed, to be appointed by the State Government:

Provided that the State Government shall ensure that not less than two of the members are persons having special knowledge or practical experience in respect of matters relating to the improvement of the quality of air or the prevention, control or abatement of air pollution.

(3) Every State Board constituted under this Act shall be a body corporate with the name specified by the State Government in the notification issued under sub-section (1), having perpetual succession and a common seal with power, subject to the provisions of this Act, to acquire and dispose of property and to contract, and may by the said name sue or be sued.

6. Central Board to exercise the powers and perform the functions of a State Board in the Union Territories

No State Board shall be constituted for a Union Territory and in relation to a Union Territory, the Central Board shall exercise the powers and perform the functions of a State Board under this Act for that Union Territory:

Provided that in relation to any Union Territory the Central Board may delegate all or any of its powers and functions under this section to such person or body of persons as the Central Government may specify.

7. Terms and conditions of service of members

(1) Save as otherwise provided by or under this Act, a member of a State Board constituted under this Act, other than the member-secretary, shall hold office for a term of three years from the date on which his nomination is notified in the Official Gazette :

Provided that a member shall, notwithstanding the expiration of his term, continue to hold office until his successor enters upon his office.

(2) The term of office of a member of a State Board constituted under this Act and nominated under clause (b) or clause (e) of sub-section (2) of Section 5 shall come to an end as soon as he ceases to hold the office under the State Government or, as the case may be, the company or corporation owned, controlled or managed by the State Government, by virtue of which he was nominated.

(3) A member of a State Board constituted under this Act, other than the member-secretary may at any time resign his office by writing under his hand addressed—

(a) in the case of the Chairman, to the State Government; and

(b) in any other case, to the Chairman of the State Board, and the seat of the Chairman or such other member shall thereupon become vacant.

(4) A member of a State Board constituted under this Act, other than the member-secretary, shall be deemed to have vacated his seat, if he is absent without reason, sufficient in the opinion of the State Board, from three consecutive meetings of the State Board or where he is nominated under Clause *(c)* of sub-section (2) of

Section 5, he ceases to be a member of the local authority and such vacation of seat shall, in either case, take effect from such date as the State Government may, by notification in the official Gazette, specify.

(5) A casual vacancy in a State Board constituted under this Act shall be filled by a fresh nomination and the person nominated to fill the vacancy shall hold office only for the remainder of the term for which the member whose place he takes was nominated.

(6) A member of a State Board constituted under this Act shall be eligible for re-nomination.

(7) The other terms and conditions of service of the Chairman and other members (except the member-secretary) of a State Board constituted under this Act shall be such as may be prescribed.

8. Disqualifications

(1) No person shall be a member of a State Board constituted under this Act, who—

(a) is, or at any time has been, adjudged insolvent, or

(b) is of unsound mind and has been so declared by a competent court, or

(c) is, or has been, convicted of an offence which, in the opinion of the State Government, involves moral turpitude, or

(d) is, or at any time has been, convicted of an offence under his Act, or

(e) has directly or indirectly by himself or by any partner, any share or interest in any firm or company carrying on the business of manufacture, sale, or hire of machinery, industrial plant, control equipment or any other apparatus for the improvement of the quality of air or for the prevention, control or abatement of air pollution, or

(f) is a director or a secretary, manager or other salaried officer or employee of any company or firm having any contract with the Board, or with the Government constituting the Board or with a local authority in the State, or with a company or corporation owned, controlled or managed by the Government, for the carrying out of programmes for the improvement of the quality of air or for the prevention, control or abatement of air pollution, or

(g) has so abused, in the opinion of the State Government, his position as a member, as to render his continuance on the State Board detrimental to the interests of the general public.

(2) The State Government shall, by order in writing, remove any

member who is or has become, subject to any disqualification mentioned in sub-section (1) :

Provided that no order of removal shall be made by the State Government under this section unless the member concerned has been given a reasonable opportunity of showing cause against the same.

(3) Notwithstanding anything contained in sub-section (1) or sub-section (6) of Section 7, a member who has been removed under this section shall not be eligible to continue to hold office until his successor enters upon his office, or, as the case may be, for re-nomination as a member.

9. Vacation of seats by members

If a member of a State Board constituted under this Act becomes subject to any of the disqualifications specified in Section 8, his seat shall become vacant.

10. Meetings of Board

(1) For the purposes of this Act, a Board shall meet at least once in every three months and shall observe such rules of procedure in regard to the transaction of business at its meetings as may be prescribed :

Provided that if, in the opinion of the Chairman, any business of an urgent nature is to be transacted, he may convene a meeting of the Board at such time as he thinks fit for the aforesaid purpose.

(2) Copies of the minutes of the meetings under sub-section (1) shall be forwarded to the Central Board and to the State Government concerned.

11. Constitutions of committees

(1) A Board may constitute as many committees consisting wholly of members or partly of members and partly of other persons and for such purpose or purposes as it may think fit.

(2) A committee constituted under this section shall meet at such time and at such place, and shall observe such rules of procedure in regard to the transaction of business at his meetings, as may be prescribed.

(3) The members of a committee other than the members of the Board shall be paid such fees and allowances, for attending its meetings and for attending to any other work of the Board as may be prescribed.

12. Temporary association of persons with Board for particular purposes

(1) A Board may associate with itself in such manner, and for such purposes, as may be prescribed, any person whom whose assistance or advice it may desire to obtain in performing any of its functions under this Act.

(2) A person associated with the Board under sub-section (1) for any purpose shall have a right to take part in the discussions of the Board relevant to that purpose, but shall not have a right to vote at a meeting of the Board and shall not be a member of the Board for any other purpose.

(3) A person associated with a Board under sub-section (1) shall be entitled to receive such fees and allowances as may be prescribed.

13. Vacancy in Board not to invalidate acts or proceedings

No act or proceeding of a Board or any committee thereof shall be called in question on the ground merely of the existence of any vacancy in or any defect in the constitution of, the Board or such committee, as the case may be.

14. Members-secretary and officers and other employees of State Boards

(1) The terms and conditions of service of the member-secretary of a State Board constituted under this Act shall be such as may be prescribed.

(2) The member-secretary of a State Board, whether constituted under this Act or not, shall exercise such powers and perform such duties as may be prescribed, or as may, from time to time, be delegated to him by the State Board of its Chairman.

(3) Subject to such rules as may be made by the State Government in this behalf, a State Board, whether constituted under this Act or not, may appoint such officers and other employees as it considers necessary for the efficient performance of its functions under this Act.

(4) The method of appointment, the conditions of service and the scales of pay of the officers (other than the member-secretary) and other employees of a State Board appointed under sub-section (3) shall be such as may be determined by regulations made by the State Board under this Act.

(5) Subject to such conditions as may be prescribed, a State Board constituted under this Act may from time to time appoint any

qualified person to be a consultant to the Board and pay him such salary and allowance or fees, as it thinks fit.

15. Delegation of powers

A Sate Board may, by general or special order, delegate to the Chairman or the member-secretary or any other officer of the Board subject to such conditions and limitations, if any, as may be specified in the order such of its powers and functions under this Act as it may deem necessary.

Chapter III

POWERS AND FUNCTIONS OF BOARDS

16. Functions of Central Board

(1) Subject to the provisions of this Act, and without prejudice to the performance of its functions under the Water (Prevention and Control of Pollution) Act, 1974, the main functions of the Central Board shall be to improve the quality of air and to prevent, control or abate air pollution in the country.

(2) In particular and without prejudice to the generality of the foregoing functions, the Central Board may—

(a) advise the Central Government on any matter concerning the improvement of the quality of air and the prevention, control or abatement of air pollution;

(b) plan and cause to be executed a nation-wide programme for the prevention, control or abatement of air pollution;

(c) co-ordinate the activities of the State Boards and resolve dispute among them;

(cc) provide technical assistance and guidance to the State Boards, carryout and sponsor investigations and research relating to problems of air pollution and prevention, control or abatement of air pollution;

(d) provide technical assistance and guidance to the State Boards, carry out and sponsor investigations and research relating to problems of air pollution and prevention, control or abatement of air pollution;

(dd) perform such of the function of any State Board as may be specified in and order made under sub-section (2) of Section 18;

(e) plan and organise the training of persons engaged or to be

engaged in programmes for the prevention, control or abatement of air pollution on such terms and conditions as the Central Board may specify;

(f) organise through mass media a comprehensive programme regarding the prevention, control or abatement of air pollution;

(g) collect, compile and publish technical and statistical data relating to air pollution and the measures devised for its effective prevention, control or abatement and prepare manuals, codes or guides relating to prevention, control or abatement of air pollution;

(h) lay down standards for the quality of air;

(i) collect and disseminate information in respect of matters relating to air pollution;

(j) perform such other functions as may be prescribed.

(3) The Central Board may establish or recognise a laboratory or laboratories to enable the Central Board to perform its functions under this section efficiently.

(4) The Central Board may—

(a) delegate any of its functions under this Act generally or specially to any of the committees appointed by it;

(b) do such other things and perform such other acts as it may think necessary for the proper discharge of its functions and generally for the purpose of carrying into effect the purposes of this Act.

17. Functions of State Boards

(1) Subject to the provisions of this Act, and without prejudice to the performance of its functions, if any, under the Water (Prevention and Control of Pollution) Act, 1974 (6 of 1974), the functions of a State Board shall be—

(a) to plan a comprehensive programme for the prevention, control or abatement of air pollution and to secure the execution thereof;

(b) to advise the State Government on any matter concerning the prevention, control or abatement of air pollution;

(c) to collect and disseminate information relating to air pollution;

(d) to collaborate with the Central Board in organising the training of persons engaged or to be engaged in programmes relating to prevention, control or abatement of air pollution and to organise mass-education programme relating thereof;

(e) to inspect, at all reasonable times, any control equipment, industrial plant or manufacturing process and to give, by

order, such directions to such persons as it may consider necessary to take steps for the prevention, control or abatement of air pollution;

(f) to inspect air pollution control areas at such intervals as it may think necessary, assess the quality of air therein and take steps for the prevention, control of abatement of air pollution in such areas;

(g) to lay down, in consultation with the central Board and having regard to the standards for the quality of air laid down by the Central Board, standards for emission of air pollutants into the atmosphere from industrial plants and automobiles or for the discharge of any air pollution into the atmosphere from any other source, whatsoever, not being a ship or an aircraft;

Provided that different standards for emission may be laid down under this clause for different industrial plants having regard to the quantity and composition of emission of air pollutants into the atmosphere from such industrial plants;

(h) to advise the State Government with respect to the suitability of any premises or location for carrying on any industry which is likely to cause air pollution;

(i) to perform such other functions as may prescribed or as may, from time to time, be entrusted to it by the Central Board or the State Government;

(j) to do such other things and to perform such other acts as it may think necessary for the proper discharge of its functions and generally for the purpose of carrying into effect the purposes of this Act.

(2) A State Board may establish or recognise a laboratory or laboratories to enable the State Board to perform its functions under this section efficiently.

18. Power to give directions

(1) In the performance of its functions under this Act—

(a) the Central Board shall be bound by such directions in writing as the Central Government may give to it; and

(b) every State Board shall be bound by such directions in writing as the Central Board or the State Government may give to it:

Provided that where a direction given by the State Government is inconsistent with the direction given by the Central Board, the matter shall be referred to the Central Government for its decision.

(2) Where the Central Government is of the opinion that any State Board has defaulted in complying with any directions given by the Central Board under sub-section (1) and as a result of such default a grave emergency has arisen and it is necessary or expedient so to do in the public interest, it may, be order, direct the Central Board to perform any of the functions of the State Board in relation to such area, for such period and for such purpose, as may be specified in the order.

(3) Where the Central Board performs any of the functions of the State Board in pursuance of a direction under sub-section (2), the expenses, if any, incurred by the Central Board with respect to the performance of such functions may, if the State Board is empowered to recover such expenses, be recovered by the Central Board with interest (at such reasonable rate as the Central Government may, by order, fix) from the date when a demand for such expenses is made until it is paid from the person or persons concerned as arrears of land revenue or of public demand.

(4) For the removal of doubts, it is hereby declared that any directions to perform the functions of any State Board given under sub-section (2) in respect of any area would not preclude the State Board from performing such functions in any other area in the State or any of its functions in that area.

Chapter IV

PREVENTION AND CONTROL OF POLLUTION

19. Power to declare air pollution control areas

(1) The State Government may, after consultation with the State Board, by notification in the Official Gazette, declare in such manner as may be prescribed, any area or areas within the State as air pollution control area or areas for the purposes of this Act.

(2) The State Government may, after consultation with the State Board, by notification in the Official Gazette—

(a) alter any air pollution control area whether by way of extension or reduction;

(b) declare a new air pollution control area in which may be merged one or more existing air pollution control areas or any part or parts thereof.

(3) If the State Government, after consultation with the State

Board,is of opinion that the use of any fuel, other than an approved fuel, in any air pollution control area or part thereof, may cause or is likely of cause air pollution, it may, be notification in the Official Gazette, prohibit the use of such fuel in such area or part thereof with effect from such date (being not less than three months from the date of publication of the notification) as may be specified in the notification.

(4) The State Government may, after consultation with the State Board, by notification in the Official Gazette, direct that with effect from such date as may be specified therein, no appliance, other than an approved appliance, shall be used in the premises situated in an air pollution control area:

Provided that different dates may be specified for different parts of an air pollution control area or for the use of different appliances.

(5) If the Government, after consultation with the State Board, is of opinion that the burning of any material (not being fuel) in any air pollution control area or part thereof may cause or is likely to cause air pollution, it may, by notification in the Official Gazette, prohibit the burning of such material in such area or part thereof.

20. Power to give instructions for ensuring standards for emission from automobiles

With a view to ensuring that the standards for emission of air pollutants from automobiles laid down by the State Board under clause *(g)* of sub-section (1) of Section 17 are complied with, the State Government shall, in consultation with the State Board, give such instructions as may be deemed necessary to the concerned authority in charge of registration of motor vehicles under the Motor Vehicles Act, 1939, and such authority shall, notwithstanding anything contained in that Act or the rules made thereunder bey bound to comply with such instructions.

21. Restrictions on use of certain industrial plants

(1) Subject to the provisions of this section, no person shall, without the previous consent of the State Board, establish or operate any industrial plant in an air pollution control area :

Provided that a person operating any industrial plant in any air pollution control area immediately before the commencement of Section 9 of the Air (Prevention and Control of Pollution) Amendment

Act, 1987 (47 of 1987), for which no consent was necessary prior to such commencement, may continue to do so for a period of three months from such commencement or, if he has made an application for such consent within the said period of three months, till the disposal of such application.

(2) An application for consent of the State Board under sub-section (1) shall be accompanied by such fees as may be prescribed and shall be made in the prescribed form and shall contain the particulars of the industrial plant and such other particulars as may be prescribed :

Provided that where any person, immediately before the declaration of any area as an air pollution control area, operates in such area any industrial plant, such person shall made the application under this sub-section within such period (being not less than three months from the date of such declaration) as may be prescribed and where such person makes such application, he shall be deemed to be operating such industrial plant with the consent of the State Board until the consent applied for has been refused.

(3) The State Board may make such inquiry as it may deem fit in respect of the application for consent referred to in sub-section (1) and in making any such inquiry, shall follow such procedure as may be prescribed.

(4) Within a period of four months after the receipt of the application for consent referred to in sub-section (1), the State Board shall, by order in writing, [and for reasons to be recorded in the order, grant the consent applied for subject to such conditions and for such period as may be specified in the order, or refuse such consent:]

Provided that it shall be open to the State Board to cancel such consent before the expiry of the period for which it is granted or refuse further consent after such expiry if the conditions subject to which such consent has been granted are not fulfilled:

[**Provided** further that before cancelling a consent or refusing a further consent under the first provision, a reasonable opportunity of being heard shall be given to the person concerned.]

(5) Every person to whom consent has been granted by the State Board under sub-section (4), shall comply with the following conditions, namely :

(i) the control equipment of such specifications as the State

Board may approve in this behalf shall be installed and operated in the premises where the industry is carried on or proposed to be carried on;

(ii) the existing control equipment, if any, shall be altered or replaced in accordance with the directions of the State Board;

(iii) the control equipment referred to in clause *(i)* or clause *(ii)* shall be kept at all times in good running condition;

(iv) chimney, wherever necessary, of such specifications as the State Board may approve in this behalf shall be erected or re-erected in such premises;

(v) such other conditions as the State Board may specify in this behalf; and

(vi) the conditions referred to in clauses *(i)*, *(ii)* and *(iv)* shall be complied with within such period as the State Board may specify in this behalf:

Provided that in the case of a person operating any industrial plant in an air pollution control area immediately before the date of declaration of such area as an air pollution control area, the period so specified shall not be less than six months:

Provided further that—

(a) after the installation of any control equipment in accordance with the specifications under clause (i), or

(b) after the alteration or replacement of any control equipment in accordance with the directions of the State Board under clause (ii), or

(c) after the erection or re-erection of any chimney under clause (iv), no control equipment or chimney shall be altered or replaced or, as the case may be, erected or re-erected except with the previous approval of the State Board.

(6) If due to any technological improvement or otherwise the State Board is of opinion that all or any of the conditions referred to in sub-section (5) require or requires variation (including the change of any control equipment, either in whole or in part), the State Board shall, after giving the person to whom consent has been granted an opportunity of being heard, vary all or any of such conditions and thereupon such person shall be bound to comply with the conditions as so varied.

(7) Where a person to whom consent has been granted by the State Board under sub-section (4) transfers his interest in the industry

to any other person, such consent shall be deemed to have been granted to such other person and he shall be bound to comply with all the conditions subject to which it was granted as if the consent was granted to him originally.

22. Persons carrying on industry, etc. not to allow emission of air pollutants in excess of the standards laid down by the State Board

No person operating any industrial plant, in any air pollution control area shall discharge or cause or permit to be discharged the emission of any air pollutant in excess of the standards laid down by the State Board under clause *(g)* of sub-section (1) of Section 17.

22A. Power of Board to make application to court for restraining persons from causing air pollution

(1) Where it is apprehended by a Board that emission of any air pollutant, in excess of the standards laid down by the State Board under clause *(g)* of sub-section (1) of Section 17, is likely to occur by reason of any person operating an industrial plant or otherwise in any air pollution control area, the Board may make an application to a court, not inferior to that of a Metropolitan Magistrate or a Judicial Magistrate of the first class for restraining such person from emitting such air pollutant.

(2) On receipt of the application under sub-section (1), the court may make such order as it deems fit.

(3) Where under sub-section (2), the court makes an order restraining any person from discharging or causing or permitting to be discharged the emission of any air pollutant, it may, in that order:

(a) direct such person to desist from taking such action as is likely to cause emission;

(b) authorise the Board, if the direction under clause *(a)* is not complied with by the person to whom such direction is issued, to implement the direction in such manner as may be specified by the Court.

(4) All expenses incurred by the Board in implementing the directions of the Court under clause *(b)* of sub-section (3) shall be recoverable from the person concerned as arrears of land revenue or of public demand.

23. Furnishing of information to State Board and other agencies in certain cases

(1) Where in any area the emission of any air pollutant into the

atmosphere in excess of the standards laid down by the State Board occurs or is apprehended to occur due to accident or other unforeseen act or event, the person in charge of the premises from where such emission occurs or is apprehended to occur shall forthwith intimate the fact of such occurrence or the apprehension of such occurrence to the State Board and to such authorities or agencies as may be prescribed.

(2) On receipt of information with respect to the fact or the apprehension of any occurrence to the nature referred to in sub-section (1), whether through intimation under that sub-section or otherwise, the State Board and the authorities or agencies shall, as early as practicable cause such remedial measures to be taken as are necessary to mitigate the emission of such air pollutants.

(3) Expenses, if any, incurred by the State Board, authority or agency with respect to the remedial measures referred to in sub-section (2) together with interest (at such reasonable rate, as the State Government may, be order, fix) from the date when a demand for the expense is made until it is paid, may be recovered by that Board, authority or agency from the person concerned, as arrears of land revenue, or of public demand.

24. Power of entry and inspection

(1) Subject to the provisions of this section, any person empowered by a State Board in this behalf shall have a right to enter, at all reasonable times with such assistance as he considers necessary, any place—

(a) for the purpose of performing any of the functions of the State Board entrusted to him;

(b) for the purpose of determining whether and if so in manner, any such functions are to be performed or whether any provisions of this Act or the rules made thereunder or any notice, order, direction or authorisation served, made, given or granted under this Act is being or has been complied with;

(c) for the purpose of examining and testing any control equipment, industrial plant, record, register, document or any other material object or for conducting a search of any place in which he has reason to believe that an offence under this Act or the rules made thereunder has been or is being or is about to be committed and for seizing any such control equipment, industrial plant, record, register, document or other material object if he has reasons to believe that it may

furnish evidence of the commission of an offence punishable under this Act or the rules made thereunder.

(2) Every person operating any control equipment or any industrial plant, in an air pollution control area shall be bound to render all assistance to the person empowered by the State Board under sub-section (1) for carrying out the functions under that sub-section and if he fails to do so without any reasonable cause of excuse, he shall be guilty of an offence under this Act.

(3) If any person willfully delays or obstructs any person empowered by the State Board under sub-section (1) in the discharge of his duties, he shall be guilty of an offence under this Act.

(4) The provisions of the Code of Criminal Procedure, 1973, or, in relation to the State of Jammu and Kashmir, or any area in which that Code is not in force, the provisions of any corresponding law in force in that State or area, shall, so far as may be, apply to any search or seizure under this section as they apply to any search or seizure made under the authority of a warrant issued under Section 94 of the said Code or, as the case may be, under the corresponding provisions of the said law.

25. Power to obtain information

For the purposes of carrying out the functions entrusted to it, the State Board or any officer empowered by it in that behalf may call for any information (including information regarding the types of air pollutant emitted into the atmosphere and the level of the emission of such air pollutants) from the occupier or any other person carrying on any industry or operating any control equipment or industrial plant and for the purpose of verifying the correctness of such information, the State Board or such officer shall have the right to inspect the premises where such industry, control equipment or industrial plant is being carried on or operated.

26. Power to take samples of air or emission and procedure to be followed in connection therewith

(1) A State Board or any officer empowered by it in this behalf shall have power to take, for the purpose of analysis, samples of air or emission from any chimney, flue or duct or any other outlet in such manner as may be prescribed.

(2) The result of any analysis of a sample or emission taken under sub-section (1) shall not be admissible in evidence in any legal proceeding unless the provisions of sub-sections (3) and (4) are complied with.

(3) Subject to the provisions of sub-section (4), when a sample of emission is taken for analysis under sub-section (1), the person

taking the sample shall—

(a) serve on the occupier or his agent, a notice, then and there, in such form as may be prescribed, of his intention to have it so analysed;

(b) in the presence of the occupier or his agent, collect a sample of emission for analysis;

(c) cause the sample to be placed in a container or containers which shall be marked and sealed and shall also be signed both by the person taking the sample and the occupier or his agent;

(d) send, without delay, the container or containers to the laboratory established or recognised by the State Board under Section 17 of, if a request in that behalf is made by the occupier or his agent when the notice is served on him under clause *(a)*, to the laboratory established or specified under sub-section (1) of Section 28.

(4) When a sample of emission is taken for analysis under sub-section (1) and the person taking the sample serves on the occupier or his agent, a notice under clause *(a)* of sub-section (3), then —

(a) in a case where the occupier or his agent willfully absents himself, the person taking the sample shall collect the sample of emission for analysis to be placed in a container or containers which shall be marked and sealed and shall also be signed by the person taking the sample, and

(b) in a case where the occupier or his agent is present at the time of taking the sample but refuses to sign the marked and sealed container or containers of the sample of emission as required under clause *(c)* of sub-section (3), the marked and sealed container or containers shall be signed by the person taking the sample, and the container or containers shall be sent without delay by the person taking the sample for analysis to the laboratory established or specified under sub-section (1) of Section 28 and such person shall inform the Government analyst appointed under sub-section (1) of Section 29, in writing, about the willful absence of the occupier or his agent, or as the case may be, his refusal to sign the container or containers.

27. Reports of the result of analysis on samples taken under Section 26

(1) Where a sample of emission has been sent for analysis to the

laboratory established or recognised by the State Board, the Board analyst appointed under sub-section (2) of Section 29 shall analyse the sample and submit a report in the prescribed form of such analysis in triplicate to the State Board.

(2) On receipt of the report under sub-section (1), one copy of the report shall be sent by the Sate Board to the occupier or his agent referred to in Section 26, another copy shall be preserved for production before the court in case any legal proceedings are taken against him and the other copy shall be kept by the State Board.

(3) Where a sample has been sent for analysis under clause *(d)* of sub-section (3) or sub-section (4) of Section 26 to any laboratory mentioned therein, the Government analyst referred to in the said sub-section (4) shall analyse the sample and submit a report in the prescribed form of the result of the analysis in triplicate to the State Board which shall comply with the provisions of sub-section (2).

(4) Any cost incurred in getting any sample analysed at the request of the occupier or his agent as provided in clause *(d)* of sub-section (3) of Section 26 or when the willfully absents himself or refused to sign the marked and sealed container or containers of sample of emission under sub-section (4) of that section, shall be payable by such occupier or his agent and in case of default the same shall be recoverable from him as arrears of land revenue or of public demand.

28. State Air Laboratory

(1) The State Government may, by notification in the Official Gazette—

(a) establish one or more State Air Laboratories; or

(b) specify one or more laboratories or institutes as State Air Laboratories to carry out the functions entrusted to the State Air Laboratory under this Act.

(2) The State Government may, after consultation with the State Board, make rules prescribing—

(a) the functions of the State Air Laboratory;

(b) the procedure for the submission to the said Laboratory of samples of air or emission for analysis or tests, the form of the Laboratory's report thereon and the fees payable in respect of such report;

(c) such other matters as may be necessary or expedient to enable

that Laboratory to carry out its functions.

29. Analysts

(1) The State Government may, by notification in the Official Gazette, appoint such persons as it thinks fit and having the prescribed qualifications to be Government analysts for the purpose of analysis of samples of air or emission sent for analysis to any laboratory established or specified under sub-section (1) of Section 28.

(2) Without prejudice to the provisions of Section 14, the State Board may, by notification in the Official Gazette, and with the approval of the State Government, appoint such persons as it thinks fit and having the prescribed qualifications to be Board analysts for the purpose of analysis of samples of air or emission sent for analysis to any laboratory established or recognised under Section 17.

30. Report of analysts

Any document purporting to be a report signed by a Government analyst or, as the case may be, a State Board analyst may be used as evidence of the facts stated therein in any proceeding under this Act.

31. Appeals

(1) Any person aggrieved by an order made by the State Board under this Act may, within thirty days from the date on which the order is communicated to him, prefer an appeal to such authority (hereinafter referred to as the Appellate Authority) as the State Government may think fit to constitute :

Provided that the Appellate Authority may entertain the appeal after the expiry of the said period of thirty days if such authority is satisfied that the appellant was prevented by sufficient cause from filing the appeal in time.

(2) The Appellate Authority shall consist of a single person or three persons as the State Government may think fit to be appointed by the State Government.

(3) The form and the manner in which an appeal may be preferred under sub-section (1), the fees payable for such appeal and the procedure to be followed by the Appellate Authority shall be such as may be prescribed.

(4) On receipt of an appeal preferred under sub-section (1), the Appellate Authority shall, after giving the appellant and the State Board an opportunity of being heard, dispose of the appeal as expeditiously as possible.

31A. Power to give directions

Notwithstanding anything contained in any other law, put subject to the provisions of this Act, and to any directions that the Central Government may give in this behalf, a Board may, in the exercise of its powers and performance of its functions under this Act, issue any directions in writing to any person, officer or authority, and such person, officer or authority shall be bound to comply with such directions.

Explanation: For the avoidance of doubts, it is hereby declared that the power to issue directions under this section includes the power to direct—

(a) the closure, prohibition or regulation of any industry, operation or process; or

(b) the stoppage or regulation of supply of electricity, water or any other service.

Chapter V

FUNDS, ACCOUNTS AND AUDIT

32. Contributions by Central Government

The Central Government may, after due appropriation made by Parliament by law in this behalf, make in each financial year such contributions to the State Boards as it may think necessary to enable the State Boards to perform their functions under this Act:

Provided that nothing in this section shall apply to any [State Board for the Prevention and Control of Water Pollution] constituted under Section 4 of the Water (Prevention and Control of Pollution) Act, 1974 (6 of 1974), which is empowered by that Act to expend money from its fund thereunder also for performing its functions, under any law for the time being in force relating to the prevention, control or abatement of air pollution.

33. Fund of Board

(1) Every State Board shall have its own fund for the purposes of this Act and all sums which may, from time to time, be paid to it by the Central Government and all other receipts (by way of contributions, if any, from the State Government, fees gifts,

grants, donations, benefactions or otherwise) of that Board shall be carried to the fund of the Board and all payment by the Board shall be made therefrom.

(2) Every State Board may expend such sums as it thinks fit for performing its functions under this Act and such sums shall be treated as expenditure payable out of the fund of that Board.

(3) Nothing in this section shall apply to any [State Board for the Prevention and Control of Water Pollution] constituted under Section 4 of the Water (Prevention and Control of Pollution) Act, 1974 (6 of 1974), which is empowered by that Act to expend money from its fund thereunder also for performing its functions, under any law for the time being in force relating to the prevention, control or abatement of air pollution.

33A. Borrowing powers of Board

A Board may, with the consent of, or in accordance with the terms of any general or special authority given to it by, the Central Government or, as the case may be, the State Government, borrow money from any source by way of loans or issue of bonds, debentures or such other instruments, as it may deem fit, for discharging all or any of its functions under this Act.]

34. Budget

The Central Board or, as the case may be, the State Board shall, during each financial year, prepare, in such form and at such time as be prescribed, a budget in respect of the financial year next ensuing showing the estimated receipt and expenditure under this Act, and copies thereof shall be forwarded to the Central Government or, as the case may be, the State Government.

35. Annual Report

(1) The Central Board shall, during each financial year, prepare, in such form as may be prescribed, an annual report giving full account of its activities under this Act during the previous financial year and copies thereof shall be forwarded to the Central Government within four months from the last date of the previous financial year and that Government shall cause every such report to be laid before both Houses of Parliament within nine months of the last date of the previous financial year.

(2) Every State Board shall, during each financial year, prepare, in such form as may be prescribed, an annual report giving full

account of its activities under this Act during the previous financial year and copies thereof shall be forwarded to the State Government within four months from the last date of the previous financial year and that Government shall cause every such report to be laid before the State Legislature within a period of nine months from the last date of the previous financial year.

36. Accounts and audit

(1) Every Board shall, in relation to its functions under this Act, maintain proper accounts and other relevant records and prepare and annual statement of accounts in such form as may be prescribed by the Central Government or, as the case may be, the State Government.

(2) The accounts of the Board shall be audited by an auditor duly qualified to act as an auditor of companies under Section 226 of the Companies Act, 1956 (1 of 1956).

(3) The said auditor shall be appointed by Central Government or, as the case may be, the State Government on the advice of the Comptroller and Auditor-General of India.

(4) Every auditor appointed to audit the accounts of the Board under this Act shall have the right to demand the production of books, accounts, connected vouchers and other documents and papers and to inspect any of the offices of the Board.

(5) Every such auditor shall send a copy of his report together with an audited copy of the accounts to the Central Government or, as the case may be, the State Government.

(6) The Central Government shall, as soon as may be after the receipt of the audit report under sub-section (5), cause the same to be laid before both Houses of Parliament.

(7) The State Government shall, as soon as may be after the receipt of the audit report under sub-section (5), cause the same to be laid before the State Legislature.

Chapter VI

PENALTIES AND PROCEDURE

37. Failure to comply with the provisions of Section 21 or Section 22 or with the directions issued under Section 31A

(1) Whoever fails to comply with the provisions of Section 21 or Section 22 or directions issued under Section 31A, shall, in

respect of each such failure be punishable with imprisonment for a term which shall not be less than one year and six months but which may extend to six years and with fine, and in case the failure continues, with and additional fine which may extend to five thousand rupees for every day during which such failure continues after the conviction for the first such failure.

(2) If the failure referred to in sub-section (1) continues beyond a period of one year after the date of conviction, the offender shall be punishable with imprisonment for a term which shall not be less than two years but which may extend to seven years and with fine

38. Penalties for certain acts

Whoever—

(a) destroys, pulls down, removes, injures or defaces any pillar, post or stake fixed in the ground or any notice or other matter put up, inscribed or placed, by or under the authority of the Board, or

(b) obstructs any person acting under the orders or directions of the Board from exercising his powers and performing his functions under this Act, or

(c) damages any works or property belonging to the Board, or

(d) fails to furnish to the Board or any officer or other employees of the Board any information required by the Board or such officer or other employee for the purpose of this Act, or

(e) fails to intimate the occurrence of the emission of air pollutants into the atmosphere in excess of the standards laid down by the State Board or the apprehension of such occurrence, to the State Board and other prescribed authorities or agencies as required under sub-section (1) of Section 23, or

(f) in giving any information which he is required to give under this Act, makes statement which is false in any material particular, or

(g) for the purpose of obtaining any consent under Section 21, makes a statement which is false in any material particular.

shall be punishable with imprisonment for a term which may extend to three months or with fine which may extend to [ten thousand rupees] or with both.

39. Penalty for contravention of certain provisions of the Act

Whoever, contravenes any of the provisions of this Act or any other or direction issued thereunder, for which no penalty has been elsewhere provided in this Act, shall be punishable with imprisonment for a term which may extend to three months or with fine which may extend to ten thousand rupees or with both, and in the case of continuing contravention, with an additional fine which may extend to five thousand rupees for every day during which such contravention continues after conviction for the first such contravention.

40. Offences by companies

(1) Where an offence under this Act has been committed by a company, every person who, at the time the offence was committed, was directly in charge of, and was responsible to, the company for the conduct of the business of the company, as well as the company, shall be deemed to be guilty of the offence and shall be liable to be proceeded against and punished accordingly :

Provided that nothing continued in this sub-section shall render any such person liable to any punishment provided in this Act, if he proves that the offence was committed without his knowledge or that he exercised all due diligence to prevent the commission of such offence.

(2) Notwithstanding anything contained in sub-section (1), where an offence under this Act has been committed by a company and it is proved that the offence has been committed with the consent or connivance of, or is attributable to any neglect on the part of any director, manager, secretary or other officer of the company, such director, manager, secretary or other officer shall also be deemed to be guilty of that offence and shall be liable to be proceeded against and punished accordingly.

Explanation: For the purposes of this section,—

(a) "company" means any body corporate, and includes a firm or other association of individuals; and

(b) "director," in relation to a firm, means a partner in the firm.

41. Offences by Government Departments

(1) Where an offence under this Act has been committed by any Department of Government, the Head of the Department shall be deemed to be guilty of the offence and shall be liable to be proceeded against and punished accordingly :

Provided that nothing contained in this section render such Head of the Department liable to any punishment if he proves that the offence was committed without his knowledge or that he exercised all due diligence to prevent the commission of such offence.

(2) Notwithstanding anything contained in sub-section (1), where an offence under this Act has been committed by a Department of Government and it is proved that the offence has been committed with the consent or connivance of, or is attributable to any neglect on the part of, any officer, other than the Head of the Department, such officer shall also be deemed to be guilty of that offence and shall be liable to be proceeded against and punished accordingly.

42. Protection of action taken in good faith

No suit, prosecution or other legal proceeding shall lie against the Government or any officer of the Government or any member or any officer or other employee of the Board in respect of anything which is done or intended to be done in good faith in pursuance of this or the rules made thereunder.

43. Cognizance of offences

(1) No court shall take cognizance of any offence under this Act except on a complaint made by—

(a) a Board or any officer authorised in this behalf by it; or

(b) any person who has given notice of not less than sixty days, in the manner prescribed, of the alleged offence and of his intention to make a complaint to the Board or officer authorised as aforesaid,

and no court inferior to that of a Metropolitan Magistrate or a Judicial Magistrate of the first class shall try any offence punishable under this Act.

(2) Where a complaint has been made under clause *(b)* of sub-section (1), the Board shall, on demand by such person, make available the relevant reports in its possession to that person:

Provided that the Board may refuse to make any such report available to such person if the same is, in its opinion, against the public interest.

44. Members, officers and employees of Board to be public servants

All the members and all officers and other employees of a Board when acting or purporting to act in pursuance of any of the provisions of this Act or the rules made thereunder shall be deemed to be public servants within the meaning of section 21 of the Indian Penal Code (45 of 1860).

45. Reports and return

The Central Board shall, in relation to its functions under this Act, furnish to the Central Government, and a State Board shall, in relation to its functions under this Act, furnish to the State Government and to the Central Board such reports, returns, statistics, accounts and other information as that Government, or, as the case may be, the Central Board may, from time to time, require.

46. Bar of jurisdiction

No civil court shall have jurisdiction to entertain any suit or proceeding in respect of any matter which an Appellate Authority constituted under this Act is empowered by or under this Act to determine, and no injunction shall be granted by any court or other authority in respect of any action taken or to be taken in pursuance of any power conferred by or under this Act.

Chapter VII

MISCELLANEOUS

47. Power of State Government to supersede State Board

(1) If at anytime the State Government is of opinion-

(a) that a State Board constituted under this Act has persistently made default in the performance of the functions imposed on it by or under this Act, or

(b) that circumstances exist which render it necessary in the public interest so to do,

the State Government may, by notification in the Official Gazette, supersede the State Board for such period, not exceeding six months, as may be specified in the notification :

Provided that before issuing a notification under this sub-section for the reasons mentioned in clause *(a)*, the State Government shall give a reasonable opportunity to the State Board to show cause why it should not be superseded and shall consider the explanations and objections, if any, of the State Board.

(2) Upon the publication of a notification under sub-section (1) superseding the State Board—

(a) all the members shall, as from the date of supersession, vacate their offices as such;

(*b*) all the powers, functions and duties which may, by or under this Act, be exercised, performed or discharged by the State Board shall, until the State Board is reconstituted under sub-section (3), be exercised, performed or discharged by such person as the State Government may direct;

(*c*) all property owned or controlled by the State Board shall, until the Board is reconstituted under sub-section (3), vest in the State Government.

(3) On the expiration of the period of supersession specified in the notification issued under sub-section (1), the State Government may—

(*a*) extend the period of supersession for such further term, nor exceeding six months, as it may consider necessary; or

(*b*) reconstitute the State Board by a fresh nomination or appointment as the case may be, and in such case any person who vacated his office under clause (*a*) of sub-section (2) shall also be eligible for nomination or appointment:

Provided that the State Government may at any time before the expiration of the period of supersession, whether originally specified under sub-section (1) or as extended under this sub-section, take action under clause (*b*) of this sub-section.

48. Special provision in the case of supersession of the Central Board or the State Boards constituted under the Water (Prevention and Control of Pollution) Act, 1974

Where the Central Board or any State Board constituted under the Water (Prevention and Control of Pollution) Act, 1974 (6 of 1974), is superseded by the Central Government or the State Government, as the case may be, under that Act, all the powers, functions and duties of the Central Board of such State Board under this Act shall be exercised, performed or discharged during the period of such supersession by the person or persons, exercising, performing or discharging the powers, functions and duties of the Central Board or such State Board under the Water (Prevention and Control of Pollution) Act, 1974 during such period.

49. Dissolution of State Boards constituted under the Act

(1) As and when the Water (Prevention and Control of Pollution) Act, 1974 (6 of 1974), comes into force in any State and the State Government constitutes a [State Board for the Prevention and Control of Water Pollution] under that Act, the State Board

constituted by the State Government under this Act shall stand dissolved and the Board first-mentioned shall exercise the powers and perform the functions of the Board second-mentioned in that State.

(2) On the dissolution of the State Board constituted under this Act—

(a) all the members shall vacate their offices as such;

(b) all money and other property of whatever kind (including the fund of the State Board) owned by, or vested in, the State Board, immediately before such dissolution, shall stand transferred to and vest in the [State Board for the Prevention and Control of Water Pollution];

(c) Every officer and other employee serving under the State Board immediately before such dissolution shall be transferred to and become an officer or other employee of the [State Board for the Prevention and Control of Water Pollution] and hold office by the same tenure and at the same remuneration and on the same terms and conditions of service as he would have held the same if the State Board constituted under this Act has not been dissolved and shall continue to do so unless and until such tenure, remuneration and terms and conditions of service are duly altered by the [State Board for the Prevention and Control of Water Pollution]:

Provided that the tenure, remuneration and terms and conditions of service of any such officer or other employee shall not be altered to his disadvantage without the previous sanction of the State Government;

(d) all liabilities and obligations of the State Board of whatever king, immediately before such dissolution, shall be deemed to be the liabilities or obligations, as the case may be, of the [State Board of the Prevention and Control of Water Pollution] and any proceeding or cause of action, pending or existing immediately before such dissolution by or against the State Board constituted under this Act in relation to such liability or obligation may be continued and enforced by or against the [State Board for the Prevention and Control of Water Pollution.]

50. *[Power to amend the Schedule,] Rep. by the Air (Prevention and Control of Pollution) Amendment Act, 1987 (47 of 1987), s.22 (w.e.f. 1.4.1988).*

51. Maintenance of register

Every State Board shall maintain a register containing particulars of the persons to whom consent has been granted under Section 21, the standards for emission laid down by it in relation to each such consent and such other particulars as may be prescribed.

(2) The register maintained under sub-section (1) shall be open to inspection at all reasonable hours by any person interested in or affected by such standards for emission or by any other person authorised by such person in this behalf.

52. Effect of other laws

Save as otherwise provided by or under the Atomic Energy Act, 1962, in relation to radioactive air pollution the Provisions of this Act shall have effect notwithstanding anything inconsistent therewith contained any enactment other than this Act.

53. Power of Central Government to make rules

(1) The Central Government may, in consultation with the Central Board by notification in the Official Gazette, make rules in respect of the following matters namely :

(a) the intervals and the time and place at which meetings of the Central Board or any committee thereof shall be held and the procedure to be followed at such meetings, including the quorum necessary for the transaction of business threat, under sub-section (1) of Section 10 and under sub-section (2) of Section 11;

(b) the fees and allowances to be paid to the members of a committee of the Central Board, not being members of the Board, under sub-section (3) of Section 11;

(c) the manner in which and the purposes for which persons may be associated with the Central Board under sub-section (1) of Section 12;

(d) the fees and allowances to be paid under sub-section (3) of Section 12 to persons associated with the Central Board under sub-section (1) of Section 12;

(e) the functions to be performed by the Central Board under clause *(i)* of sub-section (2) of Section 16;

(f) the form in which and the time within which the budget of the Central Board may be prepared and forwarded to the Central Government under Section 34;

(ff) the form in which the annual report of the Central Board may be prepared under Section 35;]

(*g*) the form in which the accounts of the Central Board may be maintained under sub-section (1) of Section 36.

(2) Every rule made by the Central Government under this Act shall be laid, as soon as may after it is made, before each House of Parliament, while it is in session, for a total period of thirty days which may be comprised in one session or in two or more successive sessions, and if, before the expiry of the session immediately following the session or the successive sessions aforesaid, both Houses agree in making any modification in the rule or both Houses agree that the rule should not be made, the rule shall thereafter have effect only in such modified form or be of no effect, as the case may be; so, however, that any such modification or annulment shall be without prejudice to the validity of anything previously done under that rule.

54. Power of State Government to make rules

(1) Subject to the provision of sub-section (3), the State Government may, by notification in the Official Gazette, make rules to carry out the purposes of this Act in respect of matters not falling within the purview of Section 53.

(2) In particular, and without prejudice to the generality of the foregoing power, such rules may provide for all or any of the following matters, namely:—

(*a*) the qualifications, knowledge and experience of scientific, engineering or management aspects of pollution control required for appointment as member-secretary of a State Board constituted under the Act;

(*aa*) the terms and conditions of service of the Chairman and other members (other than the member-secretary) of the State Board constituted under this Act under sub-section (7) of Section 7;

(*b*) the intervals and the time and place at which meetings of the State Board or any committee thereof shall be held and the proceeding to be followed at such meetings, including the quorum necessary for the transaction of business threat, under sub-section (1) of Section 10 and under sub-section (2) of Section 11;

(*c*) the fees and allowance to be paid to the members of a committee of the State Board, not being members of the Board under sub-section (3) of Section 11;

(*d*) the manner in which and the purposes for which persons may be associated with the State Board under sub-section (1) of Section 12;

(*e*) the fees and allowances to be paid under sub-section (3) of Section 12 to persons associated with the State Board under sub-section (1) of Section 12;

(*f*) the terms and conditions of service of the member-secretary of a State Board constituted under this Act under sub-section (1) of Section 14;

(*g*) the powers and duties to be exercised and discharge by the member-secretary of a State Board under sub-section (2) of Section 14;

(*h*) the conditions subject to which a State Board may appoint such officers and other employees as it considers necessary for the efficient performance of its functions under sub-section (3) of Section 14;

(*i*) the conditions subject to which a State Board may appoint a consultant under sub-section (5) of Section 14;

(*j*) the functions to be performed by the State Board under clause (*i*) of sub-section (1) of Section 17;

(*k*) the manner in which any area or areas may be declared as air pollution control area or areas under sub-section (1) of Section 19;

(*l*) the form of application for the consent of the State Board, the fees payable thereof, the period within which such application shall be made and the particulars it may contain, under sub-section (2) of Section 21;

(*m*) the procedure to be followed in respect of an inquiry under sub-section (3) of Section 21;

(*n*) the authorities or agencies to whom information under sub-section (1) of Section 23 shall be furnished;

(*o*) the manner in which samples of air or emission may be taken under sub-section (1) of Section 26;

(*p*) the form of the notice referred to in sub-section (3) of Section 26;

(*q*) the form of the report of the State Board analyst under sub-section (3) of Section 27;

(*r*) the form of the report of the Government anyalst under sub-section (3) of Section 27;

(*s*) the functions of the State Air Laboratory, the procedure for the submission to the said Laboratory of samples of air or emission for analysis or tests, the form of Laboratory's report thereon, the payable in respect of such report and other matters as may be necessary or expedient to enable that Laboratory to carry out its functions, under sub-section (2) of Section 28;

(t) the qualifications required for Government analysts under sub-section (1) of Section 29;

(u) the qualifications required for State Board analysts under sub-section (2) of Section 29;

(v) the form and the manner in which appeals may be preferred, the fees payable in respect of such appeals and the procedure to be followed by the Appellate Authority in disposing of the appeals under sub-section (3) of Section 31;

(w) the form in which and the time within which the budget of the State Board may be prepared and forwarded to the State Government under Section 34;

(ww) the form in which the annual report of the State Board may be prepared under Section 35;

(x) the form in which the accounts of the State Board may be maintained under sub-section (1) of Section 36;

(xx) the manner in which notice of intention to make a complaint shall be given under Section 43;

(y) the particulars which the register maintained under Section 51 may contain;

(z) any other matter which has to be, or may be, prescribed.

(3) After the first constitution of the State Board no rule with respect to any of the matters referred to in sub-section (2) [other than those referred to in clause *(aa)* thereof], shall be made, varied, amended or repealed without consulting that Board.

[THE SCHEDULE.] *Omitted by the Air (Prevention and Control of Pollution) Amendment Act, 1987,s . 25 (w.e.f. 1.4.1987).*

13

THE ENVIRONMENT (PROTECTION) ACT, 1986 (No.29 of 1986)

[23rd May 1986]

An Act to provide for the protection and improvement of environment and for matter connected therewith.

Whereas, decisions were taken at the United Nations Conference on the Human Environment held at Stockholm in June 1972, in which India participated, to take appropriate steps for the protection and improvement of human environment;

And whereas, it is considered necessary further to implement the decisions aforesaid insofar as they relate to the protection and improvement of environment and the prevention of hazards to human beings, other living creatures, plants and property;

Be it enacted by Parliament in the Thirty-seventh Year of the Republic of India as follows :

Chapter I

PRELIMINARY

1. Short title, extent and commencement

(1) This Act may be called the Environment (Protection) Act, 1986.

(2) It extends to the whole of India.

(3) It shall come into force on such date as the Central Government may, by notification in the Official Gazette, appoint and different dates may be appointed for different provisions of this Act and for different areas.

2. Definitions

In this Act, unless the context otherwise requires:

(a) "environment" includes water, air and land and the inter relationship which exists among and between water, air and land, and human beings, other living creatures, plants, micro-organism and property;

(b) "environmental pollutant" means any solid, liquid or gaseous substance present in such concentration as may be, or tend to be, injurious to environment;

(c) "environmental pollution" means the presence in the environment of any environmental pollutant;

(d) "handling", in relation to any substance, means the manufacture, processing, treatment, package, storage, transportation, use, collection, destruction, conversion, offering for sale, transfer or the like of such substance;

(e) "hazardous substance" means any substance or preparation which, by reason of its chemical or physico-chemical properties or handling, is liable to cause harm to human beings, other living creatures, plants, micro-organism, property or the environment;

(f) "occupier", in relation to any factory or premises, means a person who has control over the affairs of the factory or the premises and includes, in relation to any substance, the person in possession of the substance;

(g) "prescribed" means prescribed by rules made under this Act.

Chapter II

GENERAL POWERS OF THE CENTRAL GOVERNMENT

3. Power of Central Government to take measures to protect and improve environment

(1) Subject to the provisions of this Act, the Central Government shall have the power to take all such measures as it deems necessary or expedient for the purpose of protecting and improving the quality of the environment and preventing, controlling and abating environmental pollution.

(2) In particular, and without prejudice to the generality of the provisions of sub-section (1), such measures may include measures with respect to all or any of the following matters, namely :

(i) co-ordination of actions by the State Governments, Officers and other authorities—

(a) under this Act, or the rules made thereunder; or

(b) under any other law for the time being in force which is relatable to the objects of this Act;

(ii) planning and execution of a nation-wide programme for the prevention, control and abatement of environmental pollution;

(iii) laying down standards for the quality of environment in its various aspects;

(iv) laying down standards for emission or discharge of environmental pollutants from various sources whatsoever:

Provided that different standards for emission or discharge may be laid down under this clause from different sources having regard to the quality or composition of the emission or discharge of environmental pollutants from such sources;

(v) restriction of areas in which any industries, operations or processes or class of industries, operations or processes shall not be carried out or shall be carried out subject to certain safeguards;

(vi) laying down procedures and safeguards for the prevention of accidents which may cause environmental pollution and remedial measures for such accidents;

(vii) examination of such manufacturing processes, materials and substances as are likely to cause environmental pollution;

(viii) examination of such manufacturing processes, materials and substances as are likely to cause environmental pollution;

(ix) carrying out and sponsoring investigations and research relating to problems of environmental pollution;

(x) inspection of any premises, plant, equipment, machinery, manufacturing or other processes, materials or substances and giving, by order, of such directions to such authorities, officers or persons as it may consider necessary to take steps for the prevention, control and abatement of environmental pollution;

(xi) establishment or recognition of environmental laboratories and institutes to carry out the functions entrusted to such environmental laboratories and institutes under this

Act;

(xii) collection and dissemination of information in respect of matters relating to environmental pollution;

(xiii) preparation of manuals, codes or guides relating to the prevention, control and abatement of environmental pollution;

(xiv) such other matters as the Central Government deems necessary or expedient for the purpose of securing the effective implementation of the provisions of this Act.

(3) The Central Government may, if it considers it necessary or expedient so to do for the purposes of this Act, by order, published in the Official Gazette, constitute an authority or authorities by such name or names as may be specified in the order for the purpose of exercising and performing such of the powers and functions (including the power to issue directions under Section 5) of the Central Government under this Act and for taking measures with respect to such of the matters referred to in sub-section (2) as may be mentioned in the order and subject to the supervision and control of the Central Government and the provisions of such order, such authority or authorities may exercise the powers or perform the functions or take the measures so mentioned in the order as if such authority or authorities had been empowered by this Act to exercise those powers or perform those functions or take such measures.

4. Appointment of officers and their powers and functions

Without prejudice to the provisions of sub-section (3) of Section 3, the Central Government may appoint officers with such designations as it thinks fit for the purposes of this Act and may entrust to them such of the powers and functions under this Act as it may deem fit.

(2) The officers appointed under sub-section (1) shall be subject to the general control and direction of the Central Government or, if so directed by that Government, also of the authority or authorities, if any, constituted under sub-section (3) of Section 3 or of any other authority or officer.

5. Power to give directions

Notwithstanding anything contained in any other law but subject to the provisions of this Act, the Central Government may, in the exercise of its powers and performance of its functions under this Act, issue directions in writing to any person, officer or any authority and such person, officer or authority shall be bound to comply with such directions.

Explanation: For the avoidance of doubts, it is hereby declared that the power to issue directions under this Section includes the power to direct—

(a) the closure, prohibition or regulation of any industry, operation or process; or

(b) stoppage or regulation of the supply of electricity or water or any other service.

6. Rules to regulate environmental pollution

(1) The Central Government may, by notification in the Official Gazette, make rules in respect of all or any of the matters referred to in Section 3.

(2) In particular, and without prejudice to the generality of the foregoing power, such rules may provide for all or any of the following matters, namely :

(a) the standards of quality of air, water or soil for various areas and purposes;

(b) the maximum allowable limits of concentration of various environmental pollutants (including noise) for different areas;

(c) the procedures and safeguards for the handling of hazardous substances;

(d) the prohibitions and restrictions on the handling of hazardous substances in different areas;

(e) the prohibition and restrictions on the location of industries and the carrying on the process and operations in different areas;

(f) the procedures and safeguards for the prevention of accidents which may cause environmental pollution and for providing for remedial measures for such accidents.

Chapter III

PREVENTION, CONTROL AND ABETMENT OF ENVIRONMENTAL POLLUTION

7. Persons carrying on industry, operation, etc., not to allow emission or discharge of environmental pollutants in excess of the standards

No Person carrying on any industry, operation or process shall discharge or emit or permit to be discharged or emitted any environmental pollutant in excess of such standards as may be prescribed.

8. Persons handling hazardous substances to comply with procedural safeguards

No person shall handle or cause to be handled any hazardous substance except in accordance with such procedure and after complying with such safeguards as may be prescribed.

9. Furnishing of information to authorities and agencies in certain cases

(1) Where the discharge of any environmental pollutant in excess of the prescribed standards occurs or is apprehended to occur due to any accident or other unforeseen act or event, the person responsible for such discharge and the person in charge of the place at which such discharge occurs or is apprehended to occur shall be bound to prevent or mitigate the environmental pollution caused as a result of such discharge and shall also forthwith—

(a) intimate the fact of such occurrence or apprehension of such occurrence; and

(b) be bound, if called upon, to render all assistance,

to such authorities or agencies as may be prescribed.

(2) On receipt of information with respect to the fact or apprehension of any occurrence of the nature referred to in sub-section (1), whether through intimation under that sub-section or otherwise, the authorities or agencies referred to in sub-section (1) shall, as early as practicable, cause such remedial measures to be taken as are necessary to prevent or mitigate the environmental pollution.

(3) The expenses, if any, incurred by any authority or agency with respect to the remedial measures referred to in sub-section (2), together with interest (at such reasonable rates as the Government may, by order, fix) from the date when a demand for the expenses is made until it is paid, may be recovered by such authority or agency from the person concerned as arrears of land revenue or of public demand.

10. Powers of entry and inspection

(1) Subject to the provisions of this section, any person empowered by the Central Government in this behalf shall have a right to enter, at all reasonable times with such assistance as he considers necessary, any place—

(a) for the purpose of performing any of the functions of the Central Government entrusted to him;

(b) for the purpose of determining whether and if so in what

manner, any such functions are to be performed or whether any provisions of this Act or the rules made thereunder or any notice, order, direction or authorisation served, made, given or granted under this Act is being or has been complied with;

(c) for the purpose of examining and testing any equipment, industrial plant, record, register, document or any other material object or for conducting a search of any building in which he has reason to believe that an offence under this Act or the rules made thereunder has been or is being or is about to be committed and for seizing any such equipment, industrial plant, record, register, document or other material object if he has reasons to believe that it may furnish evidence of the commission of an offence punishable under this Act or the rules made thereunder or that such seizure is necessary to prevent or mitigate environmental pollution.

(2) Every person carrying on any industry, operation or process or handling any hazardous substance shall be bound to render all assistance to the person empowered by the Central Government under sub-section (1) for carrying out the functions under that sub-section and if he fails to do so without any reasonable cause or excuse, he shall be guilty of an offence under this Act.

(3) If any person willfully delays or obstructs any person empowered by the Central Government under sub-section (1) in the performance of his functions, he shall be guilty of an offence under this Act.

(4) The provisions of the Code of Criminal Procedure, 1973, or, in relation to the State of Jammu and Kashmir, or any area in which that Code is not in force, the provisions of any corresponding law in force in that State or area shall, so far as may be, apply to any search or seizure under this section as they apply to any search or seizure made under the authority of a warrant issued under Section 94 of the said Code or, as the case may be, under the corresponding provision of the said law.

11. Power to take sample and procedure to be followed in connection therewith

(1) The Central Government or any officer empowered by it in this behalf, shall have power to take, for the purpose of analysis, samples of air, water, soil or other substance from any factory, premises or other place in such manner as may be prescribed.

(2) The result of any analysis of a sample taken under sub-section (1) shall not be admissible in evidence in legal proceeding unless the

provisions of sub-sections (3) and (4) are complied with.

(3) Subject to the provisions of sub-section (4), the person taking the sample under sub-section (1) shall—

(a) serve on the occupier or his agent or person in charge of the place, a notice, then and there, in such form as may be prescribed, of his intention have it so analysed;

(b) in the presence of the occupier or his agent or person, collect a sample for analysis;

(c) cause the sample to be placed in a container or containers which shall be marked and sealed and shall also be signed both by the person taking the sample and the occupier or his agent or person;

(d) send without delay, the container or the containers to the laboratory established or recognised by the Central Government under Section 12.

(4) When a sample is taken for analysis under sub-section (1) and the person taking the sample serves on the occupier or his agent or person, a notice under clause *(a)* of sub-section (3), then—

(a) in a case where the occupier, his agent or person will fully absents himself, the person taking the sample shall collect the sample for analysis to be placed in a container or containers which shall be marked and sealed and shall also be signed by the person taking the sample, and

(b) in a case where the occupier or his agent or person present at the time of taking the sample refuses to sign the marked and sealed container or containers of the sample as required under clause (c) of sub-section (3), the marked and sealed container or containers shall be signed by the person taking the samples, and the container or containers shall be sent without delay by the person taking the sample for analysis to the laboratory established or recognised under Section 13 in writing, about the willful absence of the occupier or his agent or person, or, as the case may be, his refusal to sign the container or containers.

12. Environmental laboratories

(1) The Central Government may, by notification in the Official Gazette—

(a) establish one or more environmental laboratories;

(b) recognise one or more laboratories or institutes as environmental laboratories to carry out the functions entrusted

to an environmental laboratory under this Act.

(2) The Central Government may, by notification in the Official Gazette, make rules specifying—

(a) the functions of the environmental laboratory;

(b) the procedure for the submission to the said laboratory of samples of air, water, soil or other substance for analysis or tests, the form of the laboratory report thereon and the fees payable for such report;

(c) Such other matters as may be necessary or expedient to enable that laboratory to carry out its functions.

13. Government Analysts

The Central Government may, by notification in the Official Gazette, appoint or recognise such persons as it thinks fit and having the prescribed qualifications to be Government Analysts for the purpose of analysis of samples of air, water, soil or other substance sent for analysis to any environmental laboratory established or recognised under sub-section (1) of Section 12.

14. Reports of Government Analysts

Any document purporting to be a report signed by a Government Analyst may be used as evidence of the facts stated therein in any proceeding under this Act.

15. Penalty for contravention of the provisions of the Act and the rules, orders and directions

(1) Whoever fails to comply with or contravenes any of the provisions of this Act, or the rules made or orders or directions issued thereunder, shall, in respect of each such failure or contravention, be punishable with imprisonment for a term which may extend to five years or with fine which may extend to one lakh rupees, or with both, and in case the failure or contravention continues, with additional fine which may extend to five thousand rupees for every day during which such failure or contravention continues after the conviction for the first such failure or contravention.

(2) If the failure or contravention referred to in sub-section (1) continues beyond a period of one year after the due date of conviction, the offender shall be punishable with imprisonment for a term which may extend to seven years.

16. Offences by companies

(1) Where any offence under this Act has been committed by a

company, every person who, at the time the offence was committed, was directly incharge of, and was responsible to, the company for the conduct of the business of the company, as well as the company, shall be deemed to be guilty of the offence and shall be liable to be proceeded against and punished accordingly:

Provided that nothing contained in this sub-section shall render any such person liable to any punishment provided in this Act, if he proves that the offence was committed without his knowledge or that he exercised all due diligence to prevent the commission of such offence.

(2) Notwithstanding anything contained in sub-section (1), where an offence under this Act has been committed by a company and it is proved that the offence has been committed with the consent or connivance of, or is attributable to any neglect on the part of, any director, manager, secretary or other officer of the company, such director, manager, secretary or other officer shall also be deemed to be guilty of that offence and shall be liable to be proceeded against and punished accordingly.

Explanation: For the purposes of this section—

(a) "company" means any body corporate, and includes a firm or other association of individuals; and

(b) "director", in relation to a firm, means a partner in the firm.

17. Offence by Government Departments

(1) Where an offence under this Act has been committed by any Department of Government, the Head of the Department shall be deemed to be guilty of the offence and shall be liable to be proceeded against and punished accordingly:

Provided that nothing contained in this section shall render such Head of the Department liable to any punishment if he proves that the offence was committed without his knowledge or that he exercised all due diligence to prevent the commission of such offence.

(2) Notwithstanding anything contained in sub-section (1), when an offence under this Act has been committed by a Department of Government and it is proved that the offence has been committed with the consent or connivance of, or is attributable to any neglect on the part of, any officer, other than the Head of the Department, such officer shall also be deemed to be guilty of that offence and shall be liable to be proceeded against and punished accordingly.

Chapter IV

MISCELLANEOUS

18. Protection of action taken in good faith

No suit, prosecution or other legal proceeding shall lie against the Government or any officer or other employee of the Government or any authority constituted under this Act or any member, officer or other employee of such authority in respect of anything which is done or intended to be done in good faith in pursuance of this Act or the rules made or orders or directions issued thereunder.

19. Cognizance of offence

No court shall take cognizance of any offence under this Act except on a complaint made by—

(a) the Central Government or any authority or officer authorised in this behalf by that Government; or

(b) any person who has given notice of not less than sixty days, in the manner prescribed, of the alleged offence and of his intention to make a complaint, to the Central Government or the authority or officer authorised as aforesaid.

20. Information, reports or returns

The Central Government may, in relation to its functions under this Act, from time to time, require any person, officer, State Government or other authority to furnish to it or any prescribed authority or officer any reports, returns, statistics, accounts and other information and such person, officer, State Government or other authority shall be bound to do so.

21. Members, officers and employees of the authority constituted under Section 3 to be public servants

All the members of the authority, constituted, if any, under Section 3 and all officers and other employees of such authority when acting or purporting to act in pursuance of any provisions of this Act or the rules made or orders or directions issued thereunder shall be deemed to be public servants within the meaning of Section 21 of the Indian Penal Code.

22. Bar of jurisdiction

No civil court shall have jurisdiction to entertain any suit or proceeding in respect of anything done, action taken or order or direction issued by the Central Government or any other authority or officer in pursuance of any power conferred by or in relation to its or his functions under this Act.

23. Power to delegate

Without prejudice to the provisions of sub-section (3) of Section 3, the Central Government may, by notification in the Official Gazette, delegate, subject to such conditions and limitations as may be specified in the notification, such of its powers and functions under this Act [except the power to constitute any authority under sub-section (3) of Section 3 and to make rules under Section 25] as it may deem necessary or expedient, to any officer, State Government or other authority.

24. Effect of other laws

(1) Subject to the provisions of sub-section (2), the provisions of this Act and the rules or orders made therein shall have effect notwithstanding anything inconsistent therewith contained in any enactment other than this Act.

(2) Where any act of omission constitutes an offence punishable under this Act and also under any other Act then the offender found guilty of such offence shall be liable to be punished under the other Act and not under this Act.

25. Power to make rules

(1) The Central Government may, by notification in the Official Gazette, make rules for carrying out the purposes of this Act.

(2) In particular, and without prejudice to the generality of the foregoing power, such rules may provide for all or any of the following matters, namely :

(a) the standards in excess of which environmental pollutants shall not be discharged or emitted under Section 7;

(b) the procedure in accordance with and the safeguards in compliance with which hazardous substances shall be handled or cause to be handled under Section 8;

(c) the authorities or agencies to which intimation of the fact of occurrence or apprehension of occurrence of the discharge of any environmental pollutant in excess of the prescribed standards shall be given and to whom all assistance shall be bound to be rendered under sub-section (1) of Section 9;

(d) the manner in which samples of air, water, soil or other substance for the purpose of analysis shall be taken under

sub-section (1) of Section 11;

(e) the form in which notice of intention to have a sample analysed shall be served under clause *(a)* of sub-section (3) of Section 11;

(f) the functions of the environmental laboratories, the procedure for the submission to such laboratories of samples of air, water, soil, and other substances for analysis or test; the form of laboratory report; the fees payable for such report and other matters to enable such laboratories to carry out their functions under sub-section (2) of Section 12;

(g) the qualifications of Government Analyst appointed or recognised for the purpose of analysis of samples of air, water, soil or other substances under Section 13;

(h) the manner in which notice of the offence and of the intention to make a complaint to the Central Government shall be given under clause *(b)* of Section 19;

(i) the authority or officer to whom any reports, returns, statistics, accounts and other information shall be furnished under Section 20;

(j) any other matter which is required to be, or may be, prescribed.

26. Rules made under this Act to be laid before Parliament

Every rule made under this Act shall be laid, as soon as may be after it is made, before each House of Parliament, while it is in session, for a total period of thirty days which may be comprised in one session or in two or more successive sessions, and if, before the expiry of the session immediately following the session or the successive sessions aforesaid, both Houses agree in making any modification in the rule or both Houses agree that the rule should not be made, the rule shall thereafter have effect only in such modified form or be of no effect, as the case may be; so, however, that any such modification or annulment shall be without prejudice to the validity of anything previously done under that rule.

14

THE PUBLIC LIABILITY INSURANCE ACT. 1991 (No. 6 of 1991)

[22nd January 1991]

An Act to provide for public liability insurance for the purpose of providing-immediate relief to the persons affected by accident occurring while handling any hazardous substance and for matters connected therewith or incidental thereto.

BE it enacted by Parliament in the Forty-first Year of the Republic of India as follows:

1. (1) This Act may be called the Public Liability Insurance Act, 1991.

(2) It shall come into force on such date as the Central Government may, by notification, appoint.

2. In this Act, unless the context otherwise requires—

(a) "accident" means an accident or incident occurring while handling any hazardous substance;

(b) "Collector" means the Collector having jurisdiction over the area in which the accident occurs;

(c) "handling", in relation to any hazardous substance, means the manufacture, processing, treatment, package, storage, transportation by vehicle, use, collection, destruction, conversion, offering for sale, transfer or the like of such hazardous substance;

(d) "hazardous substance" means any substance or preparation which is defined as hazardous substance under the Environment (Protection) Act, 1986, and exceeding such quantity as may be specified, by notification, by the Central Government;

(e) "insurance" means insurance against liability under sub-

section (1) of Section 3;

(*f*) "notification" means a notification published in the Official Gazette;

(*g*) "owner" means a person who has control over handling any hazardous substance;

(*h*) "prescribed" means prescribed by rules made under this Act;

(*i*) "rules" means rules made under this Act;

(*j*) "vehicle" means any mode of surface transport other than railways.

3. (1) Where death or injury to any person (other than a workman) or damage to any property has resulted from an accident, the owner shall be liable to give such relief as is specified in the Schedule for such death, injury or damage.

(2) In any claim for relief under sub-section (1) (hereinafter referred to in this Act as claim for relief), the claimant shall not be required to plead and establish that the death, injury or damage in respect of which the claim has been made was due to any wrongful act, neglect or default of any person.

Explanation : For the purposes of this section—

(*i*) "workman" has the meaning assigned to it in the Workmen's Compensation Act, 1923;

(*ii*) "injury" includes permanent total or permanent partial disability or sickness resulting out of an accident.

4.(1) Every owner shall take out, before he starts handling any hazardous substance, one or more insurance policies providing for contracts of insurance whereby he is insured against liability to give relief under sub-section (1) of Section 3:

Provided that any owner handling any hazardous substance immediately before the commencement of this Act shall take out such insurance policy or policies as soon as may be and in any case within a period of one year from such commencement.

(2) Every owner shall get the insurance policy, referred to in sub-section (1), renewed from time to time before the expiry of the period of validity thereof so that the insurance policies may remain in force throughout the period during which such handling is continued.

(3) The Central Government may, by notification, exempt from the operation of sub-section (1) any owner, namely:

(*a*) the Central Government;

(*b*) any State Government;

(*c*) any corporation owned or controlled by the Central Government or a State Government; or

(*d*) any local authority:

Provided that no such order shall be made in relation to such owner unless a fund has been established and is maintained by that owner in accordance with the rules made in this behalf for meeting any liability under sub-section (1) of Section 3.

5. Whenever, it comes to the notice of the Collector that an accident has occurred at any place within his jurisdiction, he shall verify the occurrence of such accident and cause publicity to be given in such manner as he deems fit for inviting applications under sub-section (1) of Section 6.

6. (1) An application for claim for relief may be made—

(*a*) by the person who has sustained the injury;

(*b*) by the owner of the property to which the damage has been caused;

(*c*) where death has resulted from the accident, by all or any of the legal representatives of the deceased; or

(*d*) by any agent duly authorised by such person or owner of such property or all or any of the legal representatives of the deceased, as the case may be:

Provided that where all the legal representatives of the deceased have not joined in any such application for relief, the application shall be made on behalf of or for the benefit of all the legal representatives of the deceased and the legal representatives who have not so joined shall be impleaded as respondents to the application.

(2) Every application under sub-section (1) shall be made to the Collector and shall be in such form, contain such particulars and shall be accompanied by such documents as may be prescribed.

(3) No application for relief shall be entertained unless it is made within five years of the occurrence of the accident.

7. (1) On receipt of an application under sub-section (1) of Section 6, the Collector shall, after giving notice of the application to the owner and after giving the parties an opportunity ofbeing heard, hold an inquiry into the claim or, each of the claims, and may make an award determining the amount of relief which appears to him to be just and specifying the person or persons to whom such amount of relief shall be paid.

(2) The Collector shall arrange to deliver copies of the award to the parties concerned expeditiously and in any case within a period

of fifteen days from the date of the award.

(3) When an award is made under this section, the owner or the insurer, as the case may be, who is required to pay any amount in terms of such award shall, within thirty days of the date of announcement of the award, deposit the entire amount so awarded in such manner as the Collector may direct.

(4) In holding any inquiry under sub-section (1), the Collector may, subject to any rules made in this behalf, follow such summary procedure as he thinks fit.

(5) The Collector shall have all the powers of a Civil Court for the purpose of taking evidence on oath and of enforcing the attendance of witnesses and of compelling the discovery and production of documents and material objects and for such other purposes as may be prescribed; and the Collector shall be deemed to be a Civil Court for all the purposes of Section 195 and Chapter XXVI of the Code of Criminal Procedure, 1973.

(6) Where the insurer or the owner against whom the award is made under sub-section (1) fails to deposit the amount of such award within the period specified under sub-section (3), such amount shall be recoverable from the owner, or as the case may be, the insurer as arrears of land revenue or of public demand.

(7) A claim for relief in respect of death of, or injury to, any person or damage to any property shall be disposed of as expeditiously as possible, and every endeavour shall be made to dispose of such claim within three months of the receipt of the application for relief under sub-section (1) of Section 6.

8. (1) The right to claim relief under sub-section (1) of Section 3 in respect of death of, or injury to, any person or damage to any property shall be in addition to any other right to claim compensation in respect thereof under any other law for the time being in force.

(2) Notwithstanding anything contained in sub-section (1), where in respect of death of, or injury to, any person or damage to any property, the owner, liable to give claim for relief, is also liable to pay compensation under any other law, the amount of such compensation shall be reduced by the amount of relief paid under this Act.

9. Any person authorised by the Central Government may, for the purposes of ascertaining whether any requirements of this Act or of any rule or of any direction given under this Act have been complied with, require any owner to submit to that person such information as that person may reasonably think necessary.

10. Any person, authorised by the Central Government in this behalf, shall have a right to enter, at all reasonable times with such assistance as he considers necessary, any place, premises or vehicle, where hazardous substance is handled for the purpose of determining whether any provisions of this Act or of any rule or of any direction given under this Act is being or has been complied with and such owner is bound to render all assistance to such person.

11. (1) If a person, authorised by the Central Government in this behalf, has reason to believe that handling of any hazardous substance is taking place in any place, premises or vehicle, in contravention of sub-section (1) of Section 4, he may enter into and search such place, premises or vehicle for such handling of hazardous substance.

(2) Where, as a result of any search under sub-section (1) any handling of hazardous substance has been found in relation to which contravention of sub-section (1) of Section 4 has taken place, he may seize such hazardous substance and other things which, in his opinion, will be useful for, or relevant to, any proceeding under this Act:

Provided that where it is not practicable to seize any such substance or thing, he may serve on the owner an order that the owner shall not remove, part with, or otherwise deal with, the hazardous substance and such other things except with the previous permission of that person.

(3) He may, if he has reason to believe that it is expedient so to do to prevent an accident dispose of the hazardous substance seized under sub-section (2) immediately in such manner as he may deem fit.

(4) All expenses incurred by him in the disposal of hazardous substances under sub-section (3) shall be recoverable from the owner as arrears of land revenue or of public demand.

12. Notwithstanding anything contained in any other law but subject to the provisions of this Act, the Central Government may, in exercise of its powers and performance of its functions under this Act, issue such directions in writing as it may deem fit for the purposes of this Act to any owner or any person, officer, authority or agency and such owner, person, officer, authority or agency shall be bound to comply with such directions.

***Explanation*:** For the removal of doubts, it is hereby declared that the power to issue directions under this section includes the power to direct-

(a) prohibition or regulation of the handling of any hazardous substances; or

(b) stoppage or regulation of the supply of electricity, water or any other service.

13. (1) If the Central Government or any person authorised by that Government in this behalf has reason to believe that any owner has been handling any hazardous substance in contravention of any of the provisions of this Act, that Government or, as the case may be, that person may make an application to a Court, not inferior to that of a Metropolitan Magistrate or a Judicial Magistrate of first class for restraining such owner from such handling.

(2) On receipt of the application under sub-section (1), the Court may make such order as it deems fit.

(3) Where under sub-section (2), the Court makes an order restraining any owner from handling hazardous substance, it may, in that order—

(a) direct such owner to desist from such handling;

(b) authorise the Central Government or, as the case may be, the person referred to in sub-section (1), if the direction under clause *(a)* is not complied with by the owner to whom such direction is issued, to implement the direction in such manner as may be specified by the Court.

(4) All expenses incurred by the Central Government, or as the case may be, the person in implementing the directions of Court under clause *(b)* of sub-section (3), shall be recoverable from the owner as arrears of land revenue or of public demand.

14. (1) Whoever, contravenes any of the provisions of sub-section (1) or sub-section(2) of Section 4 or fails to comply with any direction issued under Section 12, he shall be punishable with imprisonment for a term which shall not be less than one year and six months but which may extend to six years, or with fine which shall not be less than one lakh rupees, or with both.

(2) Whoever, having already been convicted of an offence under sub-section (1), is convicted for the second offence or any offence subsequent to the second offence, he shall be punishable with imprisonment for a term which shall not be less than two years but which may extend to seven years and with fine which shall

not be less than one lakh rupees.

(3) Nothing contained in Section 360 of the Code of Criminal Procedure, 1973, or in the Probation of Offenders Act, 1958, shall apply to a person convicted of an offence under this Act unless such person is under eighteen years of age.

15. If any owner fails to comply with direction issued under Section 9 or fails to comply with order issued under sub-section (2) of Section 11, or obstructs any person in discharge of his functions under Section 10 or sub-section (1) or sub-section (3) of Section 11, he shall be punishable with imprisonment which may extend to three months, or with fine which may extend to ten thousand rupees, or with both.

16. (1) Where any offence under this Act has been committed by a company, every person who, at the time the offence was committed, was directly incharge of, and was responsible to, the company for the conduct of the business of the company, as well as the company, shall be deemed to be guilty of the offence and shall be liable to be proceeded against and punished accordingly:

Provided that nothing contained in this sub-section shall render any such person liable to any punishment provided in this Act, if he proves that the offence was committed without his knowledge or that he exercised all due diligence to prevent the commission of such offence.

(2) Notwithstanding anything contained in sub-section (1), where an offence under this Act has been committed by a company and it is proved that the offence has been committed with the consent or connivance of, or is attributable to any neglect on the part of, any director, manager, secretary or other officer of the company, such director, manager, secretary or other officer shall also be deemed to be guilty of that offence and shall be liable to be proceeded against and punished accordingly.

Explanation.- For the purposes of this section—

(a) "company" means any body corporate and includes a firm or other association of individuals;

(b) "director", in relation to a firm, means a partner in the firm.

17. Where an offence under this Act has been committed by any Department of Government, the Head of the Department shall be deemed to be guilty of the offence and shall be liable to be proceeded against and punished accordingly :

Provided that nothing contained in this section shall render such Head of the Department liable to any punishment if he proves that the offence was committed without his knowledge or that he exercised all due diligence to prevent the commission of such offence.

18. No court shall take cognizance of any offence under this Act except on a complaint made by—

(a) the Central Government or any authority or officer authorised in this behalf by that Government; or

(b) any person who has given notice of not less than sixty days in the manner prescribed, of the alleged offence and of his intention to make a complaint, to the Central Government or the authority or officer authorised as aforesaid.

19. The Central Government may, by notification, delegate, subject to such conditions and limitations as may be specified in the notification, such of its powers and functions under this Act (except the power under Section 23) as it may deem necessary or expedient to any person (including any officer, authority or other agency).

20. No suit, prosecution or other legal proceeding shall lie against the Government or the person, officer, authority or other agency in respect of anything which is done or intended to be done in good faith in pursuance of this Act or the rule made or orders or directions issued thereunder.

21. (1) The Central Government may, from time to time, constitute an Advisory Committee on the matters relating to the insurance policy under this Act.

(2) The Advisory Committee shall consist of—

(a) three officers representing the Central Government;

(b) two persons representing the insurers;

(c) two persons representing the owners; and

(d) two persons from amongst the experts of insurance or hazardous substances,

to be appointed by the Central Government.

(3) The Chairman of the Advisory Committee shall be one of the members representing the Central Government, nominated in this behalf by that Government.

22. The provisions of this Act and any rules made thereunder shall have effect notwithstanding anything inconsistent therewith contained in any other law.

23. (1) The Central Government may, by notification, make rules for carrying out the purposes of this Act.

(2) In particular, and without prejudice to the generality of the

foregoing power, such rules may provide for all or any of the following matters, namely:

(a) establishment and maintenance of fund under sub-section (3) of Section 4;

(b) the form of application and the particulars to be given therein and the documents to accompany such application under sub-section (2) of Section 6;

(c) the procedure for holding an inquiry under sub-section (4) of Section 7;

(d) the purposes for which the Collector shall have powers of a Civil Court under sub-section (5) of Section 7;

(e) the manner in which notice of the offence and of the intention to make a complaint to the Central Government shall be given under clause (b) of Section 18;

(f) any other matter which is required to be, or may be, prescribed.

(3) Every rule made under this Act shall be laid, as soon as may be after it is made, before each House of Parliament, while it is in session for a total period of thirty days which may be comprised in one session or in two or more successive sessions, and if, before the expiry of the session immediately following the session or the successive sessions aforesaid, both Houses agree in making any modification in the rule or both Houses agree that the rule should not be made, the rule shall thereafter have effect only in such modified form or be of no effect, as the case may be; so however, that any such modification or annulment shall be without prejudice to the validity of anything previously done under that rule.

THE SCHEDULE

[See Section 3(1)]

(i) Reimbursement of medical expenses incurred up to a maximum of Rs.12,500 in each case.

(ii) For fatal accidents the relief will be Rs. 25,000 per person in addition to reimbursement of medical expenses, if any, incurred on the victim up to a maximum of Rs.12,500.

(iii) For permanent total or permanent partial disability or other injury or sickness, the relief will be *(a)* reimbursement of medical expenses incurred, if any, up to a maximum of Rs. 12,500 in each case and *(b)* cash relief on the basis of percentage of disablement as certified by an authorised

physician. The relief for total permanent disability will be Rs. 25,000.

(iv) For loss of wages due to temporary partial disability which reduces the earning capacity of the victim, there will be a fixed monthly relief not exceeding Rs. 1,000 per month up to a maximum of 3 months; provided the victim has been hospitalised for a period exceeding 3 days and is above 16 years of age.

(v) Up to Rs. 6,000, depending on the actual damage, for any damage to private property.

15

THE NATIONAL ENVIRONMENT TRIBUNAL BILL 1992 (Bill No. 133 of 1992)

A Bill to provide for strict liability for damages arising out of any accident occurring while handling any hazardous substance and for the establishment of a National Environment Tribunal for effective and expeditious disposal of cases arising from such accident, with a view to giving relief and compensation for damages to persons, property and the environment and for matters connected therewith or incidental thereto.

Whereas, decisions were taken at the United Nations Conference on Environment and Development held at Rio De Janeiro in June 1992, in which India participated, calling upon the states to develop national laws regarding liability and compensation for the victims of pollution and other environmental damages;

And, whereas, it is considered expedient to implement the decisions of the aforesaid Conference so far as they relate to the protection of environment and payment of compensation for damage to persons, property and the environment while handling hazardous substances.

Be it enacted by Parliament in the Forty-third Year of the Republic of India as follows :

Chapter I

PRELIMINARY

1. (1) This Act may be called the National Environment Tribunal Act, 1992.

(2) It shall come into force on such date or dates as the Central Government may, by notification appoint and different dates may be appointed for different states and any reference in any provision of this Act to the commencement of this Act shall be

construed in relation to any State or part thereof as a reference to the coming into force of that provision in that State or part thereof.

2. In this Act unless the context otherwise requires :

(a) "accident" means an accident involving a fortuitous or sudden or unintended occurrence while handling any hazardous substance resulting in continuous or intermittent or repeated exposure to death of, or injury to any person or damage to any property or environment but does not include an accident by reason only of war or radio activity;

(b) "Bench" means a Bench of the Tribunal;

(c) "Chairman" means the Chairman of the Tribunal;

(d) "environment" includes water, air and land and the inter-relationship which exists among and between water, air and land, and human beings, other living creatures, plants, micro-organism and property;

(e) "handling", in relation to any hazardous substance, means the manufacture, processing, treatment, package, storage, transportation by vehicle, use, collection, destruction, conversion, offering for sale, transfer or the like of such hazardous substance;

(f) "hazardous substance" means any substance or preparation which is defined as hazardous substance in the Environment (Protection) Act, 1986, and exceeding such quantity as specified by the Central Government under the Public Liability Insurance Act, 1991;

(g) "Judicial Member" means a Member of the Tribunal appointed as such under this Act, and includes the Chairman or a Vice-Chairman who possesses any of the qualifications specified in sub-section (3) of Section 11;

(h) "Member" means a Member (whether Judicial or Technical) of the Tribunal, and includes the Chairman and a Vice-Chairman;

(i) "notification" means a notification published in the Official Gazette;

(j) "prescribed" means prescribed by rules made under this Act:

(k) "rules" means the rules made under this Act;

(l) "Technical Member" means a Member of the Tribunal who is not a Judicial Member within the meaning of clause *(g);*

(m) "Tribunal" means the National Environment Tribunal

established under Section 9;

(n) "Vice-Chairman" means the Vice-Chairman of the Tribunal;

Explanation **:** In the case of the Tribunal having two or more Vice-Chairman, references to the Vice-Chairman in this Act shall be construed as a reference to each of those Vice-Chairman; and

(o) "owner" means a person who owns or has control over handling any hazardous substance at the time of accident and includes :

(i) in the case of a firm any of its partners;

(ii) in the case of an association, any of its members; and

(iii) in the case of a company, any of its directors, managers, secretaries or other officers who is directly in charge of, and is responsible to the company for the conduct of the business of the company.

Chapter II

COMPENSATION FOR DEATH OF, OR INJURY TO A PERSON AND DAMAGE TO PROPERTY AND ENVIRONMENT

3. (1) Where death of, or injury to any person (other than a workman) or damage to any property or environment has resulted from an accident, the owner shall be liable to pay compensation for such death, injury or damage under all or any of the heads specified in the Schedule.

(2) In any claim for compensation under sub-section (1), the claimant shall not be required to plead and establish that the death, injury or damage in respect of which the claim has been made was due to any wrongful act neglect or default of any person.

Explanation: For the purposes of this section :

(i) "workman" has the meaning assigned to it in the Workmen's Compensation Act, 1923;

(ii) "injury" includes permanent total or permanent partial disability of sickness resulting out of an accident.

(3) If the death, injury or damage caused by an accident cannot be attributed to any individual activity but is the combined or resultant effect of several such activities, apportions and processes, the Tribunal may apportion the liability for compensation amongst

those responsible for such activities, apportions and processes on an equitable basis.

4. The Central Government may, by notification, exempt from the operation of this Act any owner, namely :

(a) by the person who has sustained the injury;

(b) any State Government;

(c) any corporation owned or controlled by the Central Government; a State Government, or

(d) any local authority.

5. (1) An application for claim for compensation may be made—

(a) by the person who has sustained the injury;

(b) by the owner of the property to which the damage has been caused;

(c) where death has resulted from the accident by all or any of the legal representatives of the deceased;

(d) by any agent duly authorised by such person or owner of such property or all or any of the legal representatives of the deceased, as the case may be;

(e) by any representative body or organisation, functioning in the field of environment and recognised in this behalf by the Central Government, under all or any of the heads specified in the Schedule; or

(f) by the Central Government or a State Government or a local authority under all or any of the heads specified in the Schedule:

Provided that where all the legal representatives of the deceased have not joined in any such application for compensation, the application shall be made on behalf of or for the benefit of all the legal representatives of the deceased and the legal representatives who have not so joined shall be implead as respondents to the application.

(2) Any claimant making an application under sub-section (1) may also make an application before the Tribunal for such relief as is provided in the Public Liability Insurance Act, 1991;

Provided that no such application shall be made if the relief has been received by the claimant earlier or an application made by the claimant to the Collector under the said Act is pending and has not been withdrawn.

(3) The Tribunal shall have, and exercise, the same jurisdiction, powers and authority in respect of the matters specified in the Public Liability Insurance Act, 1991 as the Collector has and

may exercise and, for this purpose, the provisions of that Act shall have effect subject to the modification that the reference therein to the Collector shall be construed as including a reference to the Tribunal.

(4) Every application under sub-section (1) shall be made to the Tribunal and shall contain such particulars and shall be accompanied by such documents and such fee, not exceeding one thousand rupees, as may be prescribed:

Provided that no fee shall be payable by a person whose annual income is below the prescribed limit or by a representative body or organisation referred to in clause *(e)* of sub-section (1) or by the Central Government, a State Government or a local authority.

(5) No application for compensation shall be entertained unless it is made within five years of the occurrence of the accident.

6. (1) On receipt of an application under sub-section (1) of Section 5 the Tribunal may, after such inquiry as it may deem fit reject the application summarily.

(2) Where the Tribunal does not reject the application and sub-section (1) the Tribunal may after giving notice of the application to the owner and after giving the partisan opportunity of being heard hold an inquiry into the claim or each of the claims and may make an award determining the amount of compensation which appears to be just and specifying the person or persons to whom such amount of compensation shall be paid.

(3) The Tribunal shall not be bound by the procedure laid down by the Code of Civil Procedure, 1908, but shall be guided by the principles of natural justice and, subject to the other provisions of this Act and of any rules, the Tribunal shall have power to regulate its own procedure including the fixing of places and times of its inquiry.

(4) The Tribunal shall have, for the purpose of discharging its functions under this Act, the same powers as are vested in a civil court under the Code of Civil Procedure, 1908, while trying a suit in respect of the following matters namely :

(a) summoning and enforcing the attendance of any person and examining him on oath;

(b) requiring the discovery and production of documents;

(c) receiving evidence on affidavits;

(d) subject to the provisions of Sections 123 and 124 of the Indian Evidence Act, 1872, requisitioning any public record or

document or copy of such record or document from any office;

(e) issuing commissions for the examination of witnesses or documents;

(f) reviewing its decisions;

(g) dismissing an application for default or deciding it *ex parte;*

(h) setting aside any order of dismissal of ay application for default or any order passed by it *ex parte*; and

(i) any other matter which is to be or may be prescribed.

7. Notwithstanding anything contained in any other provisions of this Act or in any other law for the time being in force, no interim order (whether by way of injunction or stay or in any other manner) shall be made on, or in any proceedings relating to an application unless—

(a) copies of such application and of all documents in support of the plea for such interim order are furnished to the party against whom such application is made or proposed to be made; and

(b) opportunity is given to such party to be heard in the matter:

Provided that the Tribunal may dispense with the requirements of clauses *(a)* and *(b)* and make an interim order as an exceptional measure if it is satisfied for reasons to be recorded in writing that it is necessary so to do for preventing any loss or damage being caused to the applicant which cannot be adequately compensated in money but any such interim order shall if it is not sooner vacated cease to have effect on the expiry of a period of fourteen days from the date on which it is made unless the said requirements have been complied with before the expiry of that period and the Tribunal has continued the operation of the interim order.

8. Where in respect of death of or injury to any person or damage to any property the owner liable to pay compensation under this Act, is also liable to pay any amount as relief under the Public Liability Insurance Act, 1991 or any other compensation under any other law, the amount of compensation payable under this Act shall be reduced by the amount of relief and other compensation paid under any other law.

Chapter III

ESTABLISHMENT OF NATIONAL ENVIRONMENT TRIBUNAL AND BENCHES THEREOF

9. The Central Government shall, by notification, establish a

Tribunal, to be known as the National Environment Tribunal, to exercise the jurisdiction, powers and authority conferred on it by or under this Act.

10. (1) The Tribunal shall consist of a Chairman and such number of Vice-Chairman, Judicial Members and Technical Members as the Central Government may deem fit and, subject to the other provisions of this Act, the jurisidiction, powers and authority of the Tribunal may be exercised by Benches thereof.

(2) Subject to the other provisions of this Act, a Bench shall consist of one Judicial Member and one Technical Member.

(3) Notwithstanding anything contained in sub-section (1), the Chairman—

(a) may, in addition to discharging the functions of the Judicial Members or the Technical Member of the Bench to which he is appointed, discharge the functions of the Judicial Member or, as the case may be, the Technical Member, of any other Bench;

(b) may transfer the Vice-Chairman or other Member from one Bench to another Bench;

(c) may authorise the Vice-Chairman or the Judicial Member or the Technical Member appointed to one Bench to discharge also the functions of the Vice-Chairman or, as the case may be, the Judicial Member or the Technical Member of another Bench; and

(d) may, for the purpose of securing that any case or cases which, having regard to the nature of the questions involved requires or require, in his opinion or under the rules made by the Central Government in this behalf, to be decided by a Bench composed of more than two members, issue such general or special orders, as he may deem fit:

Provided that every Bench constituted in pursuance of this clause shall include at least one Judicial Member and one Technical Member.

(4) Notwithstanding anything contained in the foregoing provisions of this section, it shall be competent for the Chairman or any other Member authorised by the Chairman in this behalf to function as a Bench consisting of a single Member and exercise the jurisdiction, powers and authority of the Tribunal in respect of such classes of cases or such matters pertaining to such classes of cases as the Chairman may, by general or special order, specify:

Provided that if at any stage of the hearing of any such case or matter, it appears to the Chairman or such Member that the case or matter is of such a nature that it ought to be heard by a Bench consisting of two Members, the case or matter may be transferred by the Chairman or, as the case may be, referred to him for transfer to such Bench as the Chairman may deem fit.

(5) Subject to the other provisions of this Act, the Benches of the Tribunal shall ordinarily sit at New Delhi (which shall be known as the principal Bench) and at such other places as the Central Government may, be notification, specify.

11. (1) A person shall not be qualified for appointment as the Chairman unless he—

(a) is, or has been, a Judge of the Supreme Court or a High Court; or

(b) has, for at least two years, held the office of Vice-Chairman.

(2) A person shall not be qualified for appointment as the Vice-Chairman unless he—

(a) is, or has been, a Judge of a High Court; or

(b) has, for at least two years, held the post of a Secretary to the Government of India or any other post under the Central or a State Government carrying a scale of pay which is not less than that of a Secretary to the Government of India; or

(c) *(i)* has, for at least five years, held the post of an Additional Secretary to the Government of India or any other post under the Central or a State Government carrying a scale of pay which is not less than that of an Additional Secretary to the Government of India; and

(ii) has adequate knowledge of, or experience in legal, administrative, scientific or technical aspects of the problems relating to environment; or

(d) has, for at least three years, held office as a Judicial Member or a Technical Member.

(3) A person shall not be qualified for appointment as a Judicial Member unless he—

(a) is or has been, or is qualified to be, a Judge of a High Court or

(b) has been a member of the Indian Legal Service and has next post in grade I of that Service for at least three years.

(4) A person shall not be qualified for appointment as a Technical Member unless he has adequate knowledge of, or experience in or capacity to deal with, administrative, scientific, or technical aspects of the problems relating to environment.

(5) Subject to the provisions of sub-sections (6) and (7), the Chairman, Vice-Chairman and every other Member of the Tribunal shall be appointed by the President.

(6) No appointment of a person possessing the qualifications specified in this section as the Chairman or the Vice-Chairman shall be made except after consultation with the Chief Justice of India.

(7) No appointment of a person as a Judicial Member or a Technical Member shall be made except on the recommendation of a Selection Committee appointed by the Central Government consisting of the following namely:—

(a)	Chairman of the Tribunal ;	- Chairman of the Committee *ex officio;*
(b)	Secretary to the Government of India in the Ministry of Environment and Forests;	- member *ex officio;*
(c)	Secretary to the Government of India in the Ministry of Law, Justice and Company Affairs (Department of Legal Affairs);	- member *ex officio.*
(d)	Director-General, Council of Scientific and Industrial Research;	- member *ex officio.*
(e)	an Environmentalist to be nominated by the Central Government.	- member.

12. (1) In the event of the occurrence of any vacancy in the office of the Chairman by reason of his death, resignation or otherwise, the Vice-Chairman or, as the case may be, such one of the Vice-Chairman, as the Central Government may, by notification, authorise in this behalf, shall act as the Chairman until the date on which a new Chairman, appointed in accordance with the provisions of this Act to fill such vacancy, enters upon his office.

(2) When the Chairman is unable to discharge his functions owing to absence, illness of any other cause, the Vice-Chairman or, as the case may be, such one of the Vice-Chairmen, as the Central Government may by notification authorise in this behalf, shall discharge the functions of the Chairman until the date on which the Chairman resumes his duties.

13. The Chairman, Vice-Chairman and other Members shall hold office as such for a term of five years from the date on which he enters upon his office, but shall be eligible for re-appointment for another term of five years.

Provided that no Chairman, Vice-Chairman or other Member shall hold office as such after he has attained :

(a) in the case of the Chairman the age of seventy years;

(b) in the case of the Vice-Chairman, the age of sixty-five years; and

(c) in the case of any other Member, the age of sixty-two years.

14. (1) The Chairman, Vice-Chairman or other Member may, by notice in writing under his hand addressed to the President, resign his office:

Provided that the Chairman, Vice-Chairman or other Member shall, unless he is permitted by the President to relinquish his office sooner, continue to hold office until the expiry of three months from the date of receipt of such notice or until a person duly appointed as his successor enters upon his office or until the expiry of his term of office, whichever is the earliest.

(2) The Chairman, Vice-Chairman or any other Member shall not be removed from his office except by an order made by the President on the ground of proved misbehaviour or incapacity after an inquiry made by a Judge of the Supreme Court in which such Chairman, Vice-Chairman or other Member had been informed of the charges against him and given a reasonable opportunity of being heard in respect of those charges.

(3) The Central Government may, by rules, regulate the procedure for the investigation of misbehaviour or incapacity of the Chairman, Vice-Chairman or other Member referred to in sub-section (2).

15. The salaries and allowances payable to, and the other terms and conditions of service (including pension, gratuity and other retirement benefits) of, the Chairman, Vice-Chairman and other Member shall be such as may be prescribed:

Provided that neither the salary and allowances nor the other terms and conditions of service of the Chairman, Vice-Chairman or other Member shall be varied to his disadvantage after his appointment.

16. On ceasing to hold office

(a) the Chairman of the Tribunal shall be ineligible for further employment either under the Government of India or under the Government of a State.

(b) the Vice-Chairman of the Tribunal shall, subject to the other provisions of this Act, be eligible for appointment as the Chairman of the Tribunal, but not for any other employment either under the Government of India or under the Government of State;

(c) a Member (other than the Chairman or Vice-Chairman) of the Tribunal shall subject to the other provisions of this Act be eligible for appointment as the Chairman or Vice-Chairman of the Tribunal or as the Chairman, Vice-Chairman or Member of any other Tribunal, but not for any other employment either under the Government of India or under the Government of State.

(d) the Chairman, Vice-Chairman or other Member shall not appear, act or plead before the Tribunal.

Explanation : For the purposes of this section, employment under the Government of India or under the Government of a State includes employment under any local or other authority within the territory of India or under the control of the Government of India or under any corporation or society owned or controlled by the Government.

17. The Chairman shall exercise such financial and administrative powers over the Benches as may be vested in him under the rules:

Provided that the Chairman shall have authority to delegate such of his financial and administrative power as he may think fit to the Vice Chairman or any other officer of the Tribunal, subject to the condition, that the Vice-Chairman or such officer shall, while exercising such delegated powers, continue to act under the direction, control and supervision of the Chairman.

18.(1)The Central Government shall determine the nature and categories of the officers and other employees required to assist the Tribunal in the discharge of its functions and provide the tribunal with such officers and other employees as it may think fit.

(2) The officers and other employees of the tribunal shall discharge their functions under the general superintendence of the Chairman.

(3) The salaries and allowances and conditions of service of the officers and other employee of the tribunal shall be such as may be prescribed.

19. (1) Where any Benches of the Tribunal are constituted, the Central Government may, from time to time, by notification, make provisions as to the distribution of the business of the Tribunal amongst the Benches and specify the matters which may be dealt with by each Bench.

(2) If any question arises as to whether any matter falls within the purview of the business allocated to a Bench the decision of the Chairman shall be final.

Explanation: For the removal of doubts, it is hereby declared that the expression "matters" includes applications for interim relief.

Chapter IV

JURISDICTION AND PROCEEDINGS OF THE TRIBUNAL

20. On and from the commencement of this Act, no court or other authority except the Tribunal shall have, or be entitled to exercise, any jurisdiction, powers or authority to entertain any application or action for any claim for compensation which may be entertained or dealt with by the Tribunal.

21. On the application of any of the parties and after notice to the parties, and after hearing such of them as he may desire to be heard, or on his own motion without such notice, the Chairman may transfer any case pending before one Bench, for disposal, to any other Bench.

22. If the Members of a Bench differ in opinion on any point, the point shall be decided according to the opinion of the majority, if there is a majority, but if the members are equally divided, they shall state the point or points on which they differ, and make a reference to the Chairman who shall either hear the point or points himself or refer the case for hearing on such point or points by one or more of the other members and such point or points shall be decided according to the opinion of the majority of the members who have heard the case including those who first heard it.

23. (1) Where any amount of compensation is ordered to be paid under any award by the Tribunal on the ground of any damage to environment, that amount shall be remitted to the authority specified under sub-section (3) of Section 7A of the Public Liability Insurance Act, 1991 for being credited to the Environmental Relief Fund established under that section.

(2) The amount of compensation credited to the Environmental Relief Fund under sub-section (1) may be utilised by such person or authority, in such manner and for such purposes of environment as may be prescribed.

24. (1) An award made by the Tribunal under this Act shall be executable by the Tribunal as a decree of Civil Court, and for this purpose, the Tribunal shall have all the powers of a Civil Court.

(2) Notwithstanding anything contained in sub-section (1), the Tribunal may transmit to the Collector having jurisdiction over the area in which the accident has occurred the copy of the order made by it for payment of relief as provided in the Public Liability Insurance Act, 1991 and the Collector shall execute the order in the same manner as if it were an order made by him under that Act.

(3) Where the owner against whom the award or order is made by the Tribunal fails to make the payment or deposit the amount as directed by the Tribunal within the period specified in the award or order, such amount shall be recoverable from the owner as arrears of land revenue or of public demand.

25. (1) Save as provided in sub-section (2) and notwithstanding anything contained in the Code of Civil Procedure, 1908 or in any other law, an appeal shall lie against any award or other order not being an interlocutory order, of the tribunal to the Supreme Court on one or more of the grounds specified in Section 100 of that Code.

(2) No appeal shall lied against an award or other order made by the Tribunal with the consent of the parties.

(3) Every appeal under this section shall be preferred within a period of ninety days from the date of the award or other order appealed against:

Provided that no appeal by the person who is required to pay any amount in terms of such award shall be entertained by the Supreme Court unless he has deposited with it the amount so awarded in the manner directed by the Supreme Court:

Provided further that the Supreme Court may entertain the appeal after the expiry of the said period of ninety days, if it is satisfied that the appellant was prevented by sufficient cause from preferring the appeal in time.

Chapter V

MISCELLANEOUS

26. Whoever fails to comply with any order made by the Tribunal, he shall be punishable with imprisonment for a term which may extend to three years, or with fine which may extend to ten lakh rupees, or with both.

27. (1) Where any offence under this Act has been committed by a company, every person who, at the time the offence was committed, was directly incharge of, and was responsible to, the company for the conduct of the business of the company, as well as the company, shall be deemed to be guilty of the offence and shall be liable to be proceeded against and punished accordingly:

Provided that nothing contained in this sub-section shall render any such person liable to any punishment provided in this Act, if he proves that the offence was committed without his knowledge or that he exercised all due diligence to prevent the commission of such offence.

(2) Notwithstanding anything contained in sub-section (1), where an offence under this Act has been committed by a company and it is proved that the offence has been committed with the consent or connivance of, or is attributable to any neglect on the part of any director, manager, secretary, or other officer of the company such director, manager, secretary or other officer shall also be deemed to be guilty of that offence and shall be liable to be proceeded against and punished accordingly.

Explanation : For the purposes of this section :

(a) "company" means any body corporate and includes a firm or other association of individuals; and

(b) "director", in relation to a firm, means a partner in the firm.

28. All proceedings before the Tribunal shall be deemed to be judicial proceedings within the meaning of Sections 193,219 and 228 of the Indian Penal Code.

29. The Chairman, Vice-Chairman and other members and the officers and other employees of the Tribunal shall be deemed to be public servants within the meaning of Section 21 of the Indian Penal Code.

30. No suit, prosecution or other legal proceeding shall lie against the Central Government or against the Chairman, Vice-Chairman or other Member of the Tribunal or any other person authorised by the Chairman, Vice-Chairman or other Member for anything which is in good faith done or intended to be done in pursuance of this Act or any rule or order made thereunder.

31. Save as provided in the Public Liability Insurance Act, 1991, the provisions of this Act shall have effect notwithstanding anything inconsistent therewith contained in any other law for the time being in force or in any instrument having effect by virtue of any law other than this Act.

32.(1) The Central Government may, by notification, make rules for carrying out the purposes of this Act.

(2) In particular, and without prejudice to the generality of the foregoing power, such rules may provide for all or any of the following matters, namely :

(a) the particulars which an application shall contain, the documents and the fee which shall be accompanied with it and the limit of annual income of a person so as to enable him to make application without paying any fee, under sub-section (4) of Section 5;

(b) any such matter in respect of which the Tribunal shall have powers of a civil court, under clause *(i)* of sub-section (4) of Section 6;

(c) the case of cases which, having regard to the nature of the questions involved, requires or require to be decided by a Bench of more than two members under clause *(d)* of sub-section (3) of Section 10;

(d) procedure for the investigation of misbehaviour or incapacity of the Chairman, Vice-Chairman or other Member of the Tribunal under sub-section (3) of Section 14;

(e) the salaries and allowances payable to, and the other terms and conditions of service of, the Chairman, Vice-Chairman and other members under Section 15;

(f) financial and administrative powers of the Chairman over the Benches under Section 17;

(g) the salaries and allowances and conditions of service of the officers and other employees of the Tribunal under sub-section (3) of Section 18;

(h) the person or the authority by whom, the manner in which and the purposes of environment for which the amount of compensation credited to the Environmental Relief Fund shall utilised under sub-section (2) of Section 23; and

(i) any other matter which is required to be, or may be prescribed.

(3) Every notification issued under Section 4 and every rule made under other provisions of this Act shall be laid, as soon as may be after it is made, before each House of Parliament, while it is in session for a total period of thirty days which may be comprised in one session or in two or more successive sessions, and if, before

the expiry of the session immediately following the session or the successive sessions aforesaid, both Houses agree in making any modification in the notification or the rule or both Houses agree that the notification or the rule should not be made the notification or the rule shall there after have effect only in such modified form or be of no effect, as the case may be; so, however, that any such modification or annulment shall be without prejudice to the validity of anything previously done under that notification or the rule.

THE SCHEDULE

[See Section 3(1)]

Heads under which compensation for damages may be claimed

(a) Death;

(b) Permanent, temporary, total or partial disability or other injury or sickness;

(c) Loss of wages due to total or partial disability or permanent or temporary disability;

(d) Medical expenses incurred for treatment of injuries or sickness;

(e) Damages to private property;

(j) Expenses incurred by the Government or any local authority in providing relief, aid and rehabilitation to the affected persons;

(g) Expenses incurred by Government for any administrative or legal action or to cope with any harm or damage, including compensation for environmental degradation and restoration of the quality of environment;

(h) Loss to Government or local authority arising out of, or connected with, the activity causing any damage;

(i) Claims on account of any harm, damage or destruction to the fauna including milch and draught animals and aquatic fauna;

(j) Claims on account of any harm, damage or destruction to flora including aquatic flora, crops, vegetables, trees and orchards;

(k) Claims including cost of restoration on account of any harm or damage to environment including pollution of soil, air, water, land and eco-systems.

(l) Loss and destruction of any property other than private property;

(m) Loss of business or employment or both;

(n) any other claim arising out of or connected with, any activity of handling of hazardous substance.

STATEMENT OF OBJECTS AND REASONS

The principle of strict civil liability in accident cases arising from the activities involving substances has been highlighted in a case by the Supereme Court of India. An enterprise engaged in activities with potential threat to the health and safety of the persons residing in the surrounding areas of the factory owes an absolute duty to the community to ensure that no harm is caused to anyone on account of hazardous and inherently dangerous nature of such activities. Case seeking compensation for damages to human health, property and the environment, particularly contamination of sub-surface water, are increasing. There is also an increasing trend in the number of industrial disasters.

2. The United Nations Conference on Environment and Development held as Rio de Janeiro in June, 1992, in which India participated, has also called upon the states to develop National laws regarding liability and compensation for the victims of pollution and other environmental damage.

3. It is deemed expedient to develop and codify the principle of strict civil liability in respect of all such cases where damage is caused while handling hazardous substances. It is proposed to establish a National Environmental Tribunal for effective and expenditious disposal of cases arising from certain industrial accidents and disasters with a view to provinding effective and expenditious relief and compensation for damages to human health, property and the environment.

4. The Bill seeks to achieve the aforsesaid objects.

New Delhi;
The 5th August, 1992

Kamal Nath

PRESIDENTS RECOMMENDATION UNDER ARTICLE 117 OF THE CONSTITUTION OF INDIA

[Copy of Letter No. 8/6/91/PL (CPW). dated 6th August, 1992 from Shri Kamal Nath, Minister of State of the Ministry of Environment and Forests to the Secretary-General, Lok Sabha.]

The President, having been informed of the proposed bill to provide for effective and expenditious relief, restitution and compensation for damages to human health, property and the environment to the persons affected by the accidents occuring while handling hazardous substance and for matters connected therewith or incidental thereto, recommends under Article 117(1) and (3) of the Constitution of India the introduction and consideration of the National Environment Tribunal Bill, 1992 by Lok Sabha.

Notes on clauses

Clause 3 provides for strick liability of owner for damages cuased to any person, property or the environment due to any accident occuring while handling any hazardous substances.

Clause 4 confers power on the Central Government to exempt from the operation of the Act, the Central Government, any State Government, any corporation owned or controlled by Government, or any local authority.

Clause 5 provides for making an application for claim for compensation under this Act or for relief as provided in the Public Liability Insurance Act. 1991. It also specifies five years as the limitation period.

Clause 6 provides procedure and powers of the Tribunal which shall be guided by the principles of natural justice and shall have certain, powers of a civil court.

Clause 7 empowers the Tribunal to make an interim order and provides for its procedure.

Clause 8 provides for the amount of any relief or other compensation received by any person under any other law to be reduced from the compensation awarded under this Act.

Clause 9 provides for the establishment of a National Environment Tribunal.

Clause 10 provides for the composition of the Tribunal and its Benches and also empowers the Chairman of the Tribunal to function as member on any Bench, to transfer the Vice-Chairman or other Member from one Bench to another Bench to authorise a member to discharge functions on another Bench, and to form Benches. It also empowers the Central Government to notify places others than Delhi where the Benches shall sit.

Clause 11 lays down qualifications for appointment of a person as Chairman or Vice-Chairman or Member of the Tribunal. All appointments shall be made by the President. The Chairman and Vice-Chairman shall be appointed after consultation with the Chief Justice of India and Members shall be appointed on the recommendation of a selection Committee as specified in sub-clause (7).

Clause 12 provides for appointment of Vice-Chairman as Chairman by the Government in the event of any vacancy and the authorising of Vice-Chairman and other members, respectively.

Clause 14 provides for the resignation by, and removal of, Chairman, Vice-Chairman or other members of the Tribunal, Removal may take place on the ground of proved misbehaviour or incapacity after an inquiry by a Judge of the Supreme Court.

Clause 15 empowers the Central Government to prescribe by rules the salaries, allowances and other terms and conditions of service of Chairman, Vice-Chairman and other members.

Clause 16 prohibits further employment under the Central or State Government for Chairman or Vice-Chairman or other Members. They cannot also appear. act or plead before the Tribunal.

Clause 17 provides for financial and administrative powers of the Chairman of the Tribunal as may be prescribed in the rules. He may also delegate such powers.

Clause 18 requires the Central Government to provide officers and staff to the Tribunal. Their salaries, allowances and conditions of service shall be prescribed in the rules.

Clause 19 empowers the Central Government to make provisions, by notification, for distribution of business amongst Benches. In case of doubt, decision of Chairman shall be final.

Clause 20 bars the jurisdication of courts and other authorities where the Tribunal has powers to entertain any application or action for claim.

Clause 21 empowers Chairman to transfer cases from one Bench to another Bench.

Clause 22 provides for decision in a case by majority of members of the Bench.

Clause 23 provides for the deposit and utilisation of amount payable for damage to the environment.

Clause 24 empowers the Tribunal to execute its award as a decree of civil court and also to transmit an order of interim relief to the Collector for execution. Amount of award may also be recovered as arrears of land revenue or of public demand.

Clause 25 provides for appeal to Supreme Court within 90 days on a question of law and after deposit of the money awarded and prohibits any appeal where award is given with the consent of parties.

Clause 26 provides for punishment if any person fails to comply with any order of the Tribunal.

Clause 27 provides for liability of the directors, managers, etc., of a company where an offence is committed by it.

Clause 28 provides that the proceedings before the Tribunal shall be deemed to be judicial proceedings.

Clause 29 provides that the Chairman, Vice-Chairman and Members of the Tribunal shall be deemed to be public servants.

Clause 30 provides protection for anything which is in good faith done or intended to be done under the Act or the rules.

Clause 31 provides that this Act shall have overriding effect.

Clause 32 confers powers on the Central Government to make rules to carry out the purposes of this Act.

FINANCIAL MEMORANDUM

Clause 9 of the Bill relates to the establishment of a National Environment Tribunal. Under sub-clauses (5) of clause 10. Benches of the Tribunal may sit also at such places, other than Delhi as the Central Government may, by notification, specify. Expenditure on setting up of one Bench is estimated at Rs. 15 lakh approximately. Non-recurring expenditure on four Benches, which the Government intends to set up for the time being is estimated at Rs. 18.2 lakh and recurring annual expenditure at Rs. 42.6 lakh.

MEMORADUM REGARDING DELEGATED LEGISLATION

Cluase 4 of the Bill seeks to empower the Central Government of exempt, by notification from the operation of the Act the Central Government any State Government, any corporation owned or controlled by any Government or any local authority.

2. Clause 32 empowers the Central Government to make rules regarding—

(a) the particulars which an application shall contain, the documents and the fee which shall be accompained with it and the limit of annual income of a person so as to enable him to make application without paying any fee, under sub-section (4) of Section 5;

(b) any such other matter in respect of which the tribunal shall have powers of a civil court under clause (i) of sub-section (4) of Section 6;

(c) the clause or cases which, having regard to the nature of the questions involved, requires or require to be decided by a Bench of more than two members under clause (d) of sub-section (3) of Section 10;

(d) procedure for the investigation of misbehaviour or incapacity of the Chairman, Vice-chairman or other Member of the Tribunal under sub-section (3) of Section 14;

(e) the salaries and allowances payable to and the other terms and conditions of service of the Chairman, Vice-Chairman and other members under Section 17:

(g) the salaries and allowances and conditions of service of the officers and others employees of the Tribunal under sub-section (3) of Section 18;

(h) the person or the authority by whom, the manner in which and the purposes of environment for which the amount of compensation credited to the Environmental Relief Fund shall be utilised under sub-section (2) of Section 23; and

(i) any other matter which is required to be or may be prescribed.

3. The matters with respect to which notification may be issued or rules may be made under the afforesaid provisions are matters of procedure and detail. The delegation of legislative power contained in such provisions is, therefore, or a normal character.

INDEX